NICARAGUA

Profiles of the
Revolutionary Public Sector

Table of Contents

Nicaragua: New Regional Divisions, 1982

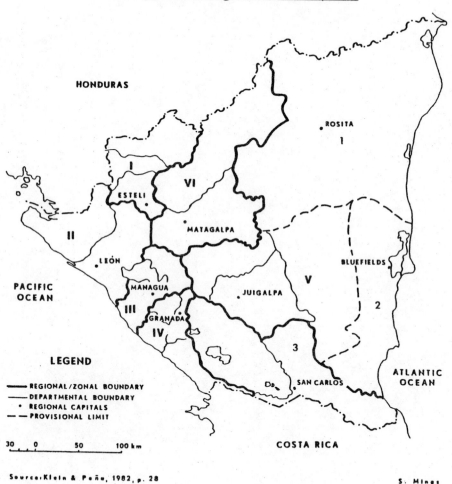

HONDURAS

• ROSITA

1

I

VI

ESTELI

II

MATAGALPA

LEÓN

BLUEFIELDS

PACIFIC
OCEAN

MANAGUA

V

JUIGALPA

III

2

GRANADA

IV

3

ATLANTIC
OCEAN

Do. SAN CARLOS

LEGEND

—— REGIONAL/ZONAL BOUNDARY
—— DEPARTMENTAL BOUNDARY
• REGIONAL CAPITALS
--- PROVISIONAL LIMIT

30   0   50   100 km

COSTA RICA

Source: Klein & Peña, 1982, p. 28

S. Mings

Glossary of Nicaraguan Acronyms

AMNLAE   Asociación de Mujeres Nicaragüenses Luisa Amanda Espinosa; Luisa Amanda Espinosa Association of Nicaraguan Women.

ANICS   Asociación Nicaragüense de Científicos Sociales; Nicaraguan Association of Social Scientists.

APP   Area de Propiedad del Pueblo; Public Property Area.

ASTC   Asociación Sandinista de Trabajadores de la Cultura; Sandinista Association of Cultural Workers.

ATC   Asociación de Trabajadores del Campo; Rural Workers' Association.

BCN   Banco Central de Nicaragua; Nicaraguan Central Bank.

BID   Banco Interamericano de Desarrollo; Interamerican Development Bank.

CAR   Centro de Abastecimiento Rural; Rural Supply Center.

CAT   Centro de Abastecimiento para los Trabajadores; Workers' Supply Center.

CDS   Comité para la Defensa Sandinista; Sandinista Defense Committee.

CEDA   Centro de Educación de Adultos; Adult Education Center.

CEP   Colectivo de Educación Popular; Popular Education Collective.

CIDCA   Centro de Investigaciones y Documentación de la Costa Atlántica; Center for Documentation and Research on the Atlantic Coast.

CIERA   Centro de Investigaciones y Estudios de la Reforma Agraria;
            Agrarian Reform Research Center.

CINASE   Centro de Investigación y Asesoría Socio-económica;
            Center for Socioeconomic Research and Consulting.

CMU   Compañía Marítima de Ultramar;
            Maritime Highseas Company.

CNES   Consejo Nacional de Educación Superior;
            National Council on Higher Education.

COIP   Corporación de Industria Popular;
            Corporation for Small-scale Industry.

COMMEMA Corporación de Mercados Municipales de Managua;
            Municipal Market Corporation for Managua.

CONAPRO Confederación Nacional de Professionales;
            National Federation of Professionals.

CORCOP   Corporación del Comercio del Pueblo;
            Public Marketing Corporation.

CORFIN   Corporación de Finanzas; Nicaraguan Finance Corporation.

CRIES   Coordinadora Regional de Investigaciones Económicas y
            Sociales; Regional Office for Social and Economic Research

CSN   Coordinadora Sindical Nicaragüense;
            Nicaraguan Union Coordinating Committee.

CST   Central Sandinista de Trabajadores;
            Sandinista Workers' Federation.

DAP   Depósito Agrícolo del Pueblo;
            Public Agricultural Warehouse.

ENABAS   Empresa Nicaragüense de Alimentos Básicos;
            Nicaraguan Basic Foodstuffs Company.

ENAL   Empresa Nicaragüense de Algodón;
            Nicaraguan Cotton Company.

ENAMARA   Empresa Nicaragüense de Matanza y Racionalización; National Slaughterhouse Company.

ENCAFE   Empresa Nicaragüense del Café; Nicaraguan Coffee Company.

ENIA   Empresa Nicaragüense de Insumos Agropecuarios; Nicaraguan Agricultural Inputs Company.

ENMAR   Empresa Nicaragüense de Productos del Mar; Nicaraguan Seafood Company.

EPB   Educación Popular Básica; Popular Basic Education.

FIR   Fondo Internacional para la Reconstrucción; International Fund for Reconstruction.

FSLN   Frente Sandinista de Liberación Nacional; Sandinista Front for National Liberation.

GRN   Gobierno de Reconstrucción Nacional; National Government for Reconstruction.

IHCA   Instituto Histórico Centroamericano; Central American Historical Institute.

INAA   Instituto Nicaragüense de Agua y Alcantarrillado; Institute for Water and Wastewater Systems.

INAP   Instituto Nicaragüense de Administración Pública; Nicaraguan Public Administration Institute.

INCAE   Instituto Centroamericano de Administración de Empresas; Central American Institute for Business Administration.

INCEI   Instituto Nicaragüense de Comercio Exterior é Interior; Nicaraguan Institute for Foreign and Domestic Trade.

INDE   Instituto Nicaragüense para el Desarrollo; Nicaraguan Institute for Development.

INE   Instituto Nicaragüense de Energía; Nicaraguan Energy Institute.

INEC   Instituto Nacional de Estadísticas y Censos;
            National Institute for Census and Statistics.

INETER   Instituto de Estudios Territoriales;
            Institute for Territorial Studies.

INIES   Instituto Nicaragüense de Investigaciones Económicas y
            Sociales; Institute for Social and Economic Research

INRA   Instituto Nicaragüense de Reforma Agraria(ahora MIDINRA);
            Nicaraguan Agrarian Reform Institute (now MIDINRA).

INSS   Instituto Nicaragüense de Seguridad Social;
            Nicaraguan Social Security Institute.

INSSBI   Instituto Nicaragüense de Seguridad Social y Bienestar;
            Institute for Social Security and Child Welfare (was INSS).

IRENA   Instituto Nicaragüense de Recursos Naturales y del Ambiente;
            Nicaraguan Institute for Natural Resources and the Environ-
            ment.

JGRN   Junta de Gobierno de Reconstrucción Nacional;
            Government Board for National Reconstruction.

JMR   Junta Municipal de Reconstrucción;
            Municipal Reconstruction Board.

MED   Ministerio de Educación; Ministry of Education.

MIC   Ministerio de Cultura; Ministry of Culture.

MICE   Ministerio de Comercio Exterior; Ministry of Foreign Trade.

MICOIN   Ministerio de Comercio Interior; Ministry of Internal Trade.

MIDINRA   Ministerio de Desarrrollo Agropecuario y Reforma Agraria;
            Ministry of Agricultural Development and Agrarian Reform.

MIFIN   Ministerio de Finanzas; Ministry of Finance.

MIND   Ministerio de Industrias; Ministry of Industry.

MINSA   Ministerio de Salud; Ministry of Health.

MINVAH   Ministerio de Vivienda y Asentamientos Humanos; Ministry of Housing and Human Settlements.

MIPLAN   Ministerio de Planificación; Ministry of Planning.

MITRAB   Ministerio del Trabajo; Ministry of Labor.

PAN   Programa Alimentario Nicaragüense; Nicaraguan Food Program.

PQAN   Plan Quinquenal para la Alimentación y Nutrición; Five-Year Food and Nutrition Plan.

SFN   Sistema Financiero Nacional; National Financial System.

SNOTS   Sistema Nacional de Ordenamiento de Trabajadores y Salarios; National System for Ordering Workers and Wages.

SNUA   Sistema Nacional Unico de Salud; National Health System.

SPP   Secretaría de Planificación y Presupuesto; Office of Planning and Budget.

SRAMU   Secretaría Regional de Asuntos Municipales; Regional Office of Municipal Affairs.

UCA   Universidad Centroamericana; Central American University.

UNAG   Unión Nacional de Agricultores y Ganaderos; National Association of Farmers and Ranchers.

UNAN   Universidad Nacional Autónoma de Nicaragua; National Autonomous University of Nicaragua.

VIMEDA   Vice-Ministerio de Educación de Adultos; Vice-Ministry of Adult Education.

Acknowledgments

This book could not have been produced, this project could not have been undertaken, and whatever positive results it may have yielded could not have been achieved without the full and open collaboration of our colleagues from INIES. Francisco Lopez and Bismarck Jaime negotiated INIES participation and fulfilled their promises to us as well as one could have expected under the circumstances. Those who worked with us on a daily basis, Martha Juárez, Tatiana González, Félix Delgado, and Herminia Valdez, "cumplieron" the tasks asked of them by INIES and by their Texas-based colleagues with a level of enthusiasm and a degree of sensitive and articulate criticism that saved us from more problems of data gathering and interpretation than I can enumerate here.

The co-coordinators of the project in Managua, Verónica Frenkel and Joanna Chataway, deserved and, I believe, received the appreciation of both North American and Nicaraguan colleagues. It was they who created the environment within which a very large amount of research became possible in very short periods of time. They would, I'm sure, also want us to recognize the assistance that we received from Apolinar and Enrique.

This book has been produced in camera-ready copy by the editor and his assistant. We used WordPerfect 4.2 wordprocessing software on Packard Bell VT-286 and Leading Edge Model D computers. The text was then printed on an Apple LaserWriter Plus. We have pushed the software to its limits and, in several cases, beyond them. A new release at the time we purchased it, the software had several serious bugs in the LaserWriter printer driver that have taken more than four months to work out. WordPerfect Corporation customer support was courteous, efficient, concerned, and cooperative. Versions of WordPerfect 4.2 dated 4/17/87 or later, and printer drivers 5/06/87 or later, are free of the underlining and right-justification problems that we encountered. The process of desk-top production was both frustrating and satisfying; but it may be the "least-alienating" way to produce a book. The bottom line: we would, in fact, do it again with the same hardware and software.

And, finally, I wish to express my indebtedness to Verónica Frenkel for the unhesitating assistance to the project and the book that she provided. Her spirit of cooperation and willingness to work long and intensive hours from the onset of the project to its very end were often above and beyond the call of a Research Assistant's duties. Without her, quite simply, the project would have been far less well organized and the book might simply never have come together.

I readily accept, however, full responsibility for any shortcomings that may be found in the book in its final form.

Michael E. Conroy

Chapter 1

The Perils and Promise
of Public Sector Research
in Nicaragua:
An Introduction

by

Michael E. Conroy

Managua. Two days after the U.S. House of Representatives voted, for the first time, to provide $100 million in mostly-military support for the anti-Sandinista contras. It was Friday, the day of a normally--massive annual demonstration celebrating the anniversary of the "Repliegue", the strategic retreat by Sandinista forces in June 1979, during the peak of the insurrection, when thousands marched overnight some 20 miles from southeastern Managua across the hills to Masaya to avoid encirclement by Somoza's National Guard. President Daniel Ortega was going to address the crowd. He had been furious, the night before, in his television commentary on the House vote. Our group of researchers (and our families back in the U.S.) wondered how we would fare, as Northamericans, in Nicaragua after the loss of hope that the U.S. Congress would block the Reagan Administration's pro-contra activities.

I was visiting the Secretaria de Planeación y Presupuesto, the closest that Managua has to a "planning ministry," looking for data on the differences across regions in fundamental levels of government services. The Secretaria, patterned on Mexico's administrative structure, maintained the most up-to-date data on most dimensions that I was researching. And very few of the data had been published.

I had been offered access, several days earlier, to any data that any of the staff at the Secretaria might have that could be useful to the study. The director of the employment and labor force division had introduced me to his staff; and he had instructed them, in my presence, to make available any and all published or unpublished data with which they were working. So I had returned to begin copying information from penciled worksheets and draft reports.

The young "compañera" who managed the data I sought had extra help that day. Two children, probably aged 7 and 9, kept her company in her 8-foot-square cubicle, squirming, giggling, drawing on pads of newsprint, and contantly questioning their mother. They had been let out of school, I learned later, to permit older students, their teachers, and other school employees a day off in preparation for the all-night trek to Masaya that some of them would choose to make. When I arrived they looked up in alarm.

I greeted their mother; we had been introduced the previous day. As I spoke to her, in my reasonably good but still accented Spanish, the kids stared at me, looked at one another, and reacted. The daughter ran behind her mother's chair and whispered in her ear.

"Is he a 'gringo'?" "Yes, my sweet, he is." "Is he one of the bad ones, mama?" "No, precious, he's a teacher who is studying our revolution. We want to know what he has to say."

Daniel Ortega was defiant in his oratory that night, asserting that not even many hundreds of millions of dollars would lead Nicaragua to bend to the will of the United States. He then turned, in a dramatic gesture, to a young U.S.-citizen woman on the platform from which he was speaking, insisted that Nicaraguans continue to distinguish between the people of the United States and the policies of the U.S. government, and invited the Northamerican woman to speak to the crowd on behalf of those in the U.S. who continued to oppose the Reagan policies.

This book represents part of the results of an experiment in collaboration between researchers at a major U.S. university and researchers at a leading Nicaraguan non-governmental research institution, the Nicaraguan Institute for Social and Economic Studies (INIES). The research reflected here was undertaken at a time of great tension in U.S.-Nicaraguan relations. It was also a time of great hardship in Nicaragua; for the first time since the 1979 insurrection, there were clear and tangible shortages of basic foods in Managua; the economy was turning each day toward the "survival mode" that President Daniel Ortega had announced earlier in the year; and Nicaraguans of all walks of life were bone-tired of the "contra" war, the fear of invasion, the momentary elation as breakthroughs appeared immanent in Contadora negotiations, and the deeper despair that followed each succeeding failure of the talks.

The experiment in collaborative research became all the more remarkable as Nicaraguan officials in more than a dozen agencies opened their files, lent staff, attended seminars by members of the team, and rearranged their schedules so that the intensive pace of the project would not be disrupted. Were it not for the war-related banners hung at workplaces, the grim reports on the nightly news, and the truckloads of young soldiers in the countryside racing to and from the more embattled areas, one might have guessed that there was no agenda more pressing than the study of some of the technical and administrative questions upon which we were working.

In fact, many of the issues studied here were considered vital by both Nicaraguan researchers and government officials. With the military balance well in hand, the survival of the revolution appeared to depend much more on the government's ability to meet the needs of the population for food and other basic commodities, health services, land, housing and education. And although Nicaraguan production remained overwhelmingly in the private sector, it was both the leadership of the public sector and the administrative problems of the public sector that would determine the principal outcomes.

Profiles. The seven studies presented here represent "profiles" of the Nicaraguan public sector, profiles of the Nicaraguan State, if you will. They cover a relatively narrow set of dimensions of the state, for the breadth was determined more by the matching of problem-areas and scholars in the project's development than by any editorial predetermination of the dimensions needed to provide complete and balanced coverage. They are inherently "snapshots" of Nicaragua in mid-1986. They do not attempt to provide a complete historical background; and they constitute descriptions and analyses of problems, programs, and policies that were undergoing continuous change. They make no pretense of proposing a comprehensive evaluation of the Nicaraguan experiment, the transition away from a particularly brutal dictatorship and toward a new vision of the developmental possibilities for a Latin American society.

The principal purpose of the research project that led to each of the chapters of this book was to grapple with a research question of general Latin American social-scientific importance which was also considered important by Nicaraguan researchers. The search for answers to those questions then served as collaborative training experiences for Nicaraguan counterparts. The chapters do offer, however, description, documentation, and evaluation that should be useful to anyone who seeks to understand the nature of the Nicaraguan revolutionary experience.

The process within which the studies were developed, furthermore, served as a fascinating learning experience for the team that traveled to Managua, mostly from Texas. Seven Latinamericanist scholars affiliated with the University of Texas at Austin and four graduate research assistants spent varying and overlapping portions of an intensive summer in Nicaragua conducting these "micro-studies" of the nature and functioning of diverse dimensions of the Nicaraguan public sector, seven years after the 1979 overthrow of the dictator Anastasio Somoza. Most of them had never been to Nicaragua before; only one of them had previously published anything on Nicaragua; but all seven of the senior researchers had established reputations in their areas of specialization in other Latin American countries.

The Project. It was Xabier Gorostiaga, the indefatigable founder of INIES, and Francisco Lopez, its Director General since 1985, who suggested the idea behind the project, nursed it through its birth pangs, and nourished it to fruition. They proposed to me in 1985 that Nicaragua offered an unusual opportunity for Northamerican scholars to study the evolution of the public sector under conditions where virtually all constraints on the form and substance of public sector activity had been removed. They noted that Nicaraguan researchers needed training in social science research methodology vis-a-vis the public sector. They felt that there was a wealth of expertise potentially available in the United States to provide that assistance. They suggested that researchers delving into these crucial issues should be willing to teach or to train young researchers in Nicaragua in the methodologies that they tended to utilize in return for Nicaraguan assistance in obtaining data and in its analysis. They further believed that outside reinforcement for the tradition of critically independent academic research would be valued in contemporary Nicaragua.

Together we identified some 15 areas of major governmental policy that badly needed evaluation and commentary and that might be areas of sufficient interest to U.S. scholars to elicit participation in a research project without high levels of salary. The potential projects ranged from questions of regional and demographic policy to evaluations of the overall direction of the nation's public administration. They included several areas of data management for administration, pricing policies, unintentionally conflicting social policies, and informatics. The only areas that were excluded were a few, such as telecommunications or direct studies of the military, that might have been considered too sensitive, under conditions of war, by the Nicaraguan government.

Motivation. The Nicaraguan public sector reflected, by 1986, some of the most innovative dimensions of the Nicaraguan Revolution. Public sector programs led to documented dramatic improvements in health conditions and levels of literacy; and they partially replaced many functions previously provided in the private sector, such as banking, grain storage and distribution, and a multitude of local, municipal, and regional services. A significant minority of agricultural production was shifted to state farms, although the agricultural sector remained the bastion of private sector production.

Neither the evolution of the Nicaraguan public sector, *per se*, nor many dimensions of its organization and functioning had been studied systematically prior to then by specialists who could take a technical view, independent of the political rhetoric swirling around Nicaragua. As had been the case in the early days of the Cuban Revolution, the practitioners of change were far too busily involved in creating that change to be able to afford the luxury of pursuing an appraisal. And, for those of us who had taken fragmentary peeks at some dimensions of Nicaraguan public policy, it was clear that there was considerable misunderstanding in the United States of the nature of the evolution of the public sector in Nicaragua, the origins of the models implemented, the scope of its activities, and the consequences of this public sector expansion for the Nicaraguan economy and society. Some of the questions not clearly answered in contemporary debates about Nicaragua included:

* Were the contemporary economic problems of Nicaragua, including scarcity of foreign exchange, medicines, and health-related resources, high rates of migration toward Managua, and slowing rates of growth of agricultural production attributable to the expansion of the public sector and to the modes of public administration that had been adopted there?

* To what extent did the evolution of the public sector in Nicaragua compare with traditional patterns in the rest of Latin America or contemporary patterns in the actually-existing socialist countries?

* Were there significant changes that might be adopted in patterns of Nicaraguan public administration that would enhance the efficiency or the equity with which the public sector was managed?

* Were there lessons in public sector growth and administration as seen in the Nicaraguan experience that could be of use to the public sector in other parts of the Third World?

It was the principal scholarly purpose of a research project to generate new answers to those questions and to contribute those answers to the international discussion of the Nicaraguan "model." Given the troubled political and financial situation which Nicaragua confronted, however, it would have been unreasonable to suggest that simple pursuit of those academic purposes would have been sufficient to justify the investment of human resources that would be necessary on the part of Nicaraguan public officials to reach new conclusions on those academic questions.

This research project offered, therefore, several dimensions beyond the normal pattern of academic research. These dimensions were not such that they might be considered specific to Nicaragua; they were, rather, dimensions that the research team considered characteristics of minimally-responsible international research in the Third World that might well be utilized elsewhere. They included preparation of immediate reports for cooperating Nicaraguan agencies on the basis of the research, a process of training Nicaraguans in each of the areas being researched, and the provision of extensive bibliographic documentation for Nicaraguan libraries in each of the areas studied.

The Experience. During late 1985 and early 1986, working through the Office of Public Sector Studies at the University of Texas' Institute of Latin American Studies, I was able to identify a team of ten researchers who were willing to work under the conditions imposed by the project for the sake of a first-hand opportunity to study and evaluate the evolution of many dimensions of the Nicaraguan public sector. None of the group, other than I, had done research on Nicaragua previously. And, in my own case, it offered the opportunity to develop a substantially different kind of fieldwork project than I had undertaken previously in my more "desktop" economic analyses.

All of the members of the research team were recognized specialists in the analysis of some dimension of the public sector, all spoke Spanish fluently, and all were free for the time needed in Nicaragua. The Ford Foundation, reflecting courage in the face of adverse political conditions at that time, then provided the funding needed for travel, per diem, and administrative support to make the project feasible.

Each of the senior researchers agreed to spend from 30 to 45 days in Nicaragua working on the project during overlapping periods between May 15th and August 31st of 1986. For most of them there was a relatively clearly-defined project outlined for them in advance (although, in two cases, the project changed totally as soon as the researcher reached Managua). During that period he or she would work out a schedule for the three basic tasks: seminars on methodology, research on a specific applied theme, and presentation of preliminary results.

Although 30-to-45 days seemed like perilously little time for undertaking a new project in a country which most had never visited before, the administrative design of the project attempted to mitigate that problem. A permanent support team, comprised of Mária Verónica Frenkel, Joanna Chataway, and four staff persons assigned by INIES (Martha Juárez, Félix Delgado, Tatiana González, and Herminia Valdes), prepared the terrain for each researcher so that he or she could, more than figuratively, "hit the ground running."

Francisco Lopez, Director General of INIES, arranged the first round of high-level contacts for each researcher; the permanent team then set up interviews, often as many as six to ten, well in advance of the arrival of the researcher. Using the Documentation Center at INIES, arguably the most complete, most accessible, and best organized in Nicaragua, the advance team prepared literal "stacks" of background materials for each researcher.

All of the Northamerican members of the team lived in a single rented house in Managua. This house eliminated time-consuming concern for daily necessities and also afforded an excellent opportunity for the team members to share the results of interviews, the discovery of new data or documentation, the analysis and interpretation of perplexing problems, and the use of vehicles hired for the project.

INIES provided office space and, frankly, shared all that it had to offer with the research team. Although the projects's continual need for haste and the unconventional accounting (required to divide costs between those covered by INIES and reimbursed to it and those paid directly by the University Texas) tested the patience of the INIES administrative staff, we received marvelous support throughout the time we were there.

We did take with us, however, virtually everything that we thought we would need. This was not just a reflection of the recognition that

Nicaragua was suffering from an acute shortage of all imported goods. It represented a decision on a separate level to make certain that the project would not be a burden on an already-plagued Nicaraguan economy, where the greatest shortages were of those products requiring foreign exchange.

"Virtually everything," in this case, meant everything from paper clips to microcomputers. The trade embargo in place in the United States in 1986 was a potential deterrent to both the participation of scholars and the provision of the supplies needed for research. The embargo decree, however, clearly permitted individuals to travel to Nicaragua for research, consulting, or other travel purposes. And it specifically exempted from the embargo provisions any materiél that individuals might take with them as personal effects when traveling to Nicaragua. The shipment of the microcomputer, however, was registered with the Commerce Department, as required, at the time that it was taken to Managua.

The Environment. Managua, in the Summer of 1986, was a difficult place for a group of foreigners to live. This was true not for the reasons that might be advanced by those who knew only the media caricatures of Nicaragua at this time. It was true because Nicaragua was then more than four years into the war with the contras, because the war was principally designed to be a war of attrition, and because the policies of the government designed to counter the effects of the war did not provide readily for stray non-Nicaraguans who happened to be in the country at that time!

This was a time of considerable food scarcity in Managua, though not in terms that compare with the scarcity of Bangladesh or the Sahelian countries. Nicaraguans had become accustomed to receiving a significant portion of their wages in "social wage" goods, food and other consumer products provided at subsidized prices through the "secure channel" of government distribution programs. And one could find an abundance of fruit and vegetables in mounds and giant baskets throughout the city. Wheat bread was scarce because wheat is all imported and because the government is deliberately encouraging people to respond to the scarcity of foreign exchange by consuming more corn products and other non-imported staples such as potatoes.

The scarcities of basic grains that have afflicted all of Central America for most of this century during the months of June, July, and August each year had been mitigated in Nicaragua by government programs from 1980 through 1985; and Chapters 4, 5, and 8 of the book describe those systems and reflect on them. The annual rainy season runs from mid-May through November in most of Central America. This means that beans that mature in 80 to 90 days become available from the new crop around mid-August; corn, with maturation for unimproved local varieties often running to 120 days, becomes abundant in September and October. For countries that depend solely on market price mechanisms for the allocation of grain supplies through the year, this seasonality means that grain prices are lowest in the Fall and highest, often prohibitively high for much of the Central American population, during the months of June and July.

The Nicaraguan government's programs for buying, storing, and redistributing across the whole population, and across the whole year, had eliminated much of the effective scarcity of most basic grains prior to 1985. The contra war, miscalculations by ENABAS, and other distribution problems discussed in the chapters below left Managua with much less than the normal supplies of basic grains and other food products during the summer of 1986; and in that sense there was dramatic scarcity.

Nicaraguans continued to have access to these programs, albeit with diminished levels of supply; but foreigners did not. The devaluation of the Córdoba that took place just before and during that summer, however, left those of us whose budgets were denominated in dollars embarassed by the copiousness of the food that we could afford to buy in the restaurants. And, although one had to ask the ubiquitous question about any menu in modest restaurants, "¿Que hay?" ("What's available?"), even the smallest comedores offered abundant supplies of vegetables for soups and broths, together with rice.

Transportation was also a problem, for the buses were as crowded as I remembered them from my days as a Peace Corps volunteer in Honduras in the early 1960's. As the U.S. economic embargo affected the Nicaraguan nation's ability to produce export products, because U.S.-made sugar-milling equipment was deteriorating without replacement or because U.S.-made agricultural machinery was more difficult to repair, the nation's bus fleet was diminishing for lack of spare parts. New buses had been purchased from Japan, Brazil, Spain, and Bulgaria, but not it numbers sufficient to meet the demand. Taxis were also scarce, most were running as "peseros" in the Mexican style, and travel to and from meetings using public conveyance would have been prohitively time-consuming. But we were able to contract the services of two car-owners who responded to the low real level of wages in salaried jobs by entering the "informal sector," offering their cars and their services as drivers for hire.

Many Northamericans distill from U.S. media treatments of Nicaragua an image of Nicaragua as a place where political intimidation is the rule, where one doesn't dare ask politically-loaded questions, or where there is an all-pervading fear of the authorities. Nicaragua is also characterized, by those who seem to know very little of it, as a nation with a monolithic and dogmatic government that would brook no criticism of its policies, whether internally or externally. During the time that this research group worked in Nicaragua, it was difficult to find evidence to support that image. It was, on the contrary, the experience of most of the researchers on this project that Nicaraguan officials, Nicaraguan researchers, and Nicaraguan people-on-the-street were exceedingly open about alternative possibilities for resolving Nicaragua's problems. The debate, in fact, never seemed to end.

Some of us were able to attend a major day-long conference on the economy, organized by CINASE (a definitely centrist private research organization), at which the full range of the domestic political opposition, including representatives of the High Council on Private Enterprise (COSEP), lambasted the government's policies and were then duly attacked by defenders of positions covering the full spectrum from theirs to the left. And it was all then duly reported in the newspapers and on the radio.

The director of the National Public Administration Institute encouraged our research in part because it provided balance, based on the Harvard Business School case-study approach, to the training that many of his staff and many government officials were receiving in alternative methods in Cuba. Representatives of the Ministry of Internal Commerce (MICOIN) were willing to admit that part of the administrative problems of public enterprises, such as ENABAS (evaluated in Chapter 5), derived from the difficulty they were having reconciling the training of their U.S.-trained staff and their Cuban-trained staff.

The complexity of Nicaragua confronted us in our research every day. For every university-educated person that we encountered on the staff of government agencies whose training had come from Eastern European countries, we found several from U.S., Latin American, and Western European universities. And many of the most skilled and dedicated professors in the universities and knowledgeable researchers in a whole gamut of research programs that we touched at one point or another were Catholic priests or nuns.

The access we were given to confidential data was aptly illustrated at ENABAS. The group working on my chapter visited the main offices of ENABAS to ask for detailed data on distribution of grains by region over the 1980-85 timespan, including both quantities and prices. The ENABAS staff indicated that they had not compiled the data, and that no one on their staff would be able to do it for us in the short time period that we had (two weeks). But the head of the statistical division then took us to the General Manager's office and, after consulting with him, indicated that the four file cabinets in the corner of the office contained the originals of all the ENABAS records for the last 6 years, including the minutes of all the Board Meetings, all internal reports, and financial data. We were welcome to sit at the boardroom table and to copy anything that we needed from them. I was convinced that this simply represented collaboration with INIES until one of our INIES collaborators, indicated, with more than a little resentfulness, that INIES had requested much of these data in times past and that they had been denied them.

And the level of interest in the limited skills that we could convey was overwhelming. The biggest shortcoming in the eventual development of the project may have been the fact that we allowed ourselves, with the encouragement of Francisco Lopez of INIES, to get spread too thin. It seemed that at each agency or office with which we worked, whether on the general information level of the National Institute of Statistics and Census (INEC) or the program-specific level of ENABAS, the staff had questions on which they earnestly sought our advice. The temptation to spend several hours or several days poring over reports and data on problems tangential to our research projects and to offer advice that should have been based on much more work was too tempting, all too often. As a result of this tendency, it is safe to suggest that the more formal training on our original projects expected by our colleagues and collaborators at INIES was substantially reduced; and by the end of the project they were legitimately (but cordially) disappointed.

For some of the members of the team, the diversity of interesting problems which they were offered was so attractive that research on their original or revised projects was severely inhibited. Even though Chandler Stolp, for example, was discouraged from his original project from the first day that he began working with the Planning Office of the Ministry of Health (as we will note below), their thirst for knowledge of microcomputer techniques for a wide variety of fundamental allocation problems left him "methodologically drained" and with less time than he had planned for the development of his paper. Partly for that reason, he offers us here an analysis of Nicaraguan health system efficiency which is as didactic as it is descriptive. It represents a novel application of linear programming technology in the context of illustrating system efficiency across 18 health centers around Managua.

The environment, in sum, was as stimulating as it was frustrating, as exciting as it was depressing, and, more than anything, fundamentally rewarding. I can't speak for all of the research team, but I have heard from most that the level of openness, the level of cooperation, the level of trust and the degree of access to raw, unprocessed, unpublished data was absolutely unprecedented in our collective research experience.

The Seven Micro-Studies

The seven low-key technical research papers that we produced constitute chapters 2 through 8 of this volume. Most of the material used here was first presented in a series of seminars in Managua to which a wide range of researchers, agency staff, students, and government officials were invited. They were then presented at a "Miniconference on the Nicaraguan Public Sector" at the University of Texas on October 21, 1986. And they were offered for critique by the scholarly community at the October 1986 XIII International Congress of the Latin American Studies Association in Boston.

Each of the seven papers provides an analysis of heretofore unreported data on specific dimensions of the Nicaraguan public sector. Each of them represents the application of established social science research techniques to issues and areas of controversy in the Nicaraguan public sector, and each provided a basis for training Nicaraguan researchers in those techniques. Each of them contains implicit and explicit critiques of the manner in which data have been analyzed by prior Nicaraguan researchers; and several of them take issue with some of the hypotheses prevailing in Nicaragua (and among many non-Nicaraguan scholars of Nicaraguan phenomena) with respect to critical contemporary issues of public sector administration in Nicaragua.

The seven papers cover widely different micro-dimensions of the Nicaraguan public sector, but they converge independently on three consensus conclusions:

a. The Nicaraguan "public sector model" is clearly different from any previous model seen in Latin America and tangibly different from Eastern European or Cuban models.

b. The "success" of the Nicaraguan "public sector model," whether measured in terms of regional decentralization and effective outreach, health-system unification and rationalization, public participation on a massive scale in many voluntary government programs, food distribution programs and policies, or the administration of public enterprises, contains, at every level, ample doses of "popular participation," important roles for the "mass organizations," and forms of "participatory democracy" seldom seen elsewhere as individual processes and, perhaps, never before seen together in one place.

c. The tangible results of the model cannot be separated from the multi-faceted impact of the "contra" war. The papers do not belabor this point; but the individual researchers found, in every case, that the impact of the war became a dominant determinant of many outcomes, distorting the direction of public sector policies in some cases, and testing them in an unusual crucible in others.

Each of the authors has responded to the demands and the opportunities of the project in a slightly different way. Each has produced a report that reflects substantially-differing experiences in the Nicaraguan research environment; and each has chosen to communicate the results of the project with a different tone and orientation. I will introduce each briefly in the order in which they follow.

The State Apparatus. Lawrence S. Graham opens the series of studies with a comparative analysis of the Nicaraguan state apparatus, the public organizations through which policies and programs are formulated and implemented. Concern with alternative modes of public administration were an early and obvious candidate for research in the project. Nicaragua has borrowed and imitated from a wide variety of sources in as many different areas of the public sector. And Nicaraguan researchers are concerned both with the simplistic characterization of their state apparatus that pervades discussion in the United States and with expert appraisal of whether their system, as it evolves, is headed toward organizational bottlenecks, institutional horseshoe canyons, or other traps that might be avoided on the basis of the collective experience of comparable societies elsewhere.

Graham looked generally into the modes of organization of the agencies providing social services in Nicaragua, and particularly into the evolution of the Ministry of Education. He sought to evaluate the organizational forms that lay behind the much-touted changes in the delivery of educational services across the country. Drawing from comparisons with other Latin American modes of organization and comparing Nicaragua to Portugal, Yugoslavia, and Rumania, he concludes that "what is most distinctive about the Nicaraguan case was the extent to which the revolutionary government has been able to create a very different state apparatus in a relatively short time." This represents, he suggests, "a new relationship between bureaucracy and society," that is "more a consequence of the popular mobilization and the participation promoted from below... than it is the result of concerted action from above."

Regionalization and Decentralization. Patricia A. Wilson assesses the achievements and the shortcomings of Nicaragua's regionalization efforts and compares what she saw in Nicaragua with the extensive previous work that she has done in Perú and Chile. She interviewed a large number of technical and administrative people throughout the government in Managua and then traveled to four major cities to speak with administrators at the municipal level. Her chapter outlines the regional administrative structure that is evolving in Nicaragua, the theoretical decentralization that has been designed and the *de facto* decentralization of administration, investment, and finances that appears to have occurred.

A skeptic about the much-vaunted promises of decentralization in other Latin American countries, Wilson finds that the Nicaraguan regionalization effort may be viewed as "a showcase for central government support for municipal development." She also suggests that Nicaragua has apparently pioneered in effective "participatory, bottom-up planning," echoing the conclusion reached by Graham. She faults the Nicaraguan regionalization, however, for the lack of "strategic spatial development planning at both regional and municipal levels"; and she notes that the continuation of regional and municipal decentralization, which could be slowed by the continuation of the contra war, might just as well be increased as an instrument for improving the productive utilization of resources in outlying regions.

The Regional Outreach of the State. Rolf Pendall and I undertook an attempt to measure and explain the rates of migration toward Managua which have been a focal point of concern for many in Nicaragua. We developed for Chapter 4 a series of measures of the extent to which the distribution of government services has varied across regions since 1980, testing to see whether an unintentional concentration of public sector goods and services in Managua and some of the other regions might explain the apparent rates of growth of Managua. What we found was a surprise to many.

Although demographic data are very weak in Nicaragua at this time, we report in the chapter that the quantifiable rates of migration toward Managua do not appear to have been as great as many have believed. We illustrate statistically a rather dramatic decentralization of access to government goods and services in health services, education, food distribution, and agrarian reform, such that the greatest gains have occurred in the outlying regions, especially in those affected by the war. There is reason to believe, we conclude, that this effective outreach has probably lessened the rates of migration toward Managua and the other more developed regions relative to what they would have been had earlier policies continued or to what they would have been, in the face of the contra war, without such regional outreach.

ENABAS, A State Trading Organization. Alfred H. Saulniers went to Nicaragua with an expectation that he would work on his area of specialization, modes of management of public enterprises, as seen in a cross-section of Nicaraguan state-trading firms. But he was invited by the Ministry of Internal Commerce (MICOIN) to conduct an in-depth study of Nicaragua's largest, most important, and most controversial public enterprise, ENABAS. His chapter provides fascinating insight into the enterprise which is at the heart of Nicaragua's basic commodities distribution program.

Saulniers illustrates the origins and evolution of ENABAS' precarious financial and administrative history, notes the tangible increases in productivity that it has shown, and discusses the conceptual problems that inhibit the development of appropriate pricing policies and, in their absence, of appropriate criteria for evalating the firm's performance. He concludes that, in the historical environment of Latin American state-owned trading organizations, ENABAS functions "surprisingly well" in the light of "the growing pains associated with a turbulent environment."

The Efficiency of Health Centers. Chandler Stolp went to Nicaragua proposing to study hospital administration and to teach about the use of microcomputers in that task. He was quickly informed that the Health Ministry, in view of the lack of microcomputers in *any* hospital at this time in Nicaragua, would prefer that he work on bolder problems, such as the planning of pharmaceutical purchases under severely constrained budgets. His chapter is, as I noted above, an application of decision science techniques to the evaluation and the planning of personnel allocation across health centers, using 18 centers around Managua as a case study.

Building on background consideration of the difficulties of allocating resources for public goods such as public health services, he describes the evolution of the Nicaraguan health care system and compares it on a number of dimensions with the health care system in El Salvador. The intriguing element of his chapter is the background theme that continues to surface: the development of a nationwide public health system, as in

Nicaragua, in which the direction of system development, a significant amount of health care resources, and reductions in the costs of providing fundamental services all emerge from widespread public participation in "popular health councils" creates a unique and challenging environment for health system evaluation, one quite distinct from any that we've seen anywhere before.

Labor Organization and Participation. The all-pervasive dimension of popular participation through the mass organizations surfaced without prior design in virtually all of the previous chapters. Scott Whiteford and Terry Hoops are anthropologists who have worked on the sugar industry in México and Argentina. They set out to explore what state ownership really means in Nicaragua in terms of the working conditions of sugar workers. They interviewed a large number of people in management, in the labor unions, and in the colonias on the farm plantations around three of the largest ingenios in the country, two that are state-owned and one that is private.

Although the private sugar mill was the largest and most modern in the country and one of the state mills had the highest productivity in the country, they found significant and somewhat surprising differences in modes and levels of participation by workers in them. They found worker participation more limited than they might have expected in the state firms and more developed, on some levels, in the private firm. Their chapter serves to illustrate in an interesting fashion how the role of the state is contradictory in its relationship to both the privately owned mill and the state-owned mill. Worker participation in the private sector places pressures on the firms that may contradict state plans or policies for them; state development of more technically sophisticated production in the public sector is creating cleavages in some of the most important of its political power bases.

Food and Agricultural Policies. The problems confronted in most of the preceeding chapters reflect implicit dilemmas that the Nicaraguan revolution has had to face. Mária Verónica Frenkel poses the food and agriculture policy problem as a series of explicit dilemmas. In the concluding chapter she provides an exhaustive survey of the literature on the problems that Nicaragua has had in meeting the food needs of its population at the same time that it has attempted to fight a war with one hand and stimulate predominantly private sector agricultural producers with the other. She highlights the conflicts and contradictions that underlay ENABAS' problems in obtaining enough food for its distribution programs at a price compatible with its budget, as analysed in Chapter 5, as well as the problems faced in providing adequate incentive to private agricultural producers.

This is a fitting concluding chapter, for it illustrates the broader policy problems faced the Nicaraguan government as it attempts to combine a large set of the concerns touched singly in the preceeding chapters. It is also an excellent illustration of the tensions between modes of public administration that remain in Nicaragua. For the conflict between those who would favor more conventional top-down, centralized planning and, in the case of agriculture, the expansion of large and state-owned production units and those favoring more decentralized and participatory processes had been resolved, by mid-1986 at least, in favor of the more democratic and participatory styles. If this is, as Graham suggested in his opening chapter, part of the very essence of the Nicaraguan experimental state apparatus, and if it permeates regional strategies, health policies, and labor relations, as succeeding chapters suggest, the Nicaraguan model is captured well by the complex and delicate interplay of potentially contradictory forces that Frenkel illustrates clearly.

Reflections on the Process

The actual experience of developing these studies was, finally, noteworthy in itself. Here was a group of "outside" Northamerican scholars, from Texas of all political places, who "landed" at the Institute for Social and Economic Studies (INIES) in Managua, almost as if by parachute, for periods ranging from two weeks to six weeks in the Summer of 1986. Each had a commitment to "produce" a serious analysis of sensitive areas of Nicaraguan government activities at precisely the time that the U.S. Congress was debating, and ultimately passing, measures providing $100 million for "counterrevolutionaries" whose explicit objective was the overthrow of the very same government. The Nicaraguans had no prior commitment with respect to the conclusions that would be reached; they didn't know any of the researchers other than me. They had ample reason to distrust and, even, to resent this group of "gringos" who arrived with everything from their own pencils and pencil sharpeners to their own microcomputers, diskettes, and programs, and trunks for carrying data, documents, and copies of final "results" back to the U.S.

The extent to which Nicaraguans on every level opened their files, their experiences, their doubts, and their concerns to the members of this group, from co-workers at INIES to government officials in ministries besieged by the public because of current economic problems, tells its own tale about Nicaragua, its public sector, and the opportunities for research there. The Summer of 1986 was a summer of great shortages, especially in Managua; the problems encountered by the group in coping with those shortages may provide methodological lessons for other scholars intent on conducting future research there.

It is very hard to communicate to an audience outside of Nicaragua how U.S.-citizen researchers could be accepted so fully, supported so completely, and encouraged so thoroughly to provide professional and critical evaluation at a time when most Nicaraguans believed that many, if not most, of their social and economic problems were directly at-tributable to U.S. aggression. Yet it is remarkably true that in all the time that I was there working on this project, among all the Nicaraguans who knew nothing of me other than the fact that I was a Northamerican, the only vaguely negative comments I received were the doubts of the young child in the SPP office, expressed to her mother, about whether I might be "one of the bad ones."

The research team, the principal authors of these studies, may have left behind some insights, some scholarly controversy, and some research technology. But, independent of our personal appraisals of the path of the Nicaraguan Revolution, we took away from Nicaragua an abiding respect for the comprehension, understanding, and international cooperation that seem to become possible, despite overwhelming difficulties, under conditions where the fundamental democratic, participatory, and self-valorizing aspirations of a people appear to have been greatly released.

Chapter 2

The Impact of the Revolution
on the State Apparatus

by

Lawrence S. Graham

Introduction

There can be no doubt that significant change has come to Nicaragua since the overthrow of the Somoza dictatorship and that a revolution has been under way since 1979. However, a revolutionary breakthrough in and of itself does not ensure sustained change in the structure and operations of a government, nor in the content of its public programs, unless there is a coherent strategy linking programmatic objectives with new organizational forms and mentalities. Far too often, lack of attention to the apparatus of the state -- the public organizations through which policies and programs are formulated and implemented -- leads to severe bottlenecks later in the state's ability to respond to and sustain mass mobilization and participation.[1] In light of these problems in other instances of revolutionary breakthrough, what this chapter seeks to ascertain is, first, whether it is possible to identify a coherent organizational strategy in the Nicaraguan Revolution, and, second, whether there is the capacity to sustain programmatically commitment to the demands for equanimity in the meeting of basic human needs.

In evaluating the impact of the Revolution on Nicaragua's state apparatus in these terms, it is important to keep in mind that creating a revolution and sustaining revolutionary change to the extent that human relations are decisively altered entail two very distinct operations. In the former, capturing control of the centers of power and staffing them with one's own partisans is essential. In the latter, transforming the structures of the state as well as the behavior and thinking of public employees definitively involves creativity and persistence of a very different sort, for which there are no uniform guidelines. Elsewhere, in the transition from capitalism to socialism, the failure to develop a coherent bureaucratic strategy for ensuring sustained change in the state apparatus and the individuals who staff it has in time led to the reappearance of many of the same administrative problems that were assumed to be the logical consequence of the old order and were automatically transcended once a revolutionary breakthrough had occurred.[2]

The conclusion I have reached after four weeks of intensive field research in Nicaragua and after comparing this fieldwork with that I have conducted elsewhere in Latin America and in East Europe is this: Seven years into the Revolution, that is, in 1986, what was most distinctive about the Nicaraguan case was the extent to which the revolutionary government had been able to create a very different state apparatus in a relatively short period of time. No matter how important this outcome is, what is even more important to stress from the outset is that this transformation of the state apparatus is more a consequence of the popular mobilization and the participation promoted from below by mass organizations than it is the result of concerted action from above by a vanguard elite. In fact, it is the thesis of this chapter that a substantial part of the debate over the nature and the thrust of the Sandinista government can best be handled by careful assessment of the internal transformations under way as a new relationship between bureaucracy and society is being established. What this entails is the analysis of actions rather than rhetoric, a task that is almost as difficult working within the regime as it is from the outside.

To assess change of this sort and to confront realistically the administrative problems that have emerged, there are two tasks at hand. One entails situating the Nicaraguan case in a broader, cross-national comparative context in order to clarify similarities and differences in the patterns of change. The other involves selection of program areas that make it possible to capture the dynamics of the changes under way. To accomplish the first task, three cases are particularly relevant: Romania, Yugoslavia, and Portugal. For the purpose of the last, social services -- especially education and health -- constitute useful measures. The former instances of revolutionary breakthrough involve problems similar to those faced by Nicaragua but very different outcomes, once implementation of new government programs related to development had to be undertaken. The program areas provide real insight into what is going on, because these are the arenas where the egalitarian aspirations inherent in revolutionary change and the competing demands for scarce resources among those concerned with the survival of the revolution, with economic progress, and with responsiveness to mass demands are most likely to be focused.

Before proceeding in either direction, however, a characterization of the state apparatus at the time transition from rule by the Somocistas to the Sandinistas took place is in order. Under the Somozas the state was limited in scope, highly centralized, and corrupt. Essentially a garrison state designed to reward a privileged minority and to exclude the majority, an autonomous state apparatus really did not exist. Created by the Somozas, that apparatus served them well and could not be separated from the personal liaisons that they had developed across the years. This does not mean, however, the absence of change, for considerable modernization in those sectors tied most closely to export-oriented commerce and the international economy did take place during the 1960s and the 1970s. As a consequence, although the majority of public employees constituted a somewhat amorphous body of civil servants serving at the discretion of the Somozas, there were pockets of expertise -- centered in the Central Bank and several of the public enterprises, such as the state-owned electrical company.

Generally speaking, however, not much policy was discussed at the presidential level under the old regime. The primary focus in the president's office lay on attending to the patronage system and to requests made in exchange for promises of loyalty. Accordingly, the last of the Somozas -- Anastasio Somoza Debayle -- delegated most questions of policy to individual ministers and they, in turn, ran things pretty much as they saw fit in the sectors under their jurisdiction. Except for the coordination of economic policy through the Central Bank, what developed was a fragmented administrative system without much coherency, employing an estimated 20,000 civil servants.[3]

The entry of the Sandinistas into power involved a two-way process of change within the state apparatus. A large percentage of what I would call sinecure-oriented bureaucrats simply shifted their loyalty with the change in regime; technical personnel -- especially the more competent economists housed in the Central Bank -- generally opted to exit as they found the revolutionary changes under way less and less to their liking. The result was pulverization of the state apparatus, with each public organization going largely its own way. Once Somoza had departed, what little coherency had existed previously dissolved. More in Nicaragua than in other societies experiencing sudden regime change, the new government was saddled with the problem of creating anew a viable state apparatus through which to design and implement policy. This challenge was further compounded by the personalized nature of the previous regime. Somoza's exit left in place considerable holdings in the economy for which nationalization was the natural recourse. When the properties of others linked closely to the regime were added in, the state acquired in a relatively short period of time a much larger number of now publicly owned enterprises than had been the case. In only a limited number of cases did the new state have the capacity to administer them effectively. To this base must be added the fact that the Sandinistas' commitment to governance for the benefit of the majority obligated them immediately to expand social services. These changes in economic and social policy, in turn, increased dramatically the new regime's administrative problems and its need for public employees. State employment rose accordingly, to an estimated 80,000.[4]

The consequence of these developments was an even more amorphous state apparatus than that which existed previously. The administrative dilemma facing the Sandinista leadership thus centered around the tension between those who would dictate the course of the Revolution from a predetermined ideological stance and those who argued for a constant redefinition of the new state in the making in light of the articulation between leadership and mass elements in the Revolution. The revolutionary project that the Sandinista leadership had in mind necessitated firm control, central direction, and coordination. Yet, the national reality that it has faced since the beginning has been a "soft state" in which neither the budgets nor the new human resources necessary to implement these goals have been available. Furthermore, as they moved ahead with the consolidation of their control and as the war with the contras has intensified, the central government found it extraordinarily difficult to get a handle on costs because of the absence of basic, reliable data and escalating demands and necessities for increasingly limited resources.

Compounding their difficulties in determining available economic resources amidst uncertainty was a severe shortage in human resources. To begin with, the reliability and competency of most of the public personnel inherited was questionable. However, even if that had not been the case, the rapid expansion of the state apparatus through nationalization and the mounting of new social services en masse meant an enormous need for new personnel committed to the goals of the Sandinista Revolution and with the capacity to administer new social and economic programs. The result was the interjection of considerable pragmatism as people learned administration by doing and responded to the demands articulated from below. In many cases, in responding to these new demands, the mass organizations simply superseded the state by attending directly to social needs at the grass-roots level. The problem was that when the state reassumed jurisdiction over these activities, conflict immediately arose between the informal methods of citizen involvement and the formal procedures established by central government officials for administering programs.

The Administration of Social Services

The tension between the restructuring of the state apparatus from above and the reshaping of public programs from below is especially visible in the administration of social services -- in education, health, social welfare, and housing. This sector is also a crucial one to examine in determining the extent of the transformation achieved in moving from a society of limited participation to one incorporating the masses. On the eve of the Sandinista Revolution, one encountered a minimal role for the state in the provision of social services and numerous private or semipublic institutions, oriented to a restricted clientele and accessible to those who paid for them. The entry of the Sandinistas into power and the staffing of central government organizations with their partisans ensured a radical reorientation in such services. Education for everyone, the right of each citizen to basic health care, the extension of social welfare benefits to the public at large were all an integral part of the transformations taking place.

Early in the Revolution the educational, health, and welfare sectors underwent basic restructuring, within the context of wider systemic changes instituted during the first ten months of the Revolution. The Ministry of Education (MED) was revamped and a national council for higher education was formed, establishing government control over universities for the first time. An integrated national health system was established and a new Ministry of Health (MINSA), was created to take responsibility for its organization and administration. The old Social Security Institute (INSS), which had provided coverage to but 16 percent of the economically active population before the Revolution, was so radically restructured that its successor organization, the Institute of Social Security and Welfare (INSSBI) became in effect a new organization. In recognition of the fact that it had taken on a whole range of new social services designed to meet basic needs, INSSBI received ministerial status. These changes are well documented in the wealth of materials published on the accomplishments and the achievements of the Revolution.[5]

Although such changes constituted an important part of the formal restructuring of the state apparatus, much more significant in terms of impact on the public at large was the role assumed by the mass organizations. As Gary Ruchwarger has demonstrated so clearly in his study of mass organizations, popular participation is the key to understanding the Nicaraguan Revolution and the transformations that have occurred since.[6] What really changed the content of education, health, and welfare programs was not so much decrees from above, couched in institutional terms, as the involvement of an enormous number of people at the grass-roots level outside the state, who took it upon themselves to see that basic social services would be made available and accessible to the poor majority.

The achievements in this area have already been so widely commented on that they need only be mentioned here briefly. Each has come to symbolize in its own way why this revolution has come to be perceived within Nicaragua as a movement of and for the masses. Two stand out: the National Literacy Campaign (the Cruzada Nacional de Alfabetización), which reduced illiteracy from 50.3 percent to 12.9 percent; and the National Health Campaigns (the Jornadas Populares de Salud), which innoculated the school-age population against infectious diseases. The primary vehicles for the success of these programs were the five major mass organizations that in 1986 were an integral part of Nicaraguan society: the Sandinista Defense Committees (CDS), the National Union of Farmers and Ranchers (UNAG), the Sandinista Workers' Federation (CST), the Rural Workers' Association (ATC), and the Luisa Amanda Espinosa Association of Nicaraguan Women (AMNLAE). These are the structures through which popular participation in the programs and activities that affected the day-to-day lives of the majority was sustained.

Accompanying these changes was an enormous increase in the beneficiaries of social services. The most dramatic illustration of this was the 406,056 people who became literate as a consequence of the 1980 campaign and the training multiplier model used in the literacy campaign to mobilize the 11,000 teachers, the 80,000 rural and urban literacy volunteers, and the 125,000 primary, secondary, and university students and adult volunteers who did the actual training.[7] Between 1981 and 1986 an estimated 140,000 adults participated in the Adult Education Program organized for workers and peasants as a follow-up to the basic literacy achieved through the campaign. The vehicle for providing such education has been the 18,000 or so informal educational centers (Colectivos de Educación Popular -- CEPs) that have been set up around the country. In these a new kind of teacher, maestros populares, offers instruction through a consolidated curriculum. As of 1986, 6,327 adults had completed the equivalency of the six years of formal education established for primary education. Overall school enrollments likewise showed a marked increase, from the 498,731 students in school in 1978 (the last full year of education before the Revolution) to 933,420 in 1986. There has been a similar increase in the number of teachers, from 12,075 employed in 1978 to the 24,142 teachers in formal education and the 15,976 maestros populares engaged in informal adult education -- a total of 40,118 teachers -- in 1985.[8]

Other indications of the priority given to education and health services for the general population are to be found in tables 2-1, 2-2, and 2-3. Generally speaking, 1983 is used as a cutoff point because this is the last year in which the new priorities of the revolutionary government can be measured without beginning to have to compensate for the effects of the war. Since that time an ever-larger percentage of the national budget has had to be reallocated to national defense. Table 2-1 reflects the increase in the educational budget from 1978 through 1983 in terms of total increase and as compared with the overall increase in governmental expenditures and growth in gross domestic product (GDP).

Although the measurements used for public health are not comparable, such indicators as number of medical appointments (consultas médicas), dental appointments (consultas odontológicas), and vaccinations (vacunaciones) in table 2-2 and use of hospital facilities in table 2-3 suggest a fundamental reorientation in the availability of health services. Missing are data comparing these patterns with pre-revolutionary health care patterns. For our purposes, it can simply be stated that the limited and fragmented character of public health facilities before the Revolution suggests the exclusion of the majority of the population.[9]

This shift in governmental services away from a privileged minority to a poor majority also entailed constant readjustment in internal organizational structures. This is because it proved to be extraordinarily difficult to arrive at the proper balance between central control and the kind of program autonomy that mass-oriented service delivery required. The record of this almost constant adjustment and readjustment of structural relationships can be traced through the numerous decree laws and reglamentos published in the Diario Oficial and in internal ministry documents -- in the constant creation of new public organizations, the continual shifting and relocation of programs, the designation and redesignation of new office titles, and unending readjustment in inter-institutional relationships.

Accompanying these changes in official forms was a much more complex set of interpersonal relations. People in the field and in substantive programs in the center had to fight a continuous battle for sufficient program autonomy to respond to their newly articulate mass clientele, against office heads and administrators with supervisory responsibilities. The latter were frequently well aware of how activities at the grass-roots level continued to outpace their capacity to provide orderly response to citizen demands in these areas or to develop new programs in accord with the policy directives developed by the new leadership; yet, they feared that open endorsement of such activities would make their oversight responsibilities all the more difficult. This was reflected as much in the constant reorganizations that had taken place in the Ministry of Education between 1979 and 1986 as it was in the difficulties encountered in the Health Ministry in developing an integrated health system from the beginning in a setting where there was virtually no prior program administration experience upon which to draw.

Table 2-1

Evolution of Educational Expenditures Relative to Gross National Product and Total Government Expenditures

	1978	1979	1980	1981	1982	1983
Educational expenditure*	363.9	430.6	732.4	1,121.1	1,228.4	1,640.0
Government expenditure*	3,286.9	2,958.6	6,363.8	8,411.7	11,108.7	14,311.5
GNP*	25,758	19,283	21,339	24,313	27,717	32,768
Govt.Exp./GNP**	12.76%	15.34%	29.82%	34.60%	40.08%	43.68%
Educ.Exp./ Govt.Exp.	11.07%	14.55%	11.51%	13.33%	11.06%	11.46%

Source: Financiamiento Educativo MED on the basis of data from MIPLAN and MIFIN; MED, La educación en cuatro años de revolución (Managua, July 19, 1983), p. 147.

Notes: These data include MED, CNES, and other ministerial education programs; 1983 numbers are preliminary.

* In millions of Córdobas

** As calculated by the author

Table 2-2
Health Services

	1980	1981	1982	1983	1984*	1985**
Medical consultations	3,013,824	3,092,595	3,853,874	4,140,008	3,982,714	4,466,587
per inhabitant	1.1	1.1	1.3	1.4	1.2	1.4
Dental Consultations	258,742	331,821	417,821	439,386	414,898	513,600
per inhabitant	0.09	0.11	0.14	0.14	0.13	0.16
Maternal-Infant examinations	71,576	622,864	1,194,583	1,636,243	1,683,478	1,818,180
prenatal exam	-	137,620	245,652	302,768	331,742	361,000
puerperal exam	-	6,635	25,235	43,045	42,278	52,800
fertility exam	-	23,528	80,725	122,400	139,789	151,820
cancer exam	-	31,063	92,429	154,495	188,195	198,640
breast exam	-	24,248	69,983	132,152	162,595	170,440
uterine/cervical exam	-	6,815	22,446	22,343	25,600	28,200
growth and development exam	-	176,072	313,958	382,768	385,082	435,000
prepartem exam	-	23,836	22,170	20,011	15,228	18,000
nutritional exam	-	128,436	287,828	438,417	410,938	417,600
U.R.O. exam	71,576	95,674	126,586	172,339	170,226	183,320
Vaccinations	1,790,343	2,544,396	3,859,174	3,495,431	4,051,395	5,603,362
BGC	81,228	139,327	210,832	195,827	219,443	305,460
measles	101,829	225,932	205,323	234,085	219,704	247,540
poliomyelitis	538,178	1,163,853	1,489,707	1,716,273	1,602,990	2,132,700
DPT	384,949	410,693	880,480	342,395	611,437	1,090,440
DT	156,411	155,229	245,210	191,735	253,491	235,440
TT	527,748	449,362	827,622	815,116	1,144,330	1,591,782
Health centers with beds						
patients discharged	7,848	9,593	13,326	14,355	16,649	30,664
patient-days	39,240	47,965	69,295	57,420	65,496	122,658
average stay (days)	5.0	5.0	5.2	4.0	3.0	4.0
occupancy rate (%)	45.7	46.1	58.9	45.0	49.0	65.0
No. of Beds	235	285	322	354	334	517
patients discharged per 100						
Inhabitants	0.3	0.3	0.4	0.5	0.5	0.9

Source: Secretaría de Planificación y Presupuesto, Plan Económico 1985 (Managua: MIPLAN, January 1985), p. 13.

* Preliminary
**Planned

Table 2-3
Hospital Services

	1980	1981	1982	1983	1984*	1985**
Medical Consultations	1,968,799	2,317,837	2,180,571	2,194,854	2,144,539	2,404,967
Consultations per Inhab.	0.7	0.8	0.7	0.7	0.7	0.7
Acute Hospitals						
Admissions	166,192	177,192	180,959	190,231	185,927	216,705
Patient-days	968,063	814,374	942,969	951,155	929,635	1,083,524
Average Stay (days)	5.8	4.5	5.2	5.0	5.0	5.0
Occupancy Rate (%)	72.0	57.0	70.8	72.0	68.0	72.0
Bed-days	1,344,660	1,428,975	1,330,060	1,398,315	1,367,110	1,504,895
No. of Beds	3,684	3,915	3,644	3,831	3,956	4,123
Admissions/100 Inhab.	6.0	6.2	6.1	6.2	5.8	6.6
Chronic Hospitals						
Admissions	3,778	3,792	3,279	2,833	2,378	2,145
Patient-days	266,727	299,947	196,740	201,143	159,177	152,293
Average Stay (days)	70.6	79.1	60.0	71.0	68.0	71.0
Ocupancy Rate (%)	90.0	101.0	77.0	76.0	86.0	76.0
Bed-days	296,745	297,110	255,506	259,880	182,764	200,385
No. of Beds	813	814	782	712	559	549
Admissions/100 Inhab.	0.20	0.20	0.10	0.10	0.10	0.06
Total Beds Available	4,497	4,729	4,426	4,543	4,515	4,672
Total Hospital Admissions	170,169	180,984	183,338	193,064	188,305	218,850

Source: Secretaría de Planificación y Presupuesto, Plan economico 1985, (Managua: MIPLAN,
January 1985), p.14.
* Preliminary
** Planned

In the search for a more adequate administrative structure through which to manage the public sector and to respond to mass demands, a great deal of consultation with the citizenry took place. The most thorough attempt along these lines comes again in the educational sector, in the national consultation -- the Consulta Nacional -- that took place throughout the country in January 1981. Involved in that process were 52,792 respondents and 33 organizations. Its objective was to gain information about citizen attitudes and expectations concerning education. From the wealth of data collected came a variety of suggestions regarding the organization of ministerial activities. The vehicle for accomplishing all this was the <u>Consejo Nacional Asesor de Educación</u>, created in November 1980. Each of the mass organizations was given representation in this body. Likewise, provision was made for representation on the Council for Higher Education (CNES), the Planning Ministry, the Education Ministry, and the universities.[10]

After a subsequent change in name and in council membership, the Consejo de Educación reached a major decision in May 1984. Education programs were to be reordered around five subsystems -- basic formal education (<u>educación básica</u>, at the primary and secondary levels), informal popular education (<u>educación popular básica</u>), technical education (<u>educación técnica</u>, involving specialization during the last three years of secondary education), higher education (<u>educación superior</u>), and training programs (<u>capacitación</u>).[11] The designation of these five basic areas produced, in turn, a new round of changes in the organization of the Education Ministry. The changes were finally settled in 1986 with the designation of two staff units -- the Dirección General de Administración (general administrative services) and the Dirección General de Planificación (planning and programming) -- plus three line units -- Direcciones General de Educación Básica (formal preschool, primary, and secondary education),[12] Educación Popular y de Adultos (informal adult education), and Educación Técnica (technical education).

Despite administrative and financial difficulties, there was an impressive increase in educational services at a nominal cost to the Nicaraguan government. This can be demonstrated by taking the raw data in table 2-1 and converting it into graphic representations (see figures 2-1 and 2-2). Figure 2-1 superimposes gross domestic product (GDP) on total government and educational expenses from 1978 -- the last full year of Somoza government expenditures -- through 1983 -- the last year in which the Sandinistas could allocate their economic resources fully to meet domestic needs. Since that time, increasingly larger percentages of the national budget have had to be reserved for fighting the war against the <u>contras</u>.[13] Figure 2-2 examines the relation between total budgeted governmental expenditures and education costs. If these two figures are compared with the last column in table 2-1 (percentage of government expenses devoted to education), they substantiate a marginal increase in education expenses compared with the size of the gross domestic product and the growth in governmental expenses. The key to explaining these developments lies in the human potential that has been released by the Revolution and the transfer of the commitment to participatory democracy into supports for expanded educational opportunities.

Figure 2-1
Education and Total Government as Share of GDP, 1978-1983

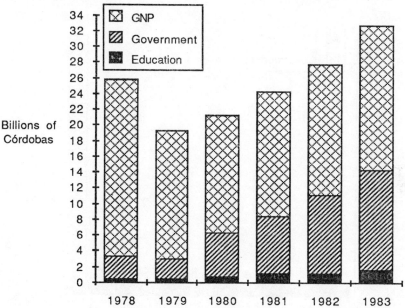

The Impact of Regionalization on Social Services Administration

Simultaneous with this continuing debate over how best to restructure the central offices of the Education Ministry was the development of another organizational dynamic: regionalization and decentralization. Again, although this pattern was a general one involving other organizations as well, the debate in education over how best to structure programs in the field can once again be used as an illustration of what was occurring in the state apparatus at large. These push/pull factors involved not only program autonomy versus control and coordination by administrative superiors, but also centralization versus decentralization pressures in center-periphery relations. In 1982 Nicaragua shifted from a subnational governmental system consisting of fifteen departments into a system of six regions and three special zones. Accordingly, each of the central ministries was expected to adjust to the new subnational arrangements, through the designation of regional delegates who would serve as representatives of the minister and at the same time would meet periodically with their regional counterparts in plannning commissions presided over by newly designated regional governmental officials. Coordination of ministerial activities in the region was, in turn, designated as the responsibility of the second-in-command in the regional government, the secretario ejecutivo.

Figure 2-2
Education as Share of Total Government Budget

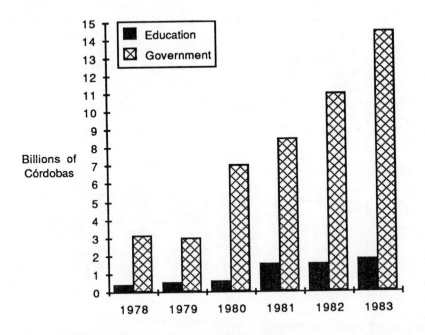

In the educational sector, experimentation with this new system began in 1983. Replacing the older system of <u>directores</u> <u>departamentales</u> and considerable separation between political and administrative jurisdictions, a new set of arrangements entered into effect in 1984. These changes paralleled a similar restructuring of the Sandinista Front (FSLN). This had the effect in education, and probably in other areas of state action as well, of minimizing the further development of parallel administrative and political organizations on a hierarchical basis, extending from center to periphery.

This particular solution developed by the Sandinista leadership to meet its own needs for flexibility and control stands in marked contrast to the problems presented by parallel organizational structures in state administration and in the Communist parties of the various East European states. The latter development -- in my opinion, after fieldwork in Romania, Poland, and Yugoslavia -- has proven to be one of the major sources of bureaucratization and decline in the effectiveness of social delivery systems in those countries. Although such practices received consideration in the single-party state under construction in Nicaragua in the early 1980s, by 1986 they had been abandoned as a consequence of the perceived need to establish more adequate communication between leaders in the FSLN and in state administration with their social bases, as represented by new mass organizations. The Sandinista leadership found that by fusing state and party roles through dual responsibilities, more coordination in governmental action could be achieved without creating the problem of excessive control and delay in action. As a consequence, each of the FSLN's territorial components in 1986 was matched by a governmental and administrative counterpart. These extend from base committees or units to zonal offices to regional offices to central organizational units. Seen in comparative perspective, what these patterns reveal is how Nicaraguan administrative practices from 1979 to 1986 fall neither into the public administration categories provided by the more pluralistic Western democratic systems -- models consciously rejected in the early stages of the Revolution -- nor into those developed under Soviet practice and replicated in varying degrees within the East European states.

Applied to the education sector, what these changes meant was increased articulation between state, party, and society. Education was thus not simply the acquisition of knowledge in a variety of subject matter areas but political education designed to enhance the individual's view of internal and external societal relations. The development of these patterns in Estelí is indicative of those occurring elsewhere. Given the limited amount of time I had available for field research, this was the region I selected for grass-roots work to offset the time spent in central government organizations in Managua. During 1983 a new regional structure was set up in Estelí for education -- one that has been replicated since in varying degrees throughout the rest of Nicaragua. Corresponding to the <u>delegado regional de educación</u> are zonal delegates in each of the thirteen zones into which the region was divided; under each, in turn, a small technical team was appointed, corresponding to the office heads in the regional office, which in turn matched the functional lines into which the central ministry was divided.

During 1984, these structural changes were accompanied by increased financial autonomy, as funds for regional programs and activities were transferred in block to regional offices. Whereas previously central financial control provided regional offices with very little flexibility to respond to regional requests and needs, under the new decentralized financial arrangements the regional delegate was given increased discretionary control over allocations for educational activities in the region under his jurisdiction. The next stage in the development of greater regional autonomy over educational activities took place during 1985, when increased control over programs and decision-making autonomy was added to the increased financial discretion given the previous year. The consequence of these innovations was a new set of administrative practices responding to Nicaraguan conditions, independent of the predetermined ideological categories so often applied to the regime in the external debate over the course of the Nicaraguan revolution.

Paralleling these developments in education were similar developments in social infrastructure policy for the Estelí region as a whole.[14] Funding and programmatic activities in Estelí had to respond to increased governmental and political pressures for coordinated regional action through predetermined priorities. This was especially important there, since this was a region that fell within the war zone, an area where the rural population was forced to live with the continual reality of incursions by the contras from across the border and deal with a war directed primarily at terrorizing and demoralizing civilians. Increasingly, as program administrators moved into 1984 and 1985, they found their operations guided by three general regional demarcations: program implementation in war zones, in the Pacific zone, where the largest percentage of the population and productive forces in the economy were concentrated, and in the Atlantic region.

The primary vehicles for reorienting ministerial programs away from functional areas (administración formalizada) and toward integrated regional policy were the new regional Casas de Gobierno, governmental organs that replicate at the regional level an analogous central government counterpart. In these, the primary function of the secretario ejecutivo was to oversee programming by institutions. Besides periodic meetings between the secretario ejecutivo and the regional delegates representing the various governmental institutions operating within the region, sectoral programming took place through regional planning commissions and accords (acuerdos) arrived at during their work sessions or as a consequence of individual meetings between the secretario ejecutivo and individual delegates. For example, in Estelí, operations in education and health were determined not only by priorities set by the regional government for integrated action on a territorial basis (as in the case of the fourteen relocated villages -- asentamientos -- in the northwest sector of Region I). A representative administrative body -- the Comisión Social -- also had a voice in determining priorities. This was a collegial organization that was set up to promote interinstitutional coordination of social infrastructure activities. Embracing the social sector would be ministerial delegates for education, health, social security and welfare, housing, and labor.

Policy dynamics, both in setting program priorities and in implementing specific sets of activities, however, led as much to cooperation as they have to conflict. Central government planning goals converted into ministerial allocations and sectoral plans and then transferred into the regional context would stand little chance of implementation without the cooperation of grass-roots components of the mass organizations. Whether one looks at policy implementation in the social services sector in the aggregate or the day-to-day administration of a primary school in an isolated village, it was apparent that what made these programs work were the grass-roots organizations that have developed outside the state. It is these organizations that had the capacity to mobilize the volunteer work on which social programs relied so heavily. Although rhetoric may at times have reflected the desire for centralized, coordinated action and a hierarchy of command, mobilization of the popular sectors of society -- especially in the countryside -- was creating a new, younger generation of self-taught, activist administrators who were learning to develop a pragmatic, flexible response to the groups closest at hand.[15]

An important part of this dynamic stemmed not from actions initiated by regional and local-level bureaucrats, but from the wider social milieu that had surrounded what has been going on in Nicarguan society since 1978. The insurrection that brought an end to the Somoza dictatorship was based on the organized, militant participation of countless numbers of individuals. The success of the literacy campaign depended on the same effective mass mobilization of the citizenry.The continued work done in mass innoculation of children to control infectious diseases achieved its successes by tapping into the same pool of mass organizations. The contra war was affecting the rural population in the areas of greatest activity but was simultaneously facilitating and consolidating the building of a new social infrastructure based on volunteer work and a sense of community that was absent in the past.

The policy integration I found in Las Segovias in education and health activities at the service delivery level was likewise being achieved by tapping into the new strength that was emerging from the grass roots, despite the absence of financial and skilled human resources. Seen from below, from isolated villages in the countryside, in the areas of greatest anxiety and conflict there was no doubt that real hardship existed and that these programs scarcely were responding to the norms articulated in more developed, urbanized settings. But where so much remains to be done and yet where so much has been accomplished in such a short period of time, one cannot come away from examining social policy without being impressed by the human resource potential that has been tapped into by giving people at large -- peasants and workers -- confidence that this is their own new society in the making and organizational vehicles through which to participate on a sustained basis.

Bureaucratic vs. Participatory Norms in Adult Education

If this is the view that one is likely to develop by tapping into the provision of social services from the bottom up, yet another view of the new state apparatus in the making can be obtained by looking at a specific program area. It is here that the greatest challenges were found in 1986 -- in giving to the Revolution a coherent organizational structure for sustained mass action without falling into the pitfall of new bureaucratization and rigidification of programs and activities, as has occurred so frequently in East Europe. The case in point is that of adult education, which belongs to the phase in mass education known as post-alfabetización, where basic literacy has been established and the adult seeks to put that new knowledge to greater use. The policy problem that emerged here was how best to institutionalize new forms of mass adult education designed to raise individual performance and productivity in such a way as to ensure continuation in these endeavors over time without destroying in the process the dynamism and involvement created by and for large numbers of people. The tension was between formalization of new educational processes on the one hand, in accord with pre-existing functional and programmatic categories set up for education policy, and the creative responses that were so much a part of the informal educational models developed over the first six years of the Revolution.

Once again, before examining the particulars of basic adult education (educación popular básica), it is helpful to see the larger picture in terms of the funds allocated to education. These particulars are to be found in table 2-4 and figure 2-3, the latter of which is a graphic representation of the raw data contained in the former table. The major resources have continued to go into formalized basic education, and it is here in that general directorate known as Basic Formal Education that the bulk of the activities and the personnel in the Education Ministry was concentrated. The other major area where fiscal resources were concentrated was higher education, but this policy area fell outside the ministry and was under the jurisdiction of the Consejo Nacional de la Educación Superior (CNES), where the commitment to dismantling the older, elitist basis of education and its reshaping in accord with the needs of a socialist society in the making was the greatest. (In consulting these figures, it should be noted that there is a problem with them, since they are based on residual data taken from table 2-1, which combines CNES funding with that set aside for professional training programs in individual government organizations, in the category known as capacitación.)

The organizational unit for informal adult education in 1986 was the Dirección de Educación Popular Básica, one of three units in the ministry's Adult Education Agency (a general directorate). As a consequence of the National Literacy Campaign of 1980, the era of greatest creativity and innovation in informal adult education was 1981 through 1983, during which the enthusiasm and the informal organizational structures developed in the literacy campaign were transferred to follow-up programs designed to move beyond basic literacy. It should be noted here that the crucial difference between pre-1981 activities, 1981-1983, and 1984-1986, is not a matter of funding (despite the percentage increase registered for 1981-1983 in table 2-4 and figure 2-3), but the degree of program autonomy and mass commitment and enthusiasm for these endeavors registered in 1981-1983. Initially, to ensure sufficient autonomy for those designing an effective informal adult educational model and to sustain the work done the previous year in the literacy campaign, this program was placed in the hands of a vice-minister for adult education (VIMEDA) and the organizational unit charged with responsibilities for these activities was given a mandate to organize its activities at the national, regional, and zonal level.[16]

Table 2-4
Expenditures on Education Programs, 1980-1983

Description	1980	1981	1982	1983	1980	1981	1982	1983*
					%	%	%	%
Central activities	82,560	37,475	67,043	47,146	12.85	4.39	7.52	4.11
Common activities	116,726	154,067	128,431	147,565	18.16	18.09	14.41	12.87
Preschool education	3,688	12,340	13,773	20,704	0.57	1.45	1.55	1.81
Primary education	259,839	360,195	383,501	526,181	40.43	42.28	43.02	45.88
Secondary education	110,509	141,768	150,596	176,335	17.20	16.64	16.89	15.37
Teacher education	10,583	15,899	15,236	24,822	1.65	1.87	1.71	2.16
Technical education:								
Commercial	9,311	11,771	12,279	13,689	1.45	1.38	1.38	1.19
Industrial	14,153	19,661	16,232	28,644	2.20	2.31	1.82	2.50
Agricultural	6,338	9,525	8,045	23,798	0.99	1.12	0.90	2.07
PRODECO	3,679	3,314	3,494	5,909	0.57	0.39	0.39	0.52
Adult education	25,251	78,570	85,544	109,800	3.93	9.22	9.60	9.57
Special education	n.a.	6,548	7,234	9,048	n.a.	0.77	0.81	0.79
Misc. expenditures	n.a.	756	n.a.	13,271	n.a.	0.09	n.a.	1.16
Total	642,637	851,888	891,408	1,146,912	100.00	100.00	100.00	100.00

Source: MED, La educación en cuatro años de revolución (MED: Managua, July 19, 1983), p. 146.
* 1983: Budgeted expenditures

In 1984 the program was reorganized: its autonomy was curtailed, and it was incorporated as a regular program unit into the Education Ministry. In 1984 work in this area reached a low point. It faced declining enrollments, a loss of dynamism and a sense of mission among those involved in implementing the program, and awareness that such work was being directly affected by a new national trajectory triggered by the recognition that the country would have to face a long-term, low-intensity war that was being felt most by the very elements of the population targeted for postliteracy adult education.

In 1985 work in this area recovered much of the autonomy it had enjoyed originally. The education minister reorganized adult education programs and consolidated them into a single organizational unit with the status of a general directorate. After recruiting a bright youth who had headed up the literacy campaign in the Managua district (Region III), experimentation began by developing a more appropriate dynamic model for postliteracy adult education. It consisted of consolidating grass-roots support through work with mass organizations, imbuing public employees working for the unit with the concept of collective work (through mobile teams moving around the country according to program priorities), and continuing reinforcement of supports for this program at the community level -- for the <u>maestros populares</u> working through Colectivos de Educación Popular (CEPs).

Figure 2-3
Priority Programs in Education

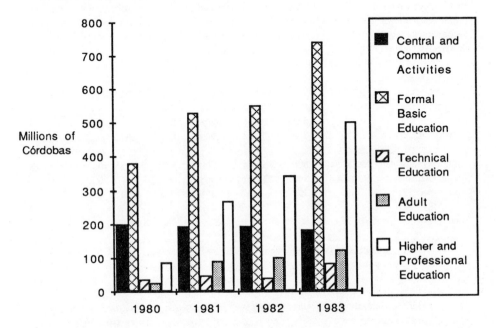

In the interim, what had developed within this office was a division for Educación Popular Básica (EPB), which had become a formalized, segmented ministerial unit subdivided into separate departments, one for curriculum and methods and the other for training and supervision. In turn, the curriculum division had been subdivided further into two sections, one for apprenticeship and instruction and the other for the preparation of teaching materials. The new administrative unit, after reorganization, sought to return to the ideas articulated originally in popular-based, informal postliteracy adult education and to dismantle the rigidities that had developed as a consequence of the new bureaucratization that had ensued. Working through two teams -- one focused on EPB activities and the other on work units established previously for adult education, the CEDAs -- the new director was reorienting the work of this unit away from stable office tasks toward ongoing program activities and was taking his staff to the field on a regular basis. At the same time, he was incorporating organizational changes to ensure that his unit would operate in accord with the country's new regional structure and with the policy established throughout the government that administrative units distinguish between programs directed at the war zone, the Pacific region, and the Atlantic coast.

The outcome of this last reorganization was to recapture in 1986 the dynamism present in these programs at the outset. Its significance, however, is much wider; for it confirms once again that when programs and endeavors by the revolutionary government departed from their new mass organization bases, especially from the wishes and the needs of the peasantry, they ran the risk not only of new rigidification and bureau-cratization but also of breaking with what was their greatest strength: their mass base (that is, their bases populares). A microcosm again of a much larger set of developments, what this particular case supports and illustrates is that the great strength of the Sandinista Revolution during its first seven years lay in its mobilization of the masses, in popular participation through mass organizations that were pursuing their own dynamic, and in continual awareness that what was under way was an on-going, fundamental revolution from below that was intensely national and that was seeking its own definition and its own trajectory, regardless of what others might wish to impose from without.

Comparison and Conclusion

At the outset I suggested that one way of evaluating the evolution of Nicaragua's state apparatus in light of the country's revolutionary experiences would be to interject a comparative dimension. To do so successfully and to heighten the saliency of that which is unique in this case, however, one must insist that analysts of the Nicaraguan scene focus their attention on action research -- that which has actually occurred independently of their value preferences -- and not rely on rhetoric. In the European context it was suggested that three sets of national experience -- Portugal's, Romania's, and Yugoslavia's -- might offer a basis for comparison and contrast. This is because they, in economic terms and in the dependency relations maintained by their own ruling elites, have closer ties with Third World realities than established scholarship is willing to accord them because of the rigidities with which we are currently saddled. There is no reason to enter into an ideological debate at this moment in the terms set either by the political and economic structures dominant in Western Europe and North America or those belonging to the Soviet Union and East Euope, because it will deflect us from the comparisons and the contrasts I wish to underscore.

The issues present in Nicaragua in 1986 concerned mass participa-tion (the incorporation of a poor majority into national life for the first time) and a national revolution seeking its own self-definition and the determination of its own priorities (the blending of Marxist political thought with the social gospel present in Liberation Theology), not the categories of ideological thought we have been working with outside Latin America for the last half century -- as much on the left as on the right.[17]

In short, if revolution in the twentieth century is defined in terms of a sudden, radical break with the past and the active incorporation of the masses into national life, and if we will return to the roots of democratic theory that lie in popular participation and not in formalistic elections that have so often lost their meaning, then there is an ample literature on all four countries -- Nicaragua, Romania, Yugoslavia, and Portugal -- to establish a new perspective on the importance of linking concepts of popular participation with national revolutions designed to provide fundamental breaks with the past.[18]   Two of these revolutions,-- in Nicaragua and Yugoslavia -- were linked in the beginning to concepts of mass mobilization and to the redefinition of social democracy in participatory terms rather than plebiscitary norms.   The Yugoslav experience is relevant to the Nicaraguan case in that the creativity and the innovation characteristic of the Yugoslav system during the 1950s and the 1960s stagnated in the 1970s as a consequence of declining economic autarky, bureaucratization, and the rigidification of accommodations made with various regional groupings, to such an extent that they rendered self-management and popular participation in the 1980s largely meaning-less.

In 1986, the administrative problems of consolidating a revolution in Nicaragua were just beginning. The task that lay ahead was the elabora-tion of programmatic solutions out of what was a unique set of experien-ces, in the context of a war economy that is making such experimentation more and more difficult. Whether or not a new administrative model will emerge remains to be seen. What was in the making between 1979 and 1986 was a new state apparatus and, consequently, the initiation for the first time in Latin American experience of an administrative system that was drawing its strength from national experiments rather than from models taken from abroad, be they capitalist or socialist. The tragedy is that such consolidation may never take place as the pressures of external aggression increase and internal cohesion decreases.

The more likely outcome, thus, is the indefinite continuation of the current situation. The administrative implication of such a situation is perpetuation of a fragmented, compartmentalized bureaucracy. Public bureaucracy, thus, will have to respond, on the one hand, to mass organizations in those instances in which the regime lacks the capacity to control its popular bases. On the other, there are pressures from above by those who would replace existing structures with institutions more akin to the formulas adopted for control and coordination in East Europe and Cuba. A third set of pressures comes from technical personnel (técnicos) identified with market-oriented public sector organizations that advocate state capitalism, decision-making structures akin to those of private enterprise, and problem-solving approaches linked to micro-decisions drawn from generic management models. If these conditions prevail, Nicaraguan public administration will remain largely reactive -- reflecting in the administrative arena the pressures and the tensions present in the system at large -- without the capacity to seize the initiative in consolidating a new social, political, and economic order.

Endnotes to Chapter 2.

1. The concept "revolutionary breakthrough" is taken from the work of Kenneth Jowitt, <u>Revolutionary Breakthroughs and National Development: The Case of Romania, 1944-1965</u> (Berkeley and Los Angeles: University of California Press, 1971). The most cogent analysis I have seen of the problem presented by rebureaucratization for state socialism is in an article by Maria Ciechocinska, "Problems in the Development of Social Infrastructure in Poland," in Lawrence S. Graham and Maria K. Ciechocinska, eds., <u>The Polish Dilemma: Views from Within</u> (Boulder, CO: Westview Press, forthcoming).

2. This problem has been especially acute in the case of Romania, where, once one transcends the rhetoric of Marxist-Leninism, one encounters in the bureaucratic structures re-created under Nicolae Ceausescu parallels with those present in the prewar dictatorship of Carol II (1930-1940). For further discussion of this point, see Lawrence S. Graham, <u>Romania: A Developing Socialist State</u> (Boulder, CO: Westview Press, 1982); and Kenneth Jowitt, ed., <u>Social Change in Romania, 1860-1940: A Debate on Development in a European Nation</u>, Research Series No. 36 (Berkeley: Institute of International Studies, University of California, 1978).

3. Francisco López, director general of the Nicaraguan Institute for Social and Economic Research (INIES), from Nicaraguan government source materials. It should be noted that Nicaragua follows standard Latin American practice in including as public employees individuals such as school teachers and health care personnel, who elsewhere are usually reported separately for statistical purposes.

4. Ibid. In this regard the Nicaraguan Revolution parallels administrative changes that accompanied the Portuguese revolution. See Lawrence S. Graham, "Changes and Continuity in Portuguese Public Administration: The Consequences of the 1974 Revolution," Technical Papers, no. 53 (Austin: Institute of Latin American Studies, University of Texas, 1986).

5. See Consejo Nacional de la Educación Superior (CNES), La educación superior en 5 años de revolución, 1979-1980 (Managua: CNES, 1984); Instituto Nicaragüense de Seguridad Social (INSS), "Informe del Instituto Nicaragüense de Seguridad Social al Consejo de Estado sobre la seguridad social y el Sistema Nacional Unico de Salud del 23 de julio de 1979 al 30 de abril de 1980" (Managua: INSS, 1980); "Intervención del ministro de educación en Nicaragua, Doctor Carlos Tunnermann Berheim, en el debate de política general" (Belgrade: 21st Meeting of the Genaral Conference of UNESCO, 1980); Ministerio de Educación (MED), Cinco años de educación en la revolución, 1979-1984 (Managua: MED, 1984); Ministerio de Salud (MINSA), "Salud: políticas, logros y limitaciones" (Managua: MINSA, 1980, mimeographed).

6. Gary Ruchwarger, People in Power: Forging a Grassroots Democracy in Nicaragua (Hadley, MA: Bergin and Garvey, forthcoming).

7. Ibid., p. 161; "Intervención del ministro de educación," p. 6; Valerie Miller, Between Struggle and Hope: The Nicaraguan Literacy Crusade (Boulder, CO: Westview Press, 1985); Rosa María Torres, "De alfabetizando a maestro popular: la post-alfabetización en Nicaragua," Cuadernos de Pensamiento Propio, Serie Ensayos, no. 4 (Managua: CRIES and INIES, 1983).

8. Juan Bautista Arrién, "Algunos logros en educación" (Managua: Dirección General de Planificación, Ministerio de Educación, 1986, mimeographed). The data he draws on in this report give a total for teachers only until 1985, while that for students extends through 1986.

9. See "Salud: políticas," p. 2, as well as Chandler Stolp's chapter in this book.

10. Miguel De Castilla Urbina, "Democracia y educación en Nicaragua" (Rio de Janeiro: Asociación Latinoamericana de Sociología, XVI Congreso Latinoamericano de Sociología, March 2-7, 1986, typescript); and Ministerio de Educación, "Consulta nacional para obtener criterios que ayudan a definir los fines y objetivos de la educación nicaragüense: informe preliminar," Documento 1 (Managua: MED, 1981).

11. De Castilla, "Democracia," pp. 45-46.

12. Educación Básica is an abbreviated designation for Dirección General de Educación General Básica, Media y Especial.

13. E. V. K. FitzGerald, "Políticas económicas de 1985 y sus perspectivas para 1986" (Managua: ANICS-INIES, Casa de CONAPRO, n.d., typescript).

14. "Social infrastructure" is a technical term used in planning to refer to all the public sector organizations involved in the determination of social policy and the delivery of social services.

15. For a general discussion of these problems and dynamics, see Ruchwarger, People in Power, pp. 213, 215-216.

16. Rosa María Torres, "Los CEP: educación popular y democracia participativa en Nicaragua," Cuadernos de Pensamiento Propio, Serie Ensayos, no. 12 (Managua: CRIES, 1985), p. 4; also see idem, "De alfabetizando," p. 13.

17. See Donald C. Hodges, Intellectual Foundations of the Nicaraguan Revolution (Austin: University of Texas Press, 1986).

18. For anyone wishing to pursue such comparison further, the relevant literature is Nancy Gina Bermeo, The Revolution within the Revolution: Workers' Control in Rural Portugal (Princeton, NJ: Princeton University Press, 1986); Eugen Pusic, ed., Participation and Self-Management, vols. 1-6 (Zagreb: Institute for Social Research, 1972); Lawrence S. Graham, "Yugoslav and Brazilian Experience with Federalism," Technical Papers Series, no. 41 (Austin: Institute of Latin American Studies, University of Texas, 1984); Michael Shafir, Romania: Politics, Economics and Society (Boulder, CO: Lynne Rienner Publishers, 1985); and Ruchwarger, People in Power.

Chapter 3

A Comparative Evaluation of Regionalization and Decentralization

by

Patricia A. Wilson

With the assistance of

Rolf Pendall

Introduction

Most political parties in Latin America -- from left to right-- agree on the need for territorially decentralizing the state apparatus. However, few have done much to achieve this mother-and-apple pie goal after taking the reins of power. Economic crisis, war, the need to consolidate political power, and the general reluctance of a government to loosen its grasp on central authority usually relegate decentralization efforts to a back burner. The current government of Nicaragua, which assumed power in 1979, has faced these same obstacles. Nevertheless, in 1982 it began a program of decentralization based on regionalization of the public sector. Shortly after beginning the regionalization effort, the country was thrust into war, which grew to occupy nearly 40 percent of the nation's budget.[1] While the exigencies of war have modified the regionalization effort, it has nonetheless gone forward.

The following analysis assesses the achievements and shortcomings of Nicaragua's regionalization effort, not only with respect to its expressed goals, but also in relationship to regionalization efforts in other Latin American countries. The political origins of decentralization, goals, methods, administrative structure, regional planning, project prioritization, project finance, sectoral coordination, the budget system, the link between budgeting and planning, the role of municipalities, and popular participation are discussed. The conclusions point out the major innovations in the Nicaraguan regionalization process compared to other Latin American countries and the major bottlenecks to be addressed in realizing the internal objectives of decentralization in Nicaragua.

The research for this project, carried out in the summer of 1986, builds on previous scholarly analyses of the regionalization process[2] and on internal government evaluations. Field interviews were conducted with high-ranking technical personnel in the presidency, central government ministries, regional governments, zonal offices, and municipal government.

Political Origins and Goals of Regionalization

In many Latin American countries, decentralization measures have been the result of broad-based regional fronts (frentes) making demands on the central government for increased resources and control (for example, the regional movements in Peru that resulted in mandatory regionalization being incorporated into the 1979 constitution).[3] In other cases decentralization measures have been initiated by the central government (for example, in Chile under Pinochet,[4] and in Peru under the military government of Morales Bermúdez).[5] This was the case in Nicaragua, where there was no regional movement demanding decentralization, except in the isolated, sparsely populated region of the Atlantic coast. Rather, regionalization was begun and backed by the central government leadership.

The government created nine regional "governments" or authorities whose principal purpose was twofold: (1) to increase the efficiency of the rapidly enlarged state apparatus; and (2) to consolidate the state apparatus politically and administratively at the local, that is to say, municipal, level. This latter goal makes Nicaragua's regionalization effort quite unusual. Most such efforts in Latin America have been aimed at creating large territorial administrative units easily controlled by the central government. In Nicaragua, in contrast, one of the two major goals of regionalization was to strengthen the municipalities, both administratively and politically.

The regionalization effort in Nicaragua is also unusual in that the government intends for the regional authorities to be more than the spatially decentralized presence of the central government. Rather, it wants eventually to decentralize resources, functions, and decision-making power to the regional level in a series of three stages: (1) voluntary coordination of the central government apparatus at the regional level; (2) a transition stage in which the regional offices of central government ministries would report to both the central ministries and the regional government; and (3) a complete transfer of the regional offices of the ministries to the jurisdiction of the regional governments, along with increased resources and power of decision. Different ministries have decentralized at different rates so that the overall regionalization process now reflects aspects of both stages 1 and 2.

Another goal of the regionalization effort is to address major regional inequalities in wealth and income by encouraging regionally based development planning and greater attention to the regional allocation of public resources in order to better realize the productive potential of each region.[6]

Determining Regional Boundaries and Capitals

The method of delimiting the new regions in Nicaragua combined both technical and political criteria. Unlike in Pinochet's Chile, existing political boundaries of departments and municipalities were respected. Given those boundaries, the central government applied technical criteria to define regions on the basis of homogeneity of the economic base, primarily, but also on the basis of geography and culture. A process of open meetings (<u>cabildos abiertos</u>) allowed municipalities located on regional boundaries the option of changing regions (which was done in at least one case).[7]

This combination of technical decisions and popular participation allowed the regionalization plan to be implemented with a minimum of controversy. In Peru, in contrast, the extreme politicization of the boundary-defining process subsumed the more important decentralization issues of control and resource allocation. The volatile issues of regionalism and territorial infighting caused the whole constitutionally mandated regionalization process in Peru to come to a standstill under the Belaúnde government.

The Nicaraguan government chose regional capitals on the pragmatic basis of least-cost location. It determined which city in each region had the greatest existing capacity to receive the regional government in terms of office space, housing, services, and communication. Given the desire to institute the regional governments quickly, the federal government rejected the longer-term strategy of locating capitals to promote development in an underdeveloped or undeveloped area.

Basic Administrative Structure and Functions

As in almost all Latin American countries, the regional authorities in Nicaragua are not created to be "governments" in the federal sense of the word, in other words, locally elected representation with broad powers to tax and spend. The regional government heads are named by the president. Unlike most Latin American regional authority heads, however, the Nicaraguan regional government head, or regional delegate (<u>delegado regional</u>, sometimes called <u>ministro delegado</u>), has a dual role. Not only is the <u>delegado</u> the head of the government administrative apparatus in the region, he or she is also the head of the regional political party structure. In most Latin American countries the directorship of a regional development authority is just one of many political appointments passed out as political favors at the regional level after a party assumes power, which reflects the modest status of the regional officials themselves. In Nicaragua, the political party head becomes the regional government head, which reflects the importance given to this body. The <u>ministro delegado</u> has had this dual administrative-political role only since

1985, when the government decided to strengthen the position's ability to coordinate the regional ministerial offices.

The principal functions of regional government in Nicaragua also differ markedly from those of most Latin American regional authorities. The typical regional authority is little more than a public works agency of the central government -- with pork barrel implications and functional overlapping with the ministries and municipalities.[8] The regional governments of Nicaragua do not execute public works at all. Their two main functions are (1) to support and assist municipalities in planning and executing investments; and (2) to coordinate the sectoral ministries at the regional level. The first function is rarely given more than lip service in regional authorities elsewhere in Latin America; the second -- although generally promoted -- is rarely achieved.

The administrative structure of the regional governments in Nicaragua reflects their two main functions (see figure 3-1). The two substantive offices of the regional governments are the Regional Office of Municipal Affairs (Secretaría Regional de Asuntos Municipales -- SRAMU), which provides support to the municipalities, and the Technical Office (Secretaría Técnica), which provides staff support to the Planning Council for coordinating the regional offices of the ministries. The Planning Council (Consejo de Planificación), which is presided over by the <u>ministro delegado</u>, combines the regional representatives of each of the sectoral ministries and other central institutions plus representatives of popular groups.

Figure 3-1
Administrative Structure of Regional Government

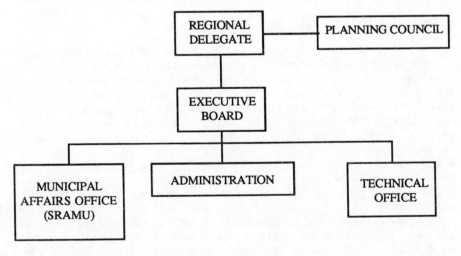

Sectoral Coordination and Decentralization

Coordination of the sectoral ministries -- for example, the Ministries of Agriculture, Industry, Transportation, and Energy -- at a spatial level is usually the Achilles' heel of a regional or departmental authority in Latin America. Even when regional offices of sectoral ministries exist, their directors are usually much more identified with, and inclined to answer to, the central office of the ministry rather than the regional authority. This loyalty is not only due to the location of individual career ladders in the ministry, but also to the central ministry's ultimate sectoral budget control.[9]

Because of this control, and despite structural efforts to strengthen the authority of the regional delegate in 1985,[10] ministerial decentralization to the regional level in Nicaragua has been voluntaristic. It depended on the motivation of individual ministry leadership at the center and the willingness of regional ministerial delegates to cooperate. Thus the degree of sectoral coordination achieved varied by sector and by region. One of the most successful regions, Estelí (see Map 1), had actually achieved an active working relationship with key ministries not only in coordinating ministerially initiated activities, but also in proposing and guiding activities executed by ministries at the regional level. In the recent regional planning literature from Latin America, this ability to influence actions through an ongoing dialogue with the various actors, rather than through a formal command structure, is called "planificación concertada."[11] A successful, albeit voluntaristic, planificación concertada puts Estelí well into phase 2 of the regionalization process. The Estelí region struck a delicate balance between the regional and ministerial authority structures. The normative and budget authority comes from the central ministries, whereas the operational authority comes largely from the regional level.

The planificación concertada is realized primarily through the Planning Council, a large advisory body headed by the regional representatives of the various ministries and the major grass-roots organizations. The real coordinating work takes place in the commissions into which the Planning Council was divided. For example, in Estelí, a basically agricultural region, the most important commission was the one on agriculture (Comisión Agropecuaria). It was composed of the regional delegate plus the regional representatives of the Ministry of Agricultural Development and Agrarian Reform (MIDINRA), the Ministry of Internal Trade (MICOIN), which oversaw the provision of basic goods, the Central Bank, and the National Union of Farmers and Ranchers (UNAG). This commission, like the other commissions of the Planning Council, is supported by a staff analyst from the Technical Office. In monthly meetings, the commission develops the technical plan for agriculture in terms of production goals and the coordination of inputs, financing, marketing, and technical support. The technical analyst also monitors plan implementation. Support committees (comités de apoyo), each dealing with a major commodity -- coffee, tobacco, cattle -- have met during critical times, such as at the harvest, and a support committee on rural credit met to evaluate credit applications.

The Basic Supplies Commission (Comisión de Abastecimientos) involved the regional delegate, the regional representative of MICOIN, and the representatives of the grass-roots organizations. These last representatives participated not in the planning of the basic supplies program, but in its execution.

The Social Commission, which should coordinate the regional activities of the Ministries of Health and Education and the Institute of Social Security and Welfare (INSSBI), did not operate as such in Estelí. Instead, the regional delegate and the analyst from the Technical Office work independently with three grass-roots groups: the Popular Health Councils (Consejos Populares de Salud), the Regional Troop Support Commission, and the local Education Councils.

Similarly, the Commission on Infrastructure and Urban Services no longer existed. The municipalities attended to its tasks at the local level, with the technical support of SRAMU.

The regional government of Estelí set up a new coordinating commission on small industry in 1985 to reflect the central government's shifting priority away from social projects and toward productive projects. This commission involved the regional delegate, the representative of the Ministry of Industry, and the MICOIN representative and was assisted by an analyst from the Technical Office. It was divided into support committees for leather, textiles, food production and wood processing, which reflectd the region's potential for small industry development.

Although some may criticize the commission structure at the regional level as being simply glorified sectoral planning devoid of territorial coordination, that criticism is quickly dispelled by looking at the very innovative subregional structure for coordinating ministerial actions: the zones. At the initiative of each region and ministry, regions have been divided into zones consisting of one to three municipalities each. In Estelí, for example, there were ten zones, each one with ministerial representatives.

The zones paralleled the regions in the way they structured intersectoral cooperation: the zonal council was divided into two working commissions through which all intersectoral interaction was channeled: the Production Commission and the Basic Supplies Commission. In Estelí the participating ministries granted substantial operating autonomy to their zonal offices in order to coordinate better with each other and to respond more efficiently to local circumstances.[12]

The principal bottleneck to sectoral coordination at the regional (and zonal) level is the voluntary nature of ministerial decentralization. Some central government institutions simply do not want to relinquish control to their regional offices. The Ministry of Labor (MINTRAB), the

Institute of Water and Wastewater Systems (INAA), and the Energy Institute (INE), for example, had very weak regional offices and no zonal offices.[13] The Ministry of Housing and Human Settlements (MINVAH) had created zones that did not correspond to those of the other ministries.[14] Given the voluntary nature of decentralization, however, it was surprising to find the willingness of some ministries to cooperate -- especially the Ministries of Health (MINSA), Agricultural Development (MIDINRA), and Education (MED).

Regional Planning

Economic planning has been a major function of the regional governments. They coordinated the production agreements between the central government and local producers, along with related programs of supplies, services, and logistics. Whereas in most Latin American countries, planning implies either the strategic allocation of scarce public resources or the preparation of voluminous indicative plans at global, sectoral, and spatial levels, it has taken on a new and special significance in Nicaragua: it means, for those portions of the economy controlled by the state, significant substitution of local, regional, and national collective decisions through the state apparatus for individual private market decisions about production, distribution, and prices. The underlying belief is that in Nicaragua the private market has been a poor allocator of goods -- socially, sectorally, and spatially -- and that collectively planned decisions about the allocation of resources could achieve a much more productive and equitable allocation. Since the state nationalized Somoza's holdings and began to turn underutilized agricultural lands over to peasant cooperatives, it has gained control of a large portion of the economy (between one-third and two-thirds of gross domestic product, depending upon the definition of "state" control).

The national -- and regional -- planning process, then, was highly important in making the economy function. The central government's Office of Planning and Budget (Secretaría de Planificación y Presupuesto --SPP) drafted a preliminary annual national production plan using global, sectoral, and territorial production objectives set by the central political leadership. It then distributed the draft plan to the sectoral ministries and the regional governments, which in turn disaggregated the objectives and channeled them down to particular productive enterprises. These productive units, after reviewing the objectives and their own production capacity, agreed to specific production quotas (metas). These quotas were then regrouped at the zonal and regional levels. The SPP prepared the final plan for approval by the political leadership. After the plan became law, the office monitored its implementation.[15]

Nicaragua's regional governments have had remarkable success in integrating a standard planning methodology, compared to similar efforts in other Latin American countries. This has been accomplished by decentralizing the staff of the SPP to the regional level (specifically the regional Technical Offices) from the very inception of the regional governments. In May 1986, the SPP entered the third and final phase of decentralization by actually relinquishing its regional staff members to the regional governments. Although these planners still look to the SPP for methodological guidance, they are employees of the regional governments. This smoothly-integrated situation contrasts sharply with the Departmental Development Corporations (CORDEs) in Peru, for example. Because of the bureaucratization and formalization of the central planning methodology developed by Peru's National Planning Institute (INP), the CORDEs either developed their own regional planning methodologies or avoided planning altogether. Even when INP planners were formally incorporated into the CORDEs, they were generally unable to integrate themselves functionally.[16]

A second type of planning by the regional governments -- the allocation of investment funds -- is much more typical of regional authorities in one sense. The only investment funds that the regional governments actually controlled, however, were for municipal-level projects to be executed by the municipalities. Thus, a major role of the regional governments -- through the SRAMUs -- was to strengthen the municipal governments by assisting them in generating and prioritizing project requests and providing technical personnel to carry out -- or assist with -- the feasibility studies for the proposed projects.

In some regions this municipal support was provided through zonal offices. For example, in Matagalpa (Region VI), the SRAMU is divided into five zonal offices, each with a SRAMU staff person. In contrast to the ministerial zonal offices, the SRAMU zonal offices were designed to work with and support the municipalities and provide an arena for local grass-roots participation in project selection and prioritization.

There was an active debate in Nicaragua about the role of the zonal offices vis-à-vis the municipalities. Some officials thought that selected municipalities should be built up as zonal seats with both administrative and political functions for the entire zone. Others thought that zonal offices should help to build up all the municipalities in a zone, both administratively and politically, then phase out. Still others thought that the municipalities should have been the administrative units, with the zones as the local political apparatus. As a result, the role of zones varied from region to region. In contrast to Matagalpa, the Estelí regional government phased out zones after building up municipal decision-making and technical capacity so that the SRAMU staff could work directly with individual municipalities.

Despite the variations among regions, a fundamental point remained: one of the main functions of the regional governments was to provide a decentralized support system to the municipalities. This emphasis on municipal support differed markedly from most regional authorities in Latin America. Typically, a regional authority had an ill-defined division of labor -- and therefore an antagonistic relationship -- with the municipalities. In those cases where regional authorities were formally charged with assisting the municipalities, they typically lack the staff or the funds to do so.[17] In the case of Peru, where the CORDEs have been charged formally with helping to improve municipal development planning, both institutional antagonisms and lack of resources prevented the CORDEs from becoming a meaningful source of support for the municipalities.

Also interfering in this relationship have been political differences between the CORDE presidents (representing the national political party in power) and local mayors. In Nicaragua the mayors were appointed by the regional delegate, so no political differences tended to exist. It will be very interesting to see whether the strong municipal support function of the regional governments continues unaltered now that the new constitution has been approved and once municipal elections are held.[18]

Another obstacle to a successful support relationship between the CORDEs and municipalities that was not present in Nicaragua was the system of dividing resources between the departmental and municipal authorities. As the municipalities gained capacity for investment planning and implementation, the CORDEs of Peru are expected to transfer functions and resources from their own budgets to the municipalities. Naturally, there has been great reluctance on the part of CORDE presidents to do that.[19] The only functioning support system for the municipalities that remains in Peru is a technical assistance office in Lima that attempts to serve the hundreds of municipalities by sending out roving teams of specialists.[20]

Besides assisting the municipalities in generating and prioritizing projects and carrying out technical studies, the regional governments in Nicaragua carried out another important planning function with respect to the municipalities: they prioritized municipal investment requests before sending them to the central government for approval. The regional governments were supposed to apply national development strategies in prioritizing municipal requests. However, the process did not lose its bottom-up nature, since the central government requires the regional governments to consider only those projects for which the municipalities had committed free communal labor. To stretch scarce resources and ensure local participation, municipal budget requests could only cover supplies and equipment.

It was at this moment of prioritizing municipal requests and applying national development strategies that regional development planning -- in the sense of strategic resource allocation -- should occur. However, the Nicaraguan prioritization process in mid-1987 involved differing degrees of project-by-project analysis -- as opposed to strategic development planning -- depending on the region. In Matagalpa, for example, the regional government simply analyzed the technical feasibility of each municipal project proposal and sent the list up to the central government for selection and approval. One official interviewed saw the regional government as a "trampoline" for sending municipal proposals to the central government -- a conduit devoid of any strategic regional planning, with no internal capacity for even doing a regional socioeconomic analysis. This official saw the regional government's main function with respect to the municipalities as one of "supervision."

In Estelí, in contrast, the regional government prioritized municipal proposals with respect to the national development strategy for the region. This strategy was both geographical and sectoral. On the one hand, the government wanted to influence migration patterns so as to repopulate the highly productive but war-stricken humid zones in the eastern portions of the region. It wanted to encourage people living in the less productive dry zones of the western part of the region to migrate eastward. Thus municipal proposals from the humid zone received higher priority than those from the arid zone.[21] Similarly, since early 1986 the regional government emphasized productive investments over social investments in keeping with the new national sectoral priority.[22] To fund projects that did not fit into the national priorities, municipalities had to raise local funds or seek direct foreign aid, such as through sister city affiliation.[23]

Because the regional government of Estelí applied these general mandates -- which were little more than rules of thumb reflecting national interests -- the central government generally adopted the regional prioritization as it was, simply assigning a total amount to the region and approving projects in order of priority until the amount was exhausted. Other than applying these rather general guidelines, however, no strategic development planning or analysis took place in the regional government of Estelí. Similarly, the region of Granada applied some general strategic geographic and sectoral priorities reflecting national goals for the region when prioritizing municipal proposals.[24]

Most regional planning (in terms of amount of public investments influenced) was done at the sectoral level by the ministries. Table 3-1 shows that 92 percent of the total public investments in the regions were planned and executed by the ministries. The less decentralized ministries planned regional investments at the central level, relying on their regional offices primarily for implementation. The more decentralized ministries gave greater authority to their regional offices for prioritizing investments and coordinating with other ministries through the Regional Planning Council. Nevertheless, since there were no sectoral budget offices at the regional level, final approval for all sectoral projects resided in the central ministries.[25]

Planning by the ministries lacked the grass-roots participation characteristic of the municipalities. A number of ministries used ad hoc forms of participation, such as public meetings and workshops at the zonal level.[26] However, most ministries viewed zones as the smallest feasible administrative unit, rather than as a means of furthering local participation.[27] Moreover, ministries as a rule did not deal with municipalities, either in project planning or in execution.

Integrated territorial planning did occur in two central government institutions: the Ministry of Housing and Human Settlements (MINVAH) and the Institute of Territorial Studies (INETER). Although producing valuable methodological guides and regional socioeconomic analyses that should be integrated into the regional planning and budgeting process, both efforts remained on an advisory level. The regional planners at INETER were totally unlinked to an operating agency, and the regional planners in the Office of Human Settlements in MINVAH were divorced from the housing side of the ministry, which is where the investment decisions were made.

Table 3-1
Ministerial vs. Municipal Development Projects,
Budgeted for 1986 (in Millions of 1985 Córdobas)

REGION	Ministerial Projects	Municipal Projects	Total	Municipal Percentage	Total Investment Per Capita (Córdobas)
Region I	457.8	207.2	665.0	31.2	200
Region II	2,557.3	143.1	2,700.4	5.3	458
Region III	4,741.8	164.0	4,905.8	3.3	540
Region IV	424.8	313.7	738.5	42.5	122
Region V	601.2	286.8	888.0	32.3	279
Region VI	2,817.9	145.9	2,963.8	4.9	688
Special Zone I	2,370.8	43.5	2,414.3	1.8	2,229
Special Zone II	2,231.1	145.5	2,376.6	6.1	4,282
Special Zone III	2,230.4	1,568.8	2,349.5	66.8	6,143
National	18,433.1	3,018.5	20,001.9	15.1	591

Source: Unpublished data from the President's Office of Regional Affairs, 1986.

There is one other level at which multisectoral regional planning takes place: the central government in conjunction with the military has special plans and projects for the conflict zones that are designed to promote economic productivity, increase standards of living, and attract migrants, for example, the General Plans (Planes Generales Unicos) for Regions I, VI, and V, and Strategic Projects such as the Carlos Fonseca Project in Waslala. These plans and projects are approved by the national party leadership and administered directly by the central government.

The Municipal Level

Resource allocation at the municipal level is a highly participatory process, especially in the development of project proposals. Whereas the municipal heads are currently chosen by the head of the regional government (usually in consensus with local grass-roots groups), the other members of the Municipal Councils (Juntas Municipales de Reconstrucción -- JMRs) are locally chosen representatives of the grass-roots groups. Projects are often proposed by the grass-roots groups themselves, such as the neighborhood Sandinista Defense Committees (Comités de Defensa Sandinista -- CDS), which act as both civil and political organizing bodies in many neighborhoods. The other important grass-roots organizations are the Sandinista Workers' Federation (Central Sandinista de Trabajadores -- CST), the Rural Workers' Association (Asociación de Trabajadores del Campo -- ATC), the National Union of Farmers and Ranchers (Unión Nacional de Agricultores y Ganaderos -- UNAG), and the Association of Nicaraguan Women (Asociación de Mujeres Nicaragüenses Luisa Amanda Espinosa -- AMNLAE).

As in most Latin American countries, the municipalities in Nicaragua rarely choose investment projects in the context of a development strategy. Rather, projects are chosen primarily in response to immediate needs and isolated requests. Ironically, this tendency may be reinforced by the active participation of grass-roots organizations in Nicaragua's municipalities. Certainly in Nicaragua the regional governments are not helping much to reverse this tendency, since they lack a well-developed, strategic, integrated planning capacity themselves. However, if an effort were made to introduce strategic development planning at the municipal level, the participatory structure already in place could make it very effective.

The central government's recent policy to emphasize productive over social investment at the municipal level may encourage municipalities to take a more strategic approach to project selection. Some municipalities have already begun a vigorous program to develop municipal enterprises that not only will create jobs but will generate profits that can be reinvested in the municipality. The municipality of León, for example, operates hotels, restaurants, and discotheques to promote tourism. The municipality of Masaya, with the technical assistance of the zonal office of the regional government (Region IV), operates a building materials factory, a building materials distributor, and a wooden furniture workshop.[28] Among smaller municipalities in Matagalpa there is a municipal chicken farm, a cereal-processing plant, and a clothing factory. New productive investments programmed for small towns in Matagalpa include bakeries, a pig farm, and covered marketplaces. These investments are designed to promote rural development in the surrounding hinterlands.

The central government is also creating innovative financial mechanisms to get the municipal governments to generate more local resources. In most Latin American countries, municipalities prefer to rely on transfers from the central government rather than antagonize their constituents with increased taxes or user fees. In Nicaragua, municipalities have been recently authorized to incur debt. This single measure created municipal access to bank credit for financing productive investments. In Peru municipalities are not allowed to incur debt and, therefore, cannot leverage financing for development projects.[29]

Municipalities are also allowed to borrow from and lend to each other. Thus richer municipalities can lend at suitable interest rates to poorer ones through a mechanism called "bridge financing" (financiamiento puente). These deals are struck either bilaterally between municipalities or arranged by the regional delegate.

The central government has proposed but not yet enacted another very innovative municipal financing tool: a severance tax of one percent of all overseas exports from a municipality, which would be returned to the municipality. This tax would encourage municipalities to promote exports and provide a significant source of income for the export-oriented municipalities. Some Latin American countries have a similar severance tax rebate, but only for certain exports (for example, petroleum in Peru and Mexico) and at a departmental -- not municipal -- level. Expanded local severance taxes have been a demand of the Peruvian regional movements for years, but to no avail.[30] Other measures being considered are a percentage municipal sales tax, as opposed to the current fixed charge per retailer that the municipality collects, and a municipal surcharge on electricity use. The government is going slowly on these proposals, however, so as not to jeopardize those exporters, retailers, and electricity consumers with the least capacity to pay.

Although municipal capacity for resource generation and self-financing is increasing, current capacity is small. Existing fees and taxes (arbitrios) do not even cover basic municipal operating costs in many cases. Only the largest municipalities have enough left over to finance any investments. In keeping with the government's emphasis on municipal development and decentralization, the central government allocates an amazingly large share of public investment resources to the municipalities (see table 3-1): nearly 8 percent (compared to less than 2 percent in Peru, for example).[31] The figures are even more remarkable on a region-by-region basis, showing regions I and V with over 30 percent of the public investment done by the municipalities, and region IV with over 40 percent.[32]

Conclusions

Compared to similar efforts in Latin America, Nicaragua's regionalization program, which began in 1982 with the creation of nine regional governments, has made remarkable strides. The major achievements of the effort have been in (1) municipal development and finance, (2) grassroots participation, and, to a lesser extent, (3) sectoral coordination at the subnational level.

The Nicaraguan regionalization effort is a showcase for central government support for municipal development. The regional governments, rather than competing with municipalities in making local investments, support the municipalities with technical and administrative assistance, including carrying out feasibility studies for municipal project proposals and providing technical assistance in project implementation. The regional governments make no investments themselves, but rather channel central government funds to the municipalities either directly or through zonal offices that service several municipalities. Moreover, compared to other Latin American countries, the central government allocates a large proportion of public investment funds to the municipalities, reaching more than 30 percent of total public investment in three regions. The central government has also been facilitating municipal resource generation by encouraging municipal enterprises and allowing municipalities to borrow from banks to make productive investments.

The Nicaraguan regionalization effort also stands out as an example of participatory, bottom-up planning. Local grass-roots organizations propose projects to the municipal councils. The municipal councils, which include grass-roots organizational representatives, prioritize projects and send their requests to the regional government (by way of the zonal office, if there is one). The regional government applies national and regional priorities in selecting projects, but chooses only among those for which there is a strong show of local support (only those projects for which the community has committed free communal labor will be considered). The regional government then sends its final priority list to the central government, which many times simply assigns an amount and approves the projects in the order given until the total amount is exhausted. Even the sectoral ministries, although much more top-down in their planning process, employ an impressive degree of public meetings and workshops.

In terms of sectoral coordination, although there remains a long way to go with the less-cooperative ministries, the achievements of some of the regional governments in coordinating the sectors through their regional planning councils have been exemplary. In some regions, for example, the regional representatives of MIDINRA, MICOIN, the Central Bank, and UNAG meet monthly along with the head of the regional government and a staff analyst to coordinate efforts to improve agricultural production and distribution. Even officials in the least-successful regional government (Region VI) reported that they had had at least some measurable success in influencing and coordinating sectoral decisions.

Despite these advances, there remain some important obstacles to achieving Nicaragua's regionalization goals. The most glaring of these is the need to introduce the concept of strategic spatial development planning at both the regional and the municipal levels. The second most important step is for the government to work on those ministries that are lagging in their decentralization efforts, in both administrative decentralization and the regional allocation of resources. The concentration of ministerial investment in Managua still gives the capital region the highest per capita public investment ratio in this country. Another issue that needs to be examined is the highly centralized control over disbursements: every regional government official interviewed complained about the tight monitoring of expenditures (for example, that each disbursement is conditioned on adequate accounting of the previous disbursement), which reduces their capability to respond to changing local circumstances and opportunities. Finally, since a significant proportion of the economy remains in the private sector, regional and local officials may want to explore ways of harnessing some of the resources of the private sector for local development by considering joint ventures.

As foreign intervention in Nicaragua escalates, some of these considerations will wane in importance until a more propitious time. Nevertheless, the Nicaraguan government has had a positive experience with regionalization, has been using the country's scarce resources more efficiently than otherwise because of it, and has been consolidating its presence at the local level. The government may well decide that as resources get even tighter, efforts at regionalization must be redoubled.

Endnotes to Chapter 3

1. Secretaría de Planificación y Presupuesto (SPP), Plan técnico económico (Managua: SPP, 1986).
2. Charles Downs, "The Development of Local and Regional Government [in Nicaragua]" (1984), manuscript, Columbia University; Charles Downs and Fernando Kusnetzoff, "The Changing Role of Local Government in the Nicaraguan Revolution," International Journal of Urban and Regional Research 6, no. 14 (1982); Fernando Kusnetzoff, "The Democratization of the State, Local Governments and Social Change: The Comparative Case Histories of Chile and Nicaragua," Revista Mexicana de Sociología 45, no. 1 (1982): 191-219; and Juan Luis Klein and Orlando Peña, "De la desestructuración a la estructuración del espacio nicaragüense: notas sobre el nuevo Plan de Regionalización de Nicaragua," paper presented to the Annual Meetings of ACELAC (Asociación Canadiense de Estudios Latino-Americanos y del Caribe), 1982.
3. See Patricia Salinas and José Garzón, "El estado, la región y la descentralización en el Perú," Revista Interamericana de Planificación 19, no. 73 (1985): 124-139: and idem, "Prospects for Political Decentralization: Peru in the 1980s," International Journal of Urban and Regional Research 9, no. 3 (1985): 330-340.
4. See Sergio Boisier, "Chile: Continuity and Change -- Variations of Centre Down Strategies under Different Political Regimes," in Walter Stohr and D. R. Fraser Taylor, eds., Development from Above or Below? The Dialectics of Regional Planning in Developing Countries

(New York: John Wiley and Sons, 1981).

5.   See Salinas and Garzón, "El estado."

6.   See Klein and Peña, "De la desestructuración a la estructuración."

7.   Interview, President's Office of Regional Affairs, June 1986.

8.   See, for example, the case of Peruvian departmental corporations in Dennis Rondinelli and Patricia Wilson, "Linking Decentralization and Regional Development Planning: The IRD Project in Peru," Journal of the American Planning Association (January 1987).

9.   Salinas and Garzón, "El estado."

10. In October 1985, after an internal evaluation showed that sectoral coordination was not being achieved, two changes were made: (1) the coordinating body (called at that time the Interinstitutional Council), which reported to the Technical Office, was substantially strengthened by having it report directly to the regional delegate, and its name was changed to the Planning Council; (2) at the same time, the regional delegates' power was strengthened by making them both the governmental and the political party heads of the region (interview, President's Office of Regional Affairs, June, 1986).

11. Jaime Johnson, Alberto García, and Fredy Monge, Estructura y gestión del estado descentralizado (Lima: Centro Peruano de Estudios para el Desarrollo Regional, 1986); see also Rondinelli and Wilson, "Linking Decentralization."

12. Interviews in Region I government, June 1986.

13. Interview with Estelí regional government, June 1986.

14. Interview with MINVAH, Managua, June 1986.

15. The 1986 National Plan (SPP, February 1986) includes not only sector-by-sector production goals but also an analysis of production bottlenecks; migration incentives necessary to get the labor force to the right areas (e.g., to the coffee fields near combat zones); the role of state enterprises in terms of quality, productivity, and resource needs; provision of productive infrastructure (e.g., for storage and distribution of basic goods); control over scarce imported inputs for priority activities and projections of needs for foreign exchange; allocation of credit; control of black market sales; means of improving labor productivity; and means for promoting nontraditional exports; means for using price controls and foreign exchange controls to influence private market production, to reduce middlemen, and to avoid excessive profit-taking. The basic agricultural productive strategy is aimed, first, at supplying internal demand and, second, at reactivating cotton and meat exports. The basic industrial strategy is to supply, first, the armed forces, second, basic final demand goods (e.g., processed food and clothing), and, third, intermediate goods for agriculture (e.g., sacks, machetes).

16. Rondinelli and Wilson, "Linking Decentralization."

17. Granted, the comparatively short distances in Nicaragua between each regional seat and the various municipalities in its region greatly simplify the logistical task of providing support at the local

level.

18. It is extremely likely, however, that municipal elections will be suspended until after the war.

19. Salinas and Garzón, "El estado."

20. Rondinelli and Wilson, "Linking Decentralization."

21. The government also sponsors direct incentives to encourage migration, such as free inspection trips, subsidies for moving, and resettlement costs.

22. After four years of building up the social infrastructure (e.g., in housing, health, and education) in the municipalities, the government began in 1985 to emphasize productive investments that generate income and promote production -- e.g., processing and marketing facilities.

23. The sister city affiliation with European and American cities is highly sought after, since such affiliation is often accompanied by sizable donations. Davis, Boulder, and Seattle have sister cities in Estelí and have raised donations ranging from a few thousand to $10,000.

24. Interview with zonal official in Masaya, Region IV (Granada), June 1986.

25. Of course, even regional budget offices can be emasculated at the national level. In Peru regional sectoral budget offices may have their budgets reworked down to the project and item level by the Ministry of Economics and Finance or the national legislature (Salinas and Garzón, "El estado").

26. Interview at MINVAH, Managua, June 1986.

27. Zonal boundaries vary from ministry to ministry, making participation even more difficult for those caught in multizonal locations.

28. The municipality bought the furniture workshop from a crafts cooperative that was having financial difficulties (interview, zonal office, Masaya, June 1986).

29. Rondinelli and Wilson, "Linking Decentralization."

30. Salinas and Garzón, "El estado."

31. Patricia Wilson and Carol Wise, "The Regional Implications of Public Investment in Peru, 1968-1983," Latin American Research Review 21, no. 2 (1986): 93-116.

32. The Special Zones are in the sparsely populated, isolated Atlantic Coast region, inhabited largely by ethnic groups who have been the source of regional autonomy movements. The central government has responded to their requests with a plan for their gradual autonomy. Only the largely undeveloped Special Zone III is operating normally. Special Zone I, the Miskito region near the Honduran border, is experiencing problems in integrating regionalization with the autonomy program. The small percentage of municipal investment in this zone (see table 3-1) probably reflects the fact that it is an active war zone. Much of the investment -- especially in resettlement villages necessitated by guerrilla activity -- is handled

directly by the central government.

Chapter 4

Internal Migration, War, and the Regional Outreach of the Nicaraguan State: 1980-1986

by

Michael E. Conroy
and
Rolf Pendall

With the assistance of
Félix Delgado Silva
and
Herminia Valdes

Introduction

Nicaragua in mid-1986 was a nation thrown spatially into turmoil. Continuing attacks on the geographical perimeter of the country by counterrevolutionary forces organized by the United States effectively reduced the available agriculturally productive area, forced thousands of rural families into resettlement villages in safer areas closer to the center of the country, and undermined numerous projects that would have incorporated the resources of peripheral regions into national reconstruction and development efforts.

There was a sense among many analysts in Nicaraguan government ministries that Managua was growing at vertigo-producing rates and that this was explicitly counterproductive for a fundamentally agricultural nation that sought to defend itself first through increases in internally oriented basic grain production. But neither the magnitude of that growth nor its causes were known with much certainty. Prior to 1979 the spatial distribution of the Nicaraguan population was undergoing processes similar to those of most of the rest of Central America: the almost total absence of significant dynamism in the domestic economy left the vast majority of the population locked into semiproletarian rural poverty.

The massive and significant transformation of the Nicaraguan economy undertaken after the 1979 revolution unleashed social forces that could have created changes in the pattern of location incentives such that Managua would become a much more attractive place for many Nicaraguans to live. Yet the principal programs implemented by the government after 1979 should have generated, at first glance, substantially increased incentives for residence in the peripheral regions and in the

countryside.   The 1981 literacy crusade that focused largely on the
countryside, agrarian reform affecting more than 50,000 families (more
than 18 percent of all rural families), dramatic improvements in rural
access to health care facilities, expansion and decentralization of
educational facilities, and programs of distribution of basic commodities
(the creation of a "secure channel") for most of the population should
have raised the relative standard of living in rural areas and peripheral
regions relative to that enjoyed by residents of Managua.   This, in turn,
should have lessened the incentive for movement of the population toward
Managua.

Higher priority was also deliberately given to several of the regions
most heavily affected by the war in order to increase government
presence, improve the conditions affecting families in those areas in
particular, repair or replace facilities damaged by contra attacks, and
counter the inroads that might be made by the contras in the absence of
vigorous government action.   These programs may or may not represent
the optimal regional distribution of government resources under peacetime
conditions, but they should have lessened the tendency for migration
toward Managua.

Yet "Managua is Nicaragua," according to a recent, much-quoted
study.[1]   It contained in 1986 a majority of the nation's industry, perhaps
as much as 30 percent of the population, and the largest share of all
public employment.   It has also consistently been the focus of the largest
proportion of all public investment.   The analytical tension in Managua
between the requirement that the nation improve its fulfillment of the
needs of the permanent and productive population of its largest city and
the national need for expanded production in rural areas became an
important political phenomenon.   Could living conditions for the city's
poorest population (an important locus of support for the government) be
improved without attracting significant numbers of new residents from
other areas?   And had that occurred?   Had there been an appropriately
"balanced" improvement in living conditions across regions such that
political and production needs were served equally?

There does not appear to have been a study to date that surveys
the effective relative regional impacts of a wide set of Nicaraguan
government programs, either before the Revolution or since.   Whether the
apparent growth of Managua after 1979 was solely or primarily the result
of the war or whether there had occurred a restructuring of the pattern
of location incentives in the country such that Managua had been turned,
unintentionally, into a significantly more attractive location for residence
will have depended, in part, on the cumulative regional impact of such
programs.   If there were substantial across-the-board disincentives
apparently associated with movement toward Managua, we would have
additional reasons for believing that Managua's growth was significantly
related to the war.   If there were major differences favoring Managua in
some government programs, the identification of the nature and magnitude
of those differences would permit further analysis of the regional varia-

tions and may have created a basis for adjustments in the policies.

Design of This Study

This microstudy in the INIES/University of Texas series was designed to analyze and evaluate several sets of interrelated phenomena. We shall first review the data available on internal migration in Nicaragua from 1979 to 1986, noting the fragility of the database and the problems that characterized all of the available indicators of rates and directions of migratory flow. We shall then review a newly gathered set of data on both the levels and the relative rates of change in levels of government programs across the major regions of the country through 1985. The programs covered include health services, education, agrarian reform, and the grain distribution programs of the Empresa Nicaragüense de Alimentos Básicos (ENABAS, the Nicaraguan Basic Foodstuffs Enterprise). We shall then consider differentials across regions in price levels and some indicators with respect to salaries. Finally, we shall look at the regional distribution of public investment programs.

The conclusions that emerge from this analysis are necessarily partial and tentative. They demonstrate, first, the remarkable decentralization of access to government services that was a major and previously less-documented accomplishment of the Revolution. They also illustrate inequalities that remained in 1986 in access across regions to government services, their coverage, and their cumulative impact. Whether these are differences that required attention is not obvious; the optimal location of the population for societies undergoing rapid and profound structural change is rarely the traditional or historical location. The appropriateness or inappropriateness of the remaining pattern of regional differences depends primarily on the goals and needs of the broader developmental process, including, in the specific case of Nicaragua, the immediate exigencies of the contra war. This study intends to illuminate the incentive structure for migration that remained in the composite of public sector programs in mid-1986 as mapped onto the regions.

A Brief Statistical Overview of the Regions

Nicaragua has been divided since 1982 into six administrative regions and three Special Zones. The delimitation is shown in Map 1 (at the start of the book). The six basic regions contained 94 percent of the population in 1985; and they differed widely in their topographical, social, and economic characteristics. Table 4-1 provides basic demographic data synthesized from the latest estimates available in mid-1986 by the Instituto Nicaragüense de Estadísticas y Censos (the Nicaraguan Census Bureau, INEC). Tables 4-2 and 4-3 present a number of those characteristics drawn from both published and unpublished data. The basic sketches of the regions that follow provide only the briefest of introductions to the characteristics of each and presuppose considerable familiarity.[2]

Table 4-1
Regional Population, According to INEC's 1985 Revisions

REGION	1980	1981	1982	1983	1984	1985
Region I	272,156	281,001	290,422	300,317	310,591	321,142
Region II	486,104	501,368	517,622	534,689	552,390	570,546
Region III	692,087	722,996	756,359	791,687	828,777	867,395
Region IV	499,228	514,904	531,597	549,125	567,305	585,953
Region V	293,898	297,664	301,469	305,485	309,595	313,689
Region VI	376,558	384,613	393,228	402,252	411,535	420,938
Special Zone I	78,666	82,876	87,399	92,216	97,312	102,666
Special Zone II	40,315	42,473	44,790	47,260	49,871	52,616
Special Zone III	31,996	32,923	33,912	34,948	36,021	37,119
Total	2,771,008	2,860,818	2,956,798	3,057,979	3,163,390	3,272,064

Percent of National Population

REGION	1980	1981	1982	1983	1984	1985
Region I	9.82	9.82	9.82	9.82	9.82	9.81
Region II	17.54	17.53	17.51	17.49	17.46	17.44
Region III	24.98	25.27	25.58	25.89	26.20	26.51
Region IV	18.02	18.00	17.98	17.96	17.93	17.91
Region V	10.61	10.40	10.20	9.99	9.79	9.59
Region VI	13.59	13.44	13.30	13.15	13.01	12.86
Special Zone I	2.84	2.90	2.96	3.02	3.08	3.14
Special Zone II	1.45	1.48	1.51	1.55	1.58	1.61
Special Zone III	1.15	1.15	1.15	1.14	1.14	1.13
Total	100.00	100.00	100.00	100.00	100.00	100.00

Source: INEC, Estimaciones de Población 1980-1987, Managua, 1985.

The "official" INEC estimates of population by region, when converted into annual population distributions across regions, as in table 4-1, tend to show stability, rather than dramatic change. If these data are trustworthy (several questions will be raised below), the regional structure of the Nicaraguan population is not changing dramatically.

Managua (Region III) contained 25 percent of the population in 1980; it contained 26.5 percent by the end of 1985, an average annual increase in its share of only 0.30 percent. Whether this is excessive or not depends on the needs of the nation, the relative productivity of the marginal labor force in Managua, and the costs of sustaining this growing population in Managua relative to the costs in other parts of the nation.

Table 4-2
Basic Characteristics of Regional Economies, 1983.

	(a) % of National Value	(b) Level of Agricultural Techni-	(c) % of National Agricultural	(d) % of Effective National	(e) % of National
REGION	Added	fication	Base	Potential	Territory
Region I	4.01	15.6	3.37	4.13	6.13
Region II	24.12	91.4	27.34	16.95	8.33
Region III	43.20	56.4	10.53	11.09	2.80
Region IV	13.25	64.5	12.49	8.03	4.19
Region V	6.34	9.6	19.76	22.46	15.12
Region VI	8.06	15.3	7.85	10.94	13.76
Special Zones	1.14	9.7	39.42	26.40	43.55
National	100.00		100.00	100.00	100.00

Source: Unpublished data from SPP/INETER.
Notes: (a) Proportions of GDP.
      (b) Proportions dedicated to exports and/or with high technification.
      (c) Proportions of national arable lands.
      (d) Uncultivated proportions of national agricultural base.
      (e) Excluding lakes and other bodies of water.

Table 4-3
Regional Distribution of the Employed Labor Force, 1982

REGION	Primary Sector % of Sector	Primary Sector % of Region	Secondary Sector % of Sector	Secondary Sector % of Region	Tertiary Sector % of Sector	Tertiary Sector % of Region
Region I	14.30	66.28	7.56	9.25	5.30	24.47
Region II	16.07	44.45	15.93	11.64	15.97	43.92
Region III	4.34	6.87	39.73	16.63	48.51	76.49
Region IV	13.40	41.71	23.25	19.12	12.65	39.17
Region V	18.70	77.70	2.56	2.81	4.72	19.49
Region VI	22.64	73.85	5.94	5.12	6.48	21.03
Special Zone I	6.10	61.62	2.12	5.65	3.26	32.73
Special Zone II	3.74	50.69	2.79	9.97	2.92	39.34
Special Zone III	0.71	76.20	0.12	3.31	0.19	20.50
Total Employed	390,186		103,061		388,141	
Percent of Total	44.26		11.69		44.04	

Urban Areas

REGION	(a) Rate of '82 Unemployment	(b) Rate of '83 Unemployment	(c) Participation Rates Male	(c) Participation Rates Female	(d) Percent Informal Sector	(e) Percent Sub-employed
Region I	7.59	27.9	66.7	33.1	19.5	22.0
Region II	9.63	22.7	61.7	40.1	19.1	13.1
Region III	13.56	22.6	66.7	41.2	14.9	11.4
Region IV	10.68	24.0	66.5	40.3	23.6	24.1
Region V	7.09	24.2	65.8	32.8	23.3	18.3
Region VI	5.75	20.5	63.9	29.5	22.4	8.4
Special Zones	12.35	6.6	65.0	40.7	23.1	19.3

Sources and notes:
(a) Ratio of unemployed to economically active population; source: INEC 1982
(b) Results of INETER's Economically Active Population projection model, 1983.
(c) Ratio of Economically Active Population to population over 9 years.
(d) Strict definition: nonfarm workers in places of five employees or fewer.
(e) Workers earning less than minimum wage or working fewer than 40 hours/week but
desiring to work full time; source, unpublished SPP/INETER data.

Region I (north-central) consists of the Departments of Nueva Segovia, Madriz, and Estelí. It contains roughly 10 percent of the national population but contributes only 4 percent of the total national value-added in production. Although the Valley of Estelí contains some agricultural production units of considerable size and sophistication, it is one of the least technified regions, contains only 3.4 percent of the "national agricultural capacity" (fondo agropecuario nacional) according to estimates from the Instituto Nacional de Estudios Territoriales (National Institute for Territorial Studies, INETER) and only 4.1 percent of INETER's estimated national "effective potential" for development.

Fully 66 percent of the Region I's labor force was employed in primary sector activities, nearly 25 percent in services, and the level of underemployment was, in 1982, one of the highest in the nation. A poor region, it was one of the first targets for contra activity in 1982 and 1983, largely because it shares a long border with the southeastern area of Honduras where contra recruitment and training first developed.

Region II (north-west) consists of the Departments of Chinandega and León, one of the richest developed agricultural areas of Nicaragua. Region II produced 24 percent of national value-added with 17.4 percent of the nation's population, 8 percent of the nation's territorial mass, and 27 percent of the fondo agropecuario. It enjoyed the highest level of technified agriculture in the nation in 1983 (91.4%). The presence of three sizable cities, León, Chinandega, and Corinto, was reflected in the fact that only 44 percent of the labor force in Region II was employed in the primary sector, with the same proportion found in the tertiary sector. The diversified nature of the regional economy may have been reflected in the relatively low 13 percent of the labor force underemployed.

Managua really is Region III. The city's population constituted in 1985 fully 84 percent of the population of the total region. The region produced 43.2 percent of the nation's total value-added, using 26.5 percent of the population, 2.8 percent of the national territory, and only 10.5 percent of the "national agricultural capacity." The agriculture outside the city limits was rated among the most highly technified (56.4 percent), as was the "garden farming" (huertos) within the city. But only 7 percent of the regional labor force was employed in the primary sector.

The service sector employed 76.5 percent of Region III's labor force, while 16 percent was employed in industry. Contrary to popular images in 1986, the region had the lowest level of employment in the "informal sector" as of 1982, 14.9 percent, and the second lowest level of under-employment, according to INEC definitions and measurements. That could have increased by 1986, of course, but there were no corroborating data available.

The south-central Region IV is composed of the Pacific coast Departments of Masaya, Granada, Carazo, and Rivas, an agriculturally rich and relatively densely populated area. It produced approximately 13 percent of the nation's value-added with 18 percent of the population, 4 percent of the national territory, and 12.5 percent of the agricultural capacity.

Region IV's labor force included the highest share in the nation in secondary, industrial activities, 19.1 percent. It was otherwise almost equally divided between agriculture and services. The small-scale agro-industrial and handicraft industries that employed its secondary-sector labor force may account for the fact that Region IV had the highest levels in the nation of both informal sector employment (23.6%) and underemployment (24.1%) in the 1982 INEC household survey.

Region V, in east-central Nicaragua, contained the Departments of Boaco and Chontales, as well as part of the Atlantic coastal plain. A distinctly agricultural area, with more small and medium-sized farms than extensive cultivation, it produced 6.3 percent of national 1982 value-added with 9.5 percent of the population, 15 percent of the nation's land mass, and 20 percent of the nation's agricultural resources, as estimated by INETER. INETER estimates suggested that Region V had the highest proportion of the agricultural development potential of any region in the nation (22.5%), in part, one presumes, because it had the lowest level of agricultural technification (9.6%). It was the most agricultural of all regions, with 78 percent of the labor force in the primary sector, and it had the lowest levels in the nation of industrial and service-sector employment. Region V had been an active war zone for several years, especially on the Atlantic side of the principal sierra.

Region VI had historically been the poorest and most remote of the six principal regions; and it was the one most troubled by the contra war from 1983 to 1986. It consists of the Departments of Jinotega and Matagalpa, the remote north-eastern departments that were for many years the agricultural frontier for migrant small-holding peasants. The region produced 8 percent of the national value-added using 12.9 percent of the population, 14 percent of the national territory, and 8 percent of the national agricultural capacity.

The employed labor force in Region VI was predominantly agricultural (74%), with only 21 percent in services. Reflecting both work patterns and statistical difficulties around agriculture, it showed the lowest levels of unemployment, according to both INEC and INETER data, the lowest level of underemployment, one of lowest levels of labor force participation for both men and women.

The three Atlantic Coast Special Zones cover 44 percent of the landmass of Nicaragua; but, according to the best available estimates, they contained only 5.8 percent of the population, and produced only 1.1 percent of the national value-added. There were very few reliable estimates of any sort that relate to these areas, whether demographic, economic, or social. If fundamental demographic data were questionable, then all subsequent attempts to relate other variables to that population base are even more questionable. The available data on the Special Zones will be reported in what follows, but little credibility can be attached to them.

The Internal Migration Conundrum

The analysis of the potential links between internal migration and the relative regional distribution of government services requires, first, reliable estimates of recent internal migration flows. There existed several sets of estimates used in government documents through 1986, but each of them suffers from flaws associated with the fundamental lack of basic demographic data. The overall trends in changes across major regions differed substantially across different estimates, both in terms of the relative magnitude of migratory flows and in terms of the actual direction of flows for at least one region, Region II. (See table 4-4.)

The dictatorship left few reliable demographic data; and Nicaragua had not undertaken a census of population since 1971. The data then published as "official" population estimates by INEC consisted of two interrelated series of estimates that provided the best available basis for total national population and for the geographical division of that population across the regions. Demographic analysis on the basis of these data required three important caveats.

Table 4-4
Alternative Estimates of Interregional Migratory Flows, 1984

REGION	INETER Estimates		Estimates Based on New INEC Regionalization		
	Absolute Migration	Implicit Migration Rate	Implicit Growth Rate	Migration Rate	Absolute Migration
Region I	-2,907	-0.91	3.40	-0.04	-124
Region II	2,523	0.49	3.28	-0.16	-883
Region III	22,619	2.74	4.66	1.22	10,111
Region IV	-1,629	-0.34	3.28	-0.16	-908
Region V	-5,903	-1.71	1.32	-2.12	-6,563
Region VI	-6,369	-1.62	2.28	-1.16	-4,774
Special Zone I			5.50	2.06	2,004
Special Zone II	9,330	4.94	5.50	2.06	1,027
Special Zone III			3.04	-0.40	-144

Source: Unpublished data from INETER and authors' calculations based on data from INEC.

One must first recognize that there was very little compatibility between INEC population data reported in the <u>Anuario Estadístico de Nicaragua</u> for years prior to 1983 and the data for national totals and major national component aggregates published thereafter. INEC received significant technical assistance in 1983 from a group of consultants for the United Nation's demographic group at the Latin American Demographic Center (CELADE). A completely new set of estimates of population growth at the national level was generated, including retrospective revisions back to 1950 and projections through 2025. These unusually bold estimates and projections became the principal basis for all subsequent INEC reports on national demographic aggregates. (The 1985 population estimates at the national level by age-cohort and sex were, in fact, identical to the 1983 projections.)

Second, the published departmental data reflected primarily prerevolutionary population processes projected up to the present. The geographical division of the population into departments and municipalities utilized no new and consistent data covering the nation with which to alter the estimates to correspond to any changes in the structure of regional incentives since well before the Revolution. The regionalized population estimates could not be used very accurately as a basis for estimates of internal migration because no subsequent data had been incorporated to adjust that prerevolutionary departmental division to reflect actual changes in patterns of location that may have occurred.

A third discontinuity was introduced in 1982 with the creation of the new regionalization of the nation. The pre-existing 15 departments were regrouped into 6 regions and 3 "special zones." Five of the six new regions consisted of complete subsets of the previous departments. But Region V was delimited to include not only the Departments of Boaco and Chontales but also three municipios of the previous Department of Zelaya: El Rama, Muelle de los Bueyes, and Nueva Guinea. The previous Department of Zelaya was divided into Special Zones I and II, excluding those three municipios; and, compounding the statistical difficulties, the new area comprising the three municipios were then also named "Zelaya."[3]

A major new set of estimates was generated by INEC in 1985 to incorporate regionalized data based on the 1984 voter registration campaign.[4] These new estimates created an additional major discontinuity, but they have been extended retroactively to 1980 and projected forward to 1987 to provide a consistent series. The technique used was innovative, if controversial.[5] INEC first produced a new set of population estimates for 1985 on the basis of ad hoc adjustments with the voter registration data. It then fitted geometric growth curves to those data to determine implicit region-specific rates of growth. These rates were utilized to derive annual region-specific estimates, but the only regionally independent data were those derived from voter registration in 1984. All of the migratory data, therefore, are captured in the differential implicit rates of regional growth.

INETER data in table 4-4 are based on a series of estimates of internal migration at the municipio level generated as part of its monumental attempt to provide a baseline for territorial planning.[6] The INETER estimates utilized a wide variety of earlier data to "grow" the population from 1980 and 1981 to 1984, subtracting INEC estimates of natural growth in each department and using 1981 estimated proportions in each municipio as the basis for updated municipal populations. They also added ad hoc adjustments for well-known cities, such as Tipitapa, shifting population only on an intradepartmental level.

Their resultant estimates of interdepartmental and interregional migration were, in effect, standard indirect estimates created by subtracting an estimate of natural growth from an estimate of total population. The reliability of such estimates depends primarily upon the accuracy of the principal assumptions: (1) constant proportions of departmental population in each municipio; (2) accurate estimates of natural growth; and (3) accurate estimates of total population. In the present statistical circumstances of Nicaragua, all three assumptions are difficult. The INETER data have the advantage of providing details at the municipal level not available from the INEC estimates, but they also have the disadvantage of not being associated with internally consistent longer term population growth projections.

The two alternative sets of migration estimates in table 4-4 provide, first, INETER estimates based on its model and, second, estimates newly derived by the authors from the latest INEC regionalized population estimates available in mid-1986 (presented in table 4-1). Although the data in both sets of estimates refer to 1984, the technique used for each makes the rates and direction of flow in both cases effectively invariant over time.

The INEC-based estimates were, first, substantially lower than those of INETER in the magnitude of estimated net interregional flows. The INEC-based estimates suggested annual migration to Region III (roughly 84 percent of which is Managua) at a rate of approximately 10,000 persons per year. INETER suggested more than twice that, 22,600 yearly. In-house estimates by the Ministry of Housing and Human Settlements (MINVAH) for the absolute size of Managua claimed a 1984 population of 900,000, approximately 20,000 more than the INEC estimate of 879,000.[7] This would be somewhat less than the size the city of Managua would have achieved under INETER net migration estimates. An average of the two, however, a rate of net in-migration to Managua of approximately 2.0 percent per year, implying 15,000 to 18,000 people per year, would provide a reasonable consensus estimate.

The INEC-based estimates and the INETER estimates differed in magnitude, but the direction of the probable migratory flows coincided in all but one of the regions. INETER data suggested that Region II was a net recipient of migrants at the rate of 2500 per year in 1984; the INEC-based estimates implied that Region II was experiencing a net out-migration at a rate under nine hundred persons per year. The difference in the estimates was exaggerated by focusing on absolute flows, for the rate of flow differed by much less. INETER indicated an inflow at a rate under 0.5 percent per year; the INEC-based estimates suggest an outflow of less than 0.2 percent per year. The available data and the techniques used in both cases were too crude for this to be a significant difference. It was safest to suggest that Region II was roughly stable with respect to migration, growing at very close to the national average rate of growth.

These extremely rough estimates, nonetheless, could be read to suggest general trends. Nicaragua was experiencing relatively clear migration away from the areas of significant contra activity, namely, the Departments of Jinotega and Matagalpa (Region VI), Boaco, Chontales, and the "new" area of Zelaya (Region V). The data would seem to suggest substantial migration toward Special Zones I and II, but this was generally believed to be an artifact of improved recent coverage of those areas. The area in and around Managua (Region III) was the principal destination for most of the interregional migration. The other regions along the Pacific coast remained relatively more stable.

Interregional migration data at this level of geographical and statistical coarseness could hide more than they reveal, because there was ample anecdotal and fragmentary evidence of much more complicated flows within and among the departments of the individual regions. Nevertheless, if much of the regionalized policy-making in Nicaragua was to be undertaken at this level, if much of the political and administrative decentralization wass effected at this level, and if most of the supplementary data on the distribution of government goods and services were collected at this level and no lower, it was at that level that we were forced to function.

What effects might government programs have had on this migratory pattern? Would the pattern have been different in the absence of public sector programs? Might the rate of out-migration from Region VI have been closer to that of Region V if it had not received "prioritized" programs and services? Or did the flow of migrants toward Managua simply reflect disproportionate availability of public programs and services there? The quality of the data available and the number of data points with which to work precluded useful sophisticated statistical analysis, but an overview of the regional distribution of governmental programs, services, and of other regional characteristics did provide insight.

The Regional Distribution of Basic Government Services

"Basic government services" is a term whose meaning in postrevolutionary Nicaragua differed from the meaning that it had in virtually any other Latin American country, with the exception of Cuba. Although all Latin American countries provide some health and educational services, the levels achieved in Nicaragua were generally viewed as dramatically different from those of most of Latin America.[8] Nicaragua had also developed a system of basic grain distribution that evolved after 1985 into a wider system of basic commodity distribution (see Chapters 5 and 8). Nicaragua carried out an agrarian reform program that had provided land to nearly 25 percent of all rural families by mid-1986. The regional dimensions of each of these programs and their composite impact upon relative regional attractiveness required analysis of the regional impact of the changes that had occurred over the years.

Educational Services. The overall achievements of the Sandinista Revolution with respect to education are illustrated, although only partially, in the five tables presented here on national and regional changes in primary and secondary education. We emphasize here the extent to which the state increased the "supply" of educational services and the regional distribution of that increase, rather than the increased "demand" reflected by increased enrollment. Increased school enrollments are an important achievement in and of themselves, but they can be obtained simply by crowding large numbers of children into a constant number of schools with a constant number of teachers. The "outreach" of the Revolution is more accurately measured in its ability to supply schools, schoolrooms, and teachers to meet the latent demand for education.

Table 4-5 presents data on employed teachers per 1000 school-age inhabitants (individuals less than 20 years old) and indicates that Nicaragua produced a continual increase in this "teacher's ratio," from 7.34 per 1000 in 1980 to 9.29 per 1000 in 1984, an increase of 26.5 percent. The regional distribution of those teachers shifted notably, reflecting reorientation of educational resources toward regions other than Managua and away from the rest of the most developed part of the Pacific Coast, Region IV (Granada, Masaya, and so on). As the total numbers of teachers increased, in both absolute terms and in terms of the teacher-to-student ratio, there has been a clear reorientation of them toward other regions. The level of this ratio in Regions III and IV fell from 117 percent of the national average to 107 percent and 115 percent, respectively. Every other region increased its position with respect to the national average, narrowing the interregional dispersion systematically.

But the relative backwardness of Regions V and VI is also illustrated in these data. In 1980 Region VI (Matagalpa and Jinotega) had less than 60 percent of the national level of primary school teachers, and Boaco had about 86 percent, the lowest levels in the nation. Resources had clearly been shifted toward Region VI, but its teacher-to-student ratio in 1984 was still the lowest in the nation, barely 72 percent of the national average. Boaco fluctuated from year to year, but finished 1984 at roughly the same relationship to the national average that it had at the outset.

The data in table 4-6 reinforce this image of distinct improvement in the outlying regions, but continued lagging in Regions V and VI. When one reviews the changes that occurred in numbers of classrooms per 1000 school-age persons (the "classroom ratio"), one finds that national average levels fell slightly from 1980 to 1984 (-3.8%) but that the regional distribution of newly-built classrooms shifted distinctly to favor the regions other than the Managua area. The shortages of construction materials and investible funds clearly restricted the rate of school construction, but it is clear from table 4-6 that Nicaragua was developing and employing its human resources, in this case teachers, with much fewer restrictions.

Table 4-5
Regional Distribution of Primary Education, 1980-1984:
Teachers per 1,000 Inhabitants under 20 Years Old

REGION	1980	1981	1982	1983	1984
Region I	6.55	7.69	9.23	8.90	10.26
Region II	6.74	7.83	8.42	9.00	9.42
Region III	8.62	8.61	8.63	9.02	9.98
Region IV	8.63	9.24	9.78	9.61	10.77
Region V	6.31	7.83	7.37	8.21	8.04
Region VI	4.31	4.42	5.40	5.99	6.73
Special Zone I	11.92	11.46	3.92	8.83	7.46
Special Zone II*	11.35	12.23	10.92	12.05	9.82
Special Zone III	7.20	10.44	12.16	8.25	7.16
National Average	7.34	7.99	8.21	8.65	9.29

Percentage of National Average

REGION	1980	1981	1982	1983	1984
Region I	89.15	96.26	112.40	102.99	110.48
Region II	91.77	98.05	102.61	104.14	101.38
Region III	117.39	107.76	105.12	104.35	107.42
Region IV	117.53	115.64	119.11	111.16	115.89
Region V*	85.88	98.07	89.84	94.97	86.50
Region VI	58.75	55.31	65.77	69.33	72.41
Special Zone I	162.37	143.51	47.77	102.08	80.31
Special Zone II/*	154.54	153.10	133.09	139.39	105.67
Special Zone III	97.99	130.69	148.12	95.44	77.09
National Average	100.00	100.00	100.00	100.00	100.00

Sources: INEC, Anuario Estadístico de Nicaragua, various issues; and table 4-1.

* For years prior to the 1982 regionalization the data for Region V refer solely to the Departments of Boaco and Chontales; those from Special Zone II refer to the old Department of Zelaya (see endnote 3).

Table 4-6
Regional Distribution of Primary Education Facilities:
Classrooms per 1,000 Inhabitants Under 20 Years Old

REGION	1980	1981	1982	1983	1984
Region I	5.15	7.13	6.67	6.29	6.21
Region II	5.65	7.53	5.68	5.70	6.24
Region III	6.08	6.54	5.13	5.48	5.24
Region IV	4.68	8.99	6.40	6.22	6.78
Region V*	3.81	7.93	5.35	5.26	4.86
Region VI	3.93	4.59	4.29	2.32	4.75
Special Zone I			6.90	5.62	4.33
Special Zone II*	14.61	10.11	7.69	6.53	5.27
Special Zone III	7.35	27.92	7.34	7.74	4.23
National	5.86	7.52	5.63	5.32	5.64

Percentage of National Average

REGION	1980	1981	1982	1983	1984
Region I	87.91	94.75	118.47	118.18	110.10
Region II	96.37	100.11	100.80	107.02	110.64
Region III	103.64	86.89	91.01	102.95	92.91
Region IV	79.85	119.51	113.66	116.88	120.31
Region V*	64.96	105.45	95.02	98.75	86.24
Region VI	66.55	61.04	76.14	43.55	84.35
Special Zone I			122.47	105.63	76.92
Special Zone II*	249.18	134.31	136.47	122.74	93.58
Special Zone III	125.30	371.04	130.35	145.46	75.15
National	100.00	100.00	100.00	100.00	100.00

Sources: INEC, Anuario Estadístico de Nicaragua, various issues; and from table 4-1.
* See note to table 4-5 for definitions of Region V and Special Zone II.

Managua (Region III) was the only region with an elementary school classroom ratio above the national average in 1980. Regions V and VI were lowest, with 65 percent and 66 percent of the national average, respectively. By 1984 those two regions had increased to 85 percent and 86 percent of the national average, and Managua had fallen to 93 percent. All of the rest of the principal Pacific Coast regions also increased, surpassing the national average. Region IV had the highest level, 120 percent of the average.

Secondary education has long been cited as an important motivation for migration toward principal cities, for high schools in Latin America have traditionally been limited to those cities. There are good reasons, including economies of scale, to justify part of that centralization. As the proportion of the population receiving secondary education increases, however, there are also reasons to support the efficiency of increasingly decentralized location.

There did not appear to be readily available time series in Nicaragua on secondary school classrooms, but the data available on secondary school teachers and on high schools are presented in tables 4-7 and 4-8. With the exception of the anomaly caused by the single high school in Puerto Cabezas (Special Zone I), Managua clearly dominated the national distribution of high school teachers. There were 70 percent more teachers per school-age resident in Region III than in the nation as a whole; and the ratio in that region was more than 4 times greater than the comparable ratio for Region VI. From 1980 to 1984 the national secondary school teacher ratio rose by 35.8 percent, from 2.18 teachers per thousand school-age persons to 2.96. Managua's relative position declined by 11 percent, from 171 percent of the national average to 160 percent. Every other region increased its position relative to the national level, although the increase in Region VI, from 40.01 percent of the average to 40.90 percent was trivial. This remained a major element of relative underservicing for the whole of Region VI.

Finally, table 4-8 depicts the regional distribution of high schools per 10,000 school-age persons in each region, a "secondary school ratio." The national levels of the ratio rose by 36.8 percent between 1980 and 1984, increasing in absolute terms from 308 centers to 467 centers, and the initial dominance of Regions III and IV lessened. Region VI apparently maintained an effectively constant number of high schools (27 in 1980 and 28 in 1984 according to INEC data), but population growth and significant construction elsewhere reduced its absolute ratio of schools to school-age population and its relationship to the national average. Region I remained constant, Region V doubled its number of high schools from 27 to 51; and the remaining regions converged on the national average.

Public Health Programs. Nicaragua's health care system achievements have been described in scores of international studies.[9] But there has been little attention to the regional distribution of those services in the context of their potential contribution toward creating or stemming migratory flows. The implicit focus here on "curative" health care facilities rather than preventive care does an injustice to the full reorganization and development of the Nicaraguan health system. (But see Chapter

6.) Within Nicaragua's historical context, however, the presence of primary health care facilities was an important physical and political symbol of government outreach. The frequent contra attacks upon clinics in towns and isolated cooperatives demonstrated this principle amply.

Table 4-7
Regional Distribution of Secondary Education, 1980-84:
Teachers per 1,000 Inhabitants under 20 Years Old

REGION	1980	1981	1982	1983	1984
Region I	1.66	1.72	1.83	2.26	2.42
Region II	1.87	2.17	2.10	2.56	2.82
Region III	3.73	4.27	4.18	4.61	4.45
Region IV	2.25	2.89	2.84	3.18	3.29
Region V	1.02	1.21	1.14	1.55	1.91
Region VI	0.87	1.13	0.92	1.07	1.21
Special Zone I	4.34	2.84	n/a	2.26	2.53
Special Zone II*	1.59	3.48	1.00	3.91	3.88
Special Zone III	0.70	0.54	0.72	1.34	1.98
National	2.18	2.53	2.38	2.84	2.96

Percentage of National Average

REGION	1980	1981	1982	1983	1984
Region I	76.20	68.03	76.87	79.58	81.74
Region II	85.78	85.82	88.27	90.14	95.36
Region III	171.22	168.77	175.89	162.32	150.32
Region IV	103.19	114.03	119.40	111.97	111.33
Region V*	46.59	47.74	47.74	54.58	64.66
Region VI	40.01	44.69	38.65	37.68	40.90
Special Zone I	198.83	112.03	n/a	79.58	85.64
Special Zone II*	72.75	137.58	41.91	137.68	131.22
Special Zone III	32.30	21.29	30.06	47.18	67.06
National	100.00	100.00	100.00	100.00	100.00

Sources: Same as tables 4-5 and 4-6.
* See note to table 4-5 for definitions of Region V and Special Zone II.

Table 4-8
Regional Distribution of Secondary Education Facilities:
Schools per 10,000 Inhabitants Under 20 Years Old

REGION	1980	1981	1982	1983	1984
Region I	1.87	1.88	2.06	2.11	2.54
Region II	1.72	2.04	2.38	1.86	2.55
Region III	2.25	2.38	2.55	2.28	2.88
Region IV	2.37	2.41	2.54	2.40	2.70
Region V	1.50	1.76	2.12	2.15	2.71
Region VI	1.18	1.12	1.22	1.53	1.13
Special Zone I	2.92	2.78	1.89	2.69	2.72
Special Zone II*	1.63	1.94	5.15	4.19	5.31
Special Zone III	1.01	0.98	0.95	3.25	4.05
National	1.90	2.01	2.24	2.15	2.55

Percentage of National Average

REGION	1980	1981	1982	1983	1984
Region I	98.56	93.56	91.86	98.08	99.44
Region II	90.26	101.69	106.27	86.59	99.99
Region III	118.30	118.62	113.67	106.08	112.90
Region IV	124.75	119.87	113.25	111.60	105.75
Region V*	78.83	87.49	94.60	100.01	106.12
Region VI	62.25	55.67	54.59	71.12	44.37
Special Zone I	153.47	168.19	84.14	124.94	106.54
Special Zone II*	85.56	96.30	229.85	195.03	207.88
Special Zone III	52.92	48.78	42.56	150.97	158.83
National	100.00	100.00	100.00	100.00	100.00

Source: Same as tables 4-5 and 4-6.
* See note to table 4-5 for definitions of Revion V and Special Zone II.

The data displayed in table 4-9 reflect the fact that major and minor health care centers increased in number from 44 in 1981 to 518 by 1984. This tenfold increase was also concretely and deliberately oriented toward the outlying areas. Eight of the 44 health centers (18%) listed by INEC in 1981 were in Region III; by 1984, 83 of the 518 (16%) were in Region III. That is, 435 of the 474 new centers were established outside of the Managua area. In Region VI, however, the number of functioning hospitals and health care centers rose to 55 by the end of 1983 but fell back to 46 by the end of 1984, a casualty of <u>contra</u> attacks on health care facilities and personnel.

The distribution of hospital beds, as seen in table 4-10, provides a measure of the distribution of more sophisticated medical services. When the demand for medical services, expressed in terms of the proportions of the population in each region, is introduced as a factor of adjustment, we find that Managua (Region III) enjoyed a marked advantage over the rest of the country in 1980, with 23.7 beds per 10,000 residents. This was 43 percent above the national average. Region V and VI demonstrated the lowest degree of advanced medical services, fully 25 -to-30 percent below the national average. The focus of the health care system upon primary care in a decentralized fashion can also be seen in the fact that total beds per 10,000 inhabitants actually fell slightly (-4.7%) from 1980 to 1984.

The dispersion across regions in the relative level of medical services of this sort, however, has been reduced significantly. Region III fell to 121 percent of the national average; Region VI rose to 85 percent of the average; only Boaco continued to lag, maintaining a level at roughly 70 percent of the national average.

Land Distribution through Agrarian Reform. The Nicaraguan government distributed more than two million <u>manzanas</u> (1.15 million acres) of arable land to more than 55,000 families during the period from 1979 through the end of 1984. The regional distribution of lands available for assignment to families and cooperatives was not necessarily coterminous with the need for land. Did unintentional bias in the regional distribution of land lead to incentives for migration toward areas where more land was being distributed or where larger plots were available?

Table 4-11 provides information on the regional distribution of lands by MIDINRA under the agrarian reform process. It shows both the number of manzanas distributed and the number and percentage of families affected. We can see from those tables that the pace of the agrarian reform increased each year from 1982 through 1984. Of the total 2 million manzanas redistributed by the end of 1984, only 6.5 percent (132,500 manzanas) had been assigned by the end of 1982. In 1983 the pace of assignments increased by nearly 400 percent, for more than 500,000 manzanas were distributed (24.9% of the total). And in 1984 the pace more than tripled again: nearly 1,400,000 manzanas were assigned.

Table 4-9
Regional Distribution of Health Care:
Hospitals and Clinics Per 10,000 Inhabitants

REGION	1981	1982	1983	1984
Region I	0.2135	2.2381	2.2976	1.8996
Region II	0.1596	1.7001	1.7206	1.7017
Region III	0.1107	0.8726	1.0484	1.0015
Region IV	0.1165	1.8623	1.8211	1.6393
Region V*	0.1069	2.8880	2.4551	2.8747
Region VI	0.1300	0.9409	1.3673	1.1178
Special Zone I	n.a.	n.a.	2.8195	2.3635
Special Zone II*	0.4275	3.6231	3.1739	3.0078
Special Zone III	0.3037	4.4232	4.8644	4.4419
National	0.1565	1.7011	1.7397	1.6375

Percentages of National Average

REGION	1981	1982	1983	1984
Region I	136.46	131.57	132.07	116.01
Region II	101.98	99.94	98.90	103.92
Region I	70.72	51.30	60.26	61.16
Region IV	74.47	109.48	104.68	100.11
Region V*	68.31	169.77	141.12	175.56
Region VI	83.08	55.31	78.59	68.26
Special Zone I	n.a.	n.a.	162.07	144.34
Special Zone II*	273.23	212.99	182.44	183.68
Special Zone III	194.12	260.02	279.61	271.26
National	100.00	100.00	100.00	100.00

Source: Same as tables 4-5 and 4-6.
* See note to Table 4.5 for definitions of Region V and Special Zone II.
n.a. = not available.

Table 4-10
Regional Distribution of Healthcare Facilities:
Beds in Hospitals and Clinics per 10,000 Inhabitants

REGION	1980	1981	1982	1983	1984
Region I	15.18	13.81	14.01	13.59	13.72
Region II	15.14	15.64	16.31	17.08	16.67
Region III	23.67	11.09	21.25	20.48	19.38
Region IV	14.08	14.57	14.86	14.97	14.93
Region V*	11.75	12.13	12.29	9.66	11.37
Region VI	12.45	12.95	12.54	12.36	13.51
Special Zone I				15.72	14.18
Special Zone II*	17.74	20.47	16.96	27.08	26.47
Special Zone III	16.88	18.22	19.76	19.46	18.60
National	16.72	13.84	16.41	16.01	15.95

Percentage of National Average

REGION	1980	1981	1982	1983	1984
Region I	90.79	99.76	85.41	84.84	86.00
Region II	90.58	112.98	99.37	106.63	104.55
Region III	141.59	80.15	129.49	127.86	121.51
Region IV	84.25	105.24	90.57	93.48	93.62
Region V*	70.31	87.65	74.88	60.30	71.29
Region VI	74.51	93.55	76.41	77.15	84.71
Special Zone I				98.19	88.92
Special Zone II*	106.12	147.88	103.37	169.13	165.97
Special Zone III	100.97	131.67	120.41	121.50	116.63
National	100.00	100.00	100.00	100.00	100.00

Sources: Same as tables 4-5 and 4-6.
* See note to table 4-5 for definitions of Region V and Special Zone II.

Table 4-11
Agrarian Reform: Area Redistributed, 1979-84

| | Area Redistributed ('000s of manzanas) | | Manzanas Distributed per Rural Family* | | Estimated Rural Families |
	1979-82	1979-84	1979-82	1979-84	
Region I	20.4	146.7	0.63	4.55	32,271
Region II	25.6	136.3	0.66	3.54	38,520
Region III	12.0	47.1	0.66	2.60	18,112
Region IV	2.8	115.9	0.08	3.24	35,732
Region V	24.0	644.6	0.64	17.13	37,640
Region VI	21.6	558.1	0.4	11.36	49,147
Special Zone I	12.1	220.3	1.13	20.62	10,686
Special Zone II	1.7	73.5	0.56	24.05	3,056
Special Zone III	5.9	66.6	1.49	16.87	3,948
National	132.5	2009.1	0.58	8.77	229,111

Percent Distribution Across Regions

| REGION | Area Redistributed | | Percent of National Average Manzanas/Family | | Percent of Rural Families Benefited |
	1979-82	1979-84	1979-82	1979-84	
Region I	15.40	7.30	109.31	51.84	14.09
Region II	19.32	6.78	114.92	40.35	16.81
Region III	9.06	2.34	114.56	29.66	7.91
Region IV	2.11	5.77	13.55	36.99	15.60
Region V	18.11	32.08	110.25	195.29	16.43
Region VI	16.30	27.78	76.00	129.50	21.45
Special Zone I	9.13	10.97	195.79	235.10	4.66
Special Zone II	1.28	3.66	96.19	274.27	1.33
Special Zone III	4.45	3.31	258.41	192.37	1.72
National	100.00	100.00	100.00	100.00	100.00

Source: INEC, Anuario Estadistico de Nicaragua, 1982 and 1984; and from table 4-1.
* Rural families in 1982; the estimates of rural population are based on rural/urban ratios drawn
   from the 1982 Anuario Estadistico, applied to the 1982 population from Table 1; we assume an
   average of six persons per family.

The regional composition of assignments of land shifted consistently away from Regions II and IV and toward Regions V and VI. These latter war-zone regions received only 34 percent of the area assigned prior to the beginning of 1983; but by the end of 1984 they had received 59.6 percent of the total area assigned.

The regional distribution of families benefiting from the agrarian reform process also reflected this shift in emphasis. Approximately 29 percent of the families benefited prior to 1983 were located in Regions V and VI; but by the end of 1984, fully 54 percent of all families benefited over the entire prior period lived in those regions.

Basic Commodities Distribution Programs. The Sandinista government created a national program to coordinate and rationalize the distribution of basic commodities soon after the victory. Many of the members of the new government, remembering the obstacles in distribution that the Chilean Popular Unity government encountered, perceived the acute necessity for such a program.[10] The functions of ENABAS, a pre-existing small state-trading organization, were dramatically increased (see Chapter 5).

The functions of ENABAS involved rationalization of basic grain distribution, purchasing the grain directly from producers, storing it in regional granaries, and reselling it to consumers, especially in the cities, at prices below the purchase price. The subsidies were explicitly intended to defend purchasing power and real wages against inflationary pressures.[11] The levels of subsidies that were paid for the four most basic food commodities (beans, rice, corn, and sorghum) rose from 3.8 million Córdobas in 1979 to 225.4 million in 1980 and up to 400 million in 1983.

The distribution of these grains represented an important contribution to the fulfillment of household needs in most of the country, even though they were simply sold, in rationed quantities, at prices below the market price. The regional distribution of ENABAS sales provided an indication of the extent to which the public sector directed the subsidies toward Managua and the more-developed regions or toward the less developed or threatened regions on the periphery.

Of the four principal ENABAS foods, sorghum was used primarily for animal feeds, and its historical distribution had consistently emphasized those regions with larger and more industrialized poultry and cattle operations. Corn, on the other hand, was less likely to be a final consumption product in urban Nicaraguan homes. Although tortillas are made for home consumption in many rural areas and poorer urban areas, tortillas are purchased ready-made from vendors in most of the country. Direct distribution of corn to individual households, therefore, was less important than the direct distribution of rice and beans, the most important staples in the Nicaraguan diet.

The data on the distribution of rice through ENABAS presented in table 4-12 illustrate both the increases in absolute quantities and the changing regional composition of the program. Average absolute quantities distributed rose from 62 pounds per person in 1980 to 100 pounds per person in 1985. In 1980 the per capita distribution in Region III was 25 percent above the national average; the otherwise lagging Region VI received precisely the national average; and all of the remaining regions received less than the national average. The lowest level of distribution occurred in Region I, a major rice-producing area, where distribution was 57 percent of the national average.

By 1984 the per capita levels of distribution had risen to 84 pounds per person. All of the regions other than Region III were close to that average or significantly above it, and Region III had fallen to 79 percent of the national level. In 1985 ENABAS made a major adjustment, increasing the allocation to Region III; at that same time the distribution in the rice-producing Region I was reduced to 70 percent of the national level.

The scenario for beans was similar in many ways. Preferential distribution of larger quantities in Region III during 1980 quickly gave way to distributions averaging 80 percent of the national norm in subsequent years. It appears, however, that highly disproportionate quantities of beans were distributed in Region VI, a major bean-producing region, from 1980 to 1985. Total national levels of distribution varied substantially over the years, with per capita ENABAS distributions rising from 23 pounds in 1980 to 43 pounds in 1983 before falling back to 21 pounds per capita by 1985.

Relative Regional Wage and Price Levels

There did not exist in Nicaragua in 1986 any data series that indicated effective mean or median wages by region. The national social security institute, INSSBI, presumably possessed the capability of generating such estimates for workers in some portions of the formal sector, but it had not done so.

The wage scales set by the national labor classification system (SNOTS) were not regionalized. They were, in theory, applied equally across all regions in the country. There was much anecdotal information among government workers about extra benefits available to those who were willing to work in outlying regions. But, again, there was no systematic information available. The 1985 National "Demo-laboral" Survey was expected to yield important information in this area, but its results were not expected until late 1986.

If the SNOTS wage scales were being applied uniformly across all regions, the principal determinant of relative regional wage levels for workers in any given SNOTS category would be the relative regional price level. In order to determine the magnitude of the differences in cost of living across regions and the trends in those differences, we created a special "market basket" designed to permit interregional comparisons.

Table 4-12
Food Distribution: Pounds of Rice Distributed Per Capita, 1980-1985
(In Relation to Urban Population Only)

REGION

	1980	1981	1982	1983	1984	1985
Region I	35.85	59.36	61.72	74.82	77.84	70.02
Region II	47.06	39.22	44.12	56.56	82.56	117.18
Region III	78.02	66.57	50.79	53.49	66.19	104.56
Region IV	51.54	72.33	163.50	84.62	91.98	92.52
Region V*	67.09	93.63	127.47	148.47	131.95	120.19
Region VI	62.78	84.03	49.18	65.64	116.92	108.84
Special Zone I			122.13	107.96	196.72	99.84
Special Zone II*	86.30	173.63	84.41	115.81	90.40	0.92
Special Zone III	28.45	62.26	0.00	94.61	104.78	0.00
National	63.14	68.28	91.54	69.09	84.00	100.60

Percent of National Averages

REGION	1980	1981	1982	1983	1984	1985
Region I	56.77	86.94	67.43	108.30	92.66	69.60
Region II	74.54	57.44	48.20	81.87	98.29	116.48
Region III	123.58	97.50	55.48	77.42	78.80	103.94
Region IV	81.63	105.93	178.62	122.49	109.50	91.96
Region V*	106.26	137.14	139.26	214.90	157.08	119.47
Region VI	99.44	123.07	53.73	95.01	139.18	108.19
Special Zone I			133.43	156.27	234.18	99.24
Special Zone II*	136.68	254.30	92.21	167.64	107.61	0.91
Special Zone III	45.06	91.19	0.00	136.95	124.73	0.00
National	100.00	100.00	100.00	100.00	100.00	100.00

Source: Table 4-1 and unpublished data from ENABAS.
* For years prior to the 1982 regionalization, the data from Region V refer solely to the
  Departments of Boaco and Chontales; those from Special Zone II refer to the Department of
  Zelaya.

Table 4-13
Food Distribution: Pounds of Beans Distributed Percapita, 1980-1985
(In Relation to Urban Population Only)

REGION	1980	1981	1982	1983	1984	1985
Region I	23.03	35.40	38.75	53.01	73.96	47.42
Region II	12.90	25.48	26.21	51.08	29.58	17.34
Region III	28.44	24.94	23.72	28.21	30.94	17.43
Region IV	12.58	19.90	18.27	24.67	20.14	11.12
Region V*	21.87	23.94	54.19	77.20	56.35	55.85
Region VI	62.78	109.28	101.84	134.85	134.67	45.67
Special Zone I			48.10	47.35	84.78	14.96
Special Zone II*	17.42	43.00	23.81	39.04	38.46	0.92
Special Zone III	32.66	28.06	27.29	32.12	74.33	32.83
National	23.68	30.53	30.69	42.51	40.05	21.34

Percent of National Averages

REGION	1980	1981	1982	1983	1984	1985
Region I	97.26	115.98	126.26	120.05	184.67	222.24
Region II	54.49	83.46	85.39	120.17	73.86	81.26
Region III	120.13	81.71	77.28	66.36	77.25	81.67
Region IV	53.14	65.20	59.52	58.02	50.29	52.12
Region V*	92.38	78.43	176.54	181.62	140.70	261.73
Region VI	265.16	357.97	331.81	317.22	336.28	214.01
Special Zone I			156.70	111.39	211.69	70.10
Special Zone II*	73.56	140.87	77.59	91.84	96.03	4.31
Special Zone III	137.96	91.91	88.90	75.56	185.60	153.88
National	100.00	100.00	100.00	100.00	100.00	100.00

Source: Table 4-1 and unpublished data from ENABAS.
* For years prior to the 1982 regionalization, the data from Region V refer solely to the
   Departments of Boaco and Chontales; those from Special Zone II refer to the Department of
   Zelaya.

The special regional pricing commodity basket consists of a set of 20 food items that met the following criteria. First, they were drawn directly from the basket then monitored monthly by INIES for the sake of producing an independent estimate of changes in the cost of living. In fact, the 20 items selected represented 65.7 percent of the total costs of "food products" in the March 1986 benchmark INIES estimate. Each of the products selected was also a part of the set of food products for which INEC had been monitoring prices in the principal cabeceras municipales from 1980 to 1985. Finally, each of the products in the special basket had to be measured in the same units of measurement in both the INEC price series and in an interministerial report on consumption levels by major commodity.[12] Some goods are measured in units in one and in pounds in the other; for the sake of minimal reliability, consistency in measurement unit was also required.[13]

The 20 food items are listed in table 4-14, along with the quantities of each utilized in the MICOIN/SPP/MITRAB Canasta Básica. This is the canasta that represents the highest level of consumption in the combined inter-ministerial studies, but it is the only level for which benchmark INIES data were available. The "absolute weights" of table 4-14 represent the total cost of the quantities indicated in the March 1986 benchmark; the "relative weights" indicate the percentile contribution of each to the canasta. The total cost of the special basket created here constituted 51.9 percent of the total cost of the canasta básica portion of the INIES price study; so total costs for the full canasta would be roughly twice the cost of this selection. No data were available on comparable costs for housing, clothing, entertainment, and the other items in more complete price indices.

To the extent that this canasta especial reflects important components of the relative cost of living, Managua was the most expensive place to live in Nicaragua in 1981, and it continued to be the most expensive in 1985. Table 4-15 demonstrates that all of the regions outside of Managua (with the exception of the Atlantic Coast) had cost levels in 1981 for this illustrative selection of foods that were only 40 percent of the cost of the same products in Managua (Region III). Although the estimated monthly cost of the "special basket" for a family of six in Region III rose from 2,400 Córdobas in 1981 to 24,000 Córdobas in 1985, the relative price level in regions other than Managua remained essentially static in 1982, 1983, and 1984, well below those of Managua. From 1984 to 1985, however, prices of foodstuffs in outlying regions jumped to an average of 77% of the price level in Managua.

The migration to Region III noted for the period through 1984 was occurring, then, despite continued dramatic differences in the costs of basic foodstuffs. Whether wage differences existed that offset those price differences was doubted by most of the SPP staff and field employees as well. The answer will not be known, however, until the results of the "Demo-laboral" Survey are released.

Table 4-14
Special Basket of Goods for Regional Price Analysis
(Monthly Family Budget, Selected Food Items)

PRODUCT	Quantity	Unit	Absolute Weighting	Relative Weighting
Beef	1	Pounds	500	1.555
Ground beef	2	Pounds	600	1.866
Pork	5	Pounds	1700	5.286
Whole chicken	1	Each	270	0.840
Rice (ENABAS)	31	Pounds	1240	3.856
French bread	12	Pounds	2560	7.960
Tortillas	17	Pounds	2000	6.219
Red beans (ENABAS)	20	Pounds	3200	9.951
Onion	10	Pounds	1778	5.529
Tomato	15	Pounds	3000	9.329
Potatoes	10	Pounds	2000	6.219
Eggs	120	Each	2800	8.707
Milk (past.)	67.5	Liters	2696	8.383
Cheese (fresh)	4	Pounds	1600	4.975
Vegetable oil	4	Liters	2000	6.219
Refined salt	4	Pounds	60	0.187
Tomato sauce	1 1/2	Bottle	250	0.777
Vinegar	1	Bottle	275	0.855
Ground coffee	4	Pounds	780	2.425
Sugar	15	Pounds	2850	8.862
TOTAL			32159	100.000

Notes: The quantities are from MICOIN's canasta básica; the weighting is based on prices from March of 1986, gathered by INIES; the special basket represents 65.7 percent of the total of the "food" category and 51.9 percent of the total value of INIES' canasta básica.

The Regional Distribution of Investment Projects

There are two levels on which investment planning can affect relative regional standards of living and the relative locational attractiveness of an area. Large-scale, multiyear investment projects may be located in a specific region and may affect it differentially, and year-to-year government budgeting for investment may affect regions differentially. No usable time series for regionalized investments existed in 1986, either on the major project level or the annual investment planning level. Recent single-period data on both levels, however, were available.

Table 4-15
Differential Costs of Living by Region*
Special Basket of Goods (Food Only), 1981-1985
(Monthly Costs in Córdobas, Family of Six Persons)

REGION	1981	1982	1983	1984	1985
Region I	967.54	1,089.86	1,431.54	2,103.37	8,651.01
Region II	1,091.92	1,146.63	1,467.93	2,932.01	9,127.27
Region III	2,434.76	2,703.60	3,201.05	4,832.30	11,698.20
Region IV	1,071.80	1,165.00	1,461.08	2,200.03	9,282.65
Region V	n/a	n/a	1,452.91	2,090.23	9,390.87
Region VI	1,034.33	1,121.54	1,380.97	1,940.63	8,524.56
Atlantic Coast	1,527.31	1,502.86	2,067.29	3,401.93	9,291.78

Percentages of the Managua (Region III) Cost of Living

REGION	1981	1982	1983	1984	1985
Region I	39.74	40.31	44.72	43.53	73.95
Region II	44.85	42.41	45.86	60.68	78.02
Region III	100.00	100.00	100.00	100.00	100.00
Region IV	44.02	43.09	45.64	45.53	79.35
Region V	n/a	n/a	45.39	43.26	80.28
Region VI	42.48	41.48	43.14	40.16	72.87
Atlantic Coast	62.73	55.59	64.58	70.40	79.43

Source: INEC, Anuario Estadístico de Nicaragua, various issues; and from table 4-1.
* Regional prices derived from prices in the departmental capitals; prices on the Atlantic Coast based solely on prices in Bluefields. No data were available for prices in 1981 or 1982 for the departmental capitals of Region V (Boaco and Juigalpa).

Table 4-16 presents regionalized data drawn from a recent study by the Fondo Nicaragüense de Inversiones, a Nicaraguan Central Bank institution, that detailed and evaluated a portfolio of 40 major investment projects under way in mid-1985. The regionalization of the data provided only first-round impacts, that is, an indication of the region for which (or in which) the project was being developed. It did not incorporate the secondary effects, such as the impacts on other regions from which inputs were purchased. As it stands, the portfolio of projects provides an indication of where the government is placing its long-term investment projects, where each project is implicitly weighted by its total Cordoba cost.

The investment per inhabitant was highest in Region VI, with the exception of the Special Zones. Investment projects in the portfolio of 40 as of late 1985 provided nearly 27,000 Córdobas per person in Region VI. The lowest level of investment per capita pertained to Region V, with only 3,400 Córdobas per capita. Investment projects for Region III, the largest in absolute amount (C$ 858 million), yielded a percapita level of C$ 14,530, 84 percent of the national average.

Table 4-16
Regional Distribution of Principal Investment Projects,
Underway as of July 1985*

REGION	1982 Population (Thousands)	Total Invested (Millions of of Córdobas)	Regional Percent Distribution	Thousands of Córdobas Invested Percapita	Percent in Relation to National Average
Region I	290.3	1939.2	3.84	6.68	38.61
Region II	490.3	8957.8	17.75	18.27	105.61
Region III	858.3	12471.1	24.71	14.53	83.99
Region IV	491.2	1974.6	3.91	4.02	23.24
Region V	263.8	896.9	1.78	3.40	19.65
Region VI	355.2	9661.4	19.14	27.20	157.23
Special Zone I	96.2	2953.3	5.85	30.70	177.46
Special Zone II	41.8	2353.8	4.66	56.31	325.49
Special Zone III	30.2	1603.9	3.18	53.11	306.99
National	2917.8	7655.1	15.17	2.62	15.14
TOTALS	2917.8	50477.9	99.98	17.30	100.00

Source: FNI, Fondo Nacional de Inversiones, Inversiones 1979 1984; Análisis del Proceso Inversionista Nicaragüense, Segundo Avance, October 1985, Table No. 16.2.

* Data based on a portfolio of 40 projects ongoing in July 1985 that represent 89 percent of productive investment for 1984 and 87 percent of that category for the 1985 program.

Table 4-17 presents a regionalization of the 1985 Public Investment Program as an illustration of year-to-year investment programming. The 1985 program concentrated heavily on Region III, both in absolute terms and in per capita terms. The largest absolute investment plan for infrastructure and the largest per capita budget, by a large margin, were programmed for Region VI. Once again, the public sector gave exceptional priority to that war-torn region.

Table 4-17
Regional and Sectoral Distribution
of the 1985 "Programa de Inversiones"
(Thousands of Córdobas)

REGION	Total Investment Córdobas	Per capita	Agriculture Córdobas	Per capita (Rural)	Infrastructure Córdobas	Per capita
Region I	399,276	1.243	326,828	1.566	51,968	0.162
Region II	488,718	0.857	108,500	0.432	184,348	0.323
Region III	4,033,545	4.650	2,129,181	17.534	464,418	0.535
Region IV	371,133	0.633	128,267	0.576	43,210	0.074
Region V	202,480	0.645	53,900	0.235	64,180	0.205
Region VI	1,833,892	4.357	939,640	3.058	644,767	1.532
Special Zones	2,716,508	14.119	529,427	4.443	1,407,147	7.314
National	9,843,028	3.008	4,215,743	2.889	2,859,948	0.874

Percent Distribution

REGION	Total Investment Total	Average	Agriculture Total	Average	Infrastructure Total	Average
Region I	4.06	41.33	7.75	54.20	1.82	18.51
Region II	4.97	28.47	2.57	14.96	6.45	36.97
Region III	40.98	154.58	50.51	606.94	16.24	61.26
Region IV	3.77	21.06	3.04	19.94	1.51	8.44
Region V	2.06	21.46	1.28	8.15	2.24	23.41
Region VI	18.63	144.83	22.29	105.85	22.54	175.25
Special Zones	27.60	469.35	12.56	153.80	49.20	836.75
National	100.00	100.00	100.00	100.00	100.00	100.00

Source: Unpublished data from the Secretaría de Planificación y Presupuesto.

A Summary Measure for Regional Outreach

There is no obvious manner of combining public sector outreach across regions in programs as diverse as public health, basic grain distribution, education, agrarian reform, public investment, and their consequences for relative levels of salaries and prices. Nor did there exist the data that would have been needed to relate each of those dimensions to internal migration in a statistically reliable fashion. This was especially true when there were only six regions and relatively unreliable estimates of the rates of flow for only a single point in time.

Nevertheless, the qualitative dimension of each of these measures is relatively clear. Higher levels of accomplishment on each of the measures that have been surveyed here, with the exception of prices, can be conceptually linked to improvements in relative regional conditions and a lessening of the incentive for migration.

We have generated above estimates of the status of each region for each of the variables, measured in terms of percentage variation from the national average. In table 4-18 we present a summary of those measures for a selection of 12 variables at two points in time, 1980-81 and 1984-85. The simple arithmetic mean of the levels of achievement relative to the national average for each variable provides a single index of overall relative outreach by the public sector to each region. The change in that index from the earlier period to the latter in any given region indicates overall change across time. Changes in the dispersion of the index across regions indicate the success with which the public sector outreach has widened or lessened interregional inequality.

The index has one glaring weakness. It carries an implicit assumption that each of the measures is equally important or that three measures for education give a weighting that is appropriate relative to two measures for public health and one for prices. There is no reason to believe that weighting to be inherently more appropriate than one that gives three times the weight to prices and one-third as much weight to education. The only basis for choosing a clearly more appropriate weighting would be a sample survey indicating national weighted preferences across these programs or an indication of the de facto weights implicit in the public sector planning.

Table 4-18 also provides an opportunity to see, program by program, where any given region has made progress and where it may have slipped. Managua was clearly the region in 1980-81 with the highest average regional levels of the public sector programs analyzed here. Regions I, II, and IV were approximately equal, with an average of 83 percent to 85 percent of the national average level overall. By 1984-85, however, Managua's average level was the lowest of any region, having fallen from 97.09 to 71.51.

Table 4-18
Summary Regional Distribution of Public Sector Services
(Percentile Relationship to National Average Levels
Six Core Regions: 1980 and 1984-85)

Sector (1980)	Region I	Region II	Region III	Region IV	Region V	Region VI
Primary education						
Teachers	89.15	91.77	117.39	117.53	85.88	58.75
Classrooms	87.91	96.37	103.64	79.85	64.96	66.55
Schools	119.78	83.75	59.03	96.66	147.31	86.73
Secondary education						
Teachers	76.20	85.78	171.22	103.19	46.59	40.01
Schools	98.56	90.26	118.30	124.75	78.83	62.25
Health care						
Hospital beds	91.95	91.75	143.41	85.33	70.31	75.47
Centers ('81)	138.83	103.75	71.94	75.76	68.31	84.52
Agrarian reform (up to '82)						
Area	109.31	114.92	114.56	13.55	110.25	76.00
Families	94.46	153.78	119.75	99.33	57.54	91.24
Grain distribution						
Rice	57.25	75.16	124.61	82.31	136.68	100.27
Beans	98.13	54.99	121.22	53.62	92.38	267.56
Prices (-) ('81)	-39.74	-44.85	-100.00	-44.02	n/a	-42.48
AVERAGE	85.15	83.12	97.09	73.99	87.19	80.57

Sector (1984-85	Region I	Region II	Region III	Region IV	Region V	Region VI
Primary education ('84)						
Teachers	110.48	101.38	107.42	115.89	86.50	72.41
Classrooms	110.10	110.64	92.91	120.31	86.24	84.35
Schools	127.59	111.56	58.71	104.68	128.60	119.76
Secondary education ('84)						
Teachers	81.74	95.36	150.32	111.33	64.66	40.90
Schools	99.44	99.99	112.90	105.75	106.12	44.37
Health care ('84)						
Hospital beds	86.00	104.55	121.51	93.62	71.29	84.71
Centers	116.01	103.92	61.16	100.11	175.56	68.26
Agrarian reform (thru '84)						
Area	51.84	40.35	29.66	36.99	195.29	129.50
Families	73.45	67.81	37.97	88.54	114.09	140.15
Grain distribution						
Rice	69.60	116.48	103.94	91.96	119.47	108.19
Beans	222.24	81.26	81.67	52.12	261.73	214.01
Prices (-)	-73.95	-78.02	-100.00	-79.35	-80.28	-72.87
AVERAGE	89.55	79.61	71.51	78.50	110.77	86.15

Source: Previous tables.

Conclusions

Nicaragua appears to have accomplished a remarkable reorientation of public sector resources, between 1980 and 1985, toward outlying regions, especially those most severely affected by the contra war. The acute and disproportionate migration toward Managua that was believed to have occurred could not be corroborated with data available through mid-1986. The burgeoning of the city on its periphery, the filling-in of previously unsettled central city lands, and the confrontations over land in the city that were occurring in 1986, pitting Sandinista worker and neighborhood organizations against governmental offices, may have reflected more clearly the relocation of Managua-area population and reductions in density in existing Managua neighborhoods.

We have tried to stress throughout the study the tentative nature of our faith in the statistics available; further, we have emphasized that, apart from the data we did have, much remained hidden. Nonetheless, we could draw some conclusions.

First, there was evidence to suggest that regional outreach, resettlement programs in the peripheral regions, and continued commitment of the population to residence in endangered zones had led to far less migration toward Managua than one might have expected under the circumstances. Managua continued to attract more people than any other area in the country, both absolutely and as a percentage of its overall population. The city appeared to have grown at a rate of little more than 0.25 percent annually since the Sandinista victory.

Second, by 1985 Managua no longer dominated social and economic investment nearly to the extent that it did in 1980; the central government had actively pursued this decentralization, seeking a more equitable dispersal of services to the outlying parts of the country. In all the areas we examined, from health care to prices, except in that of sectoral investments (table 4-17), we observed an overall leveling across the regions of public service provision.

If, however, agrarian reform, health service, education, and food prices have begun to provide people incentives to remain in the remote regions, why did they continue to migrate to Managua at even the perceived pace?

Much of the answer lay with the contra war. Changes in the style of the war, from one of large strikes with substantial numbers of invading forces to a "low-intensity war" characterized by economic sabotage in remote areas has struck the small farmers in the outlying regions harder than anyone else. If those farmers and the residents of smaller towns felt threatened, keeping them in the countryside may have demanded even more incentives.

Another part of the answer undoubtedly lay in the attraction of the informal sector in Managua. Since we had no data on wages in the informal sector, we could not include it in our analysis. Nevertheless, anecdotal evidence pointed overwhelmingly to the attraction of higher wages in that sector.

Finally, many observers in Managua noted that there had been practically no repression of land invasions in urban areas after 1979. It may well be that the rate of movement toward Managua will continue to be high so long as migrants face a much less hostile government as they arrive in Managua.

Given the data we collected, which showed a consistent attempt to direct services out of Region III, one would have expected migration to Managua to slow down. In fact, this was not the case. One thing was certain: the counterrevolutionary war, which killed and displaced Nicaraguans in the remotest regions, provided a strong incentive to leave them. The fact that so many remained in those areas speaks volumes that we cannot about the fuller effects of the Sandinista revolution and the commitments of farmers and townspeople in the outlying regions to defend it.

Endnotes to Chapter 4

1. CIERA (Centro de Investigaciones y Estudios de la Reforma Agraria) and UNRISD (United Nations Research Institute for Social Development), <u>Managua Es Nicaragua: El Impacto de la Capital en el Sistema Alimentario Nacional</u>, Managua, October 1984.

2. For more detailed information and an analysis of the regionalization rationale, see: Juan-Luis Klein and Orlando Peña, "De la Destructuración a la Estructuración del Espacio Nicaraguense: Notas Sobre el Plan de Regionalización de Nicaragua," Departament des Sciences Humaines, Universite de Quebec a Chicoutimi (October 1982).

3. From a regional science perspective, it was perfectly reasonable to include those three <u>municipios</u> in one of the basic regions, for they are linked to the national economy and the Pacific area of the nation by all-weather roads and by development history, more than any of the areas icoporated into the Special Zones. This regionalization presents a problem, however, in that there are virtually no data available on a municipal basis for the period prior to 1983, when the regionalization was first implemented for data reporting, that would permit rectifying the departmental deata of the "old Zelaya" so that Region V and the Special Zones are covered accurately for periods prior to that date. The adjustment adopted here for the period prior to 1983, unless otherwise indicated, is to use data for Boaco and Chontales alone to represent Region V and to use all of the "old Zelaya" to reprsent Special Zones I and II.

4. INEC, Instituto Nacional de Estadísticas y Censos, <u>Estimaciones de Poblacion 1980-1987, Sexo - Grupo de Edad - Region</u>, Agosto de 1985.

5. The precise form in which the adjustment was made has not been described in written documents; the reconstruction presented here is based on conversations with INEC statistical methods staff in June 1986.
6. INETER (Instituto Nacional de Estudios Territoriales), Marco Nacional de Regionalización para la Planficación Física (2do Adelantado), 1986.
7. SPP/INETER, Borrador Resumen Diagnostico Territorial..., op.cit., p. 12.
8. See, for example, Carlos Tunnerman Bernheim, Hacia una Nueva Educación en Nicaragua, Managua: Ministro de Educación, 1981, and chapters in Thomas Walker, ed., Nicaragua--The First Five Yars, New York: Praeger, 1985.
9. See, for example, Paula Braveman, "Primary Health Care Takes Root in Nicaragua," in the World Health Organization's World Health Forum, 6 (1985) 4: 368-372; also Halperin, D. & Garfield, R., New England Journal of Medicine, 307 (1982): 388-392.
10. See, for example, MICOIN (Ministerio de Comercio Interior), Sistemas de Comercialización: Productos Básicos de Consumo Popular, Volume I, "Aspectos Globales."
11. Ibidem, p. C-2.
12. The ministries involved are those of Interior Commerce (MICOIN) and Labor (MITRAB) and the Office of Planning and Budget (SPP).
13. The data published by INEC is based upon surveys in selected "cabeceras municipales." For 1981 and 1982 only six outlying "cabeceras" were surveyed in addition to Managua, but they were fortunately distributed such that there was one in each of the future regions, except for Region V. The data in Table 18 are based, therefore, on data for a single "cabecera" in each region for 1981 and 1982. For the remaining years they consist of weighted averages of the prices provided for any "cabecera" listed in the respective region. Missing data in the INEC price reports were interpolated by applying the average rate of growth of all prices for the respective region.

Chapter 5

State Trading Organizations in Expansion: A Case Study of ENABAS

by

Alfred H. Saulniers

With the assistance of Félix Delgado Silva

Introduction

On coming to power on July 19, 1979, the Nicaraguan Junta set the stage for a massive increase in the portfolio of government-owned corporations. Decree No. 3, issued the following day, confiscated all goods pertaining to the Somoza family, to high officials of the National Guard, and to government officials who had abandoned the country after December 1977. Decree No. 38, issued six weeks later, widened the circle of people whose properties were subject to confiscation by including those linked to Somocismo. As an immediate consequence of these measures, the government became owner of 23.3 percent of the nation's arable land,[1] of a variety of industrial firms, and of many small retailers or other companies in the service sector.

The new Nicaraguan state also adapted its existing public enterprises to better fit its new policy of controlling internal resource allocation. Overall, this resulted in an increased government presence in the economy through added provision of basic goods and services. It shifted the emphasis of existing providers and tightened control of the environmental context for decision making. Consequently, some existing government organizations were faced with major shifts away from their long-standing objectives of supporting the production of agro-export crops and were subsequently reoriented to the provision of basic agricultural products. This chapter examines in detail one such company, ENABAS, the Nicaraguan Basic Foodstuffs Enterprise. A brief historical background to the company is provided, followed by an economic and financial analysis of company operations from 1980 to 1985. An intragovernmental, interlinkage framework serves as the basis for examining the management environment and context for company action and for studying the network of relations that link ENABAS to other government agencies.

Historical Background

The government of Nicaragua had a long tradition in marketing of foodstuffs for agro-export and for local consumption. Both aspects were reflected in ENABAS's institutional bases. First, ENABAS arose, in part, from a standard state trading organization (STO).[2] In 1942, the Compañía Marítima de Ultramar (CMU) was established under the Law of Mercantile Societies and incorporated in the United States with the objective of marketing Nicaragua's chief export crop, coffee.[3] Later, the Banco Nacional absorbed the CMU, downgrading it in the process to the status of an import-export department operating in the bank without any independent legal existence.

ENABAS's other institutional base came from the Granero Nacional Número 1, which acted as a small marketing board to dampen price fluctuations for farmers and customers. Organized without any separate legal identity as a special program administered by the Instituto de Fomento Nacional, it accomplished both objectives by providing farmers with higher prices than could otherwise be expected at harvest time and by releasing stocks to consumers at lower prices than would be expected in the immediate preharvest shortages.[4] The double-barreled subsidy mission resulted in substantial losses.[5]

The two institutional bases joined in 1960 with the creation of the National Institute of Foreign and Domestic Trade, INCEI, which was designed to resolve the management problem of providing autonomy in decision making to two institutions whose current administrative structure impeded action.[6] INCEI's law of creation granted it full administrative autonomy, which included a distinct legal identity, financial independence, and contractual freedom, all elements missing from its two parent organizations.[7] INCEI's goals were clearly economic, not social, and stressed selling Nicaragua's export products in the most advantageous international markets; developing local markets for Nicaraguan and foreign merchandise received low priority.[8] The list of possible actions available to the company reflects the clear bias toward export agriculture: of the eleven areas specified in INCEI's law of creation, only three dealt with the marketing of basic grains, namely, cleaning and preserving, establishing a warehouse and sales system, and providing preharvest credit to farmers.[9]

INCEI has been criticized as having the goal of supplying cheap foodstuffs to agricultural workers to hold down real wages, thereby maintaining high profits for agro-exporters.[10] At the time of its creation, however, keeping profits high by closely monitoring export markets and by using the market analysis information to time Nicaragua's sales in markets and on terms to maximize contract prices clearly overshadowed any real wage effects. Only later, in the 1970s, after

INCEI had been stripped of authority over two key export crops, cotton and coffee, did its real wage effects through imports, local purchases, and sales of basic grains assume importance.[11]

By the end of the decade, INCEI's distribution system comprised 322 agencies scattered throughout the country.[12] Notwithstanding this national presence, INCEI had only a limited impact; it accounted for barely 5 percent of the national grain market during the late 1970s, too marginal a presence to regulate or control the market properly.[13] Its drying facilities were low-efficiency and its storage facilities were low-capacity, crippling any effective efforts at expansion.[14] The entrepreneurial policies of the new government shifted policy dramatically during 1979, placing greater emphasis on the social interest.[15] Consequently, exactly two months after the new government came to power, INCEI was reorganized as ENABAS.

A New Mission - Helping the Nicaraguan People

ENABAS received a new mission along with its new name: to act as the government's sole authorized agent in importing and exporting basic grains and as the government's discretionary agent in buying and selling basic grains in the local market.[16] To carry out those functions, ENABAS retained the standard attributes of independent legal personality, financial independence, and contractual freedom.[17] As company officials interpreted the objectives, ENABAS would act as the government's wholesaler in basic necessities to assure the Nicaraguan people secure lines of supply at low prices.[18] To fulfill its new mission, ENABAS would buy grains through a network of state agricultural warehouses (DAPs), import supplies in the event of a shortfall in local production, provide warehousing and drying functions for farmers, and distribute its production in the new, secure channels comprising local retailers (expendios populares), marketplaces, the nationalized supermarkets, and commisaries at major workplaces.

As befitting its expanded state-trading role, ENABAS was placed under the Ministry of Foreign Trade, MICE;[19] but in 1980, to group ENABAS with other firms involved in domestic trade and services along functional lines, the government created MICOIN[20] to simplify the "irrational and chaotic" organization of the country's commercial activity.[21] The shift in ministerial ascription supports the McCalla and Schmitz hypothesis that state trading in temperate zone agricultural products, including maize, is generally undertaken by nations as an element of domestic policy, rather than as an explicit international trade policy.[22] Indeed, one of the major MICOIN attributes was to apply all dispositions of Nicaragua's Law in Defense of Consumers.[23]

ENABAS Economic and Financial Growth: 1980-1985

Table 5-1 reviews aggregate physical measures of ENABAS operations from 1980 to 1985. Basic grains purchases rose from slightly more than 4 million quintales (hundred-pound sacks) in 1980 to almost 7.5 million in 1983. The two following years witnessed sharp drops as foreign exchange shortages notably curbed ENABAS's import capabilities. Sales of basic grains rose similarly, peaking in 1984, then dropping to a 5.5 million quintal level in 1985. The labor force employed by ENABAS rose 15 percent from 1982 to 1983, reflecting increased numbers of temporary workers hired at years' end to help with postharvest drying and storage. The drop by 1985 to less than 2,200 workers represents a decrease of more than 150 permanent workers.

Storage capacity remained close to 5 million quintales after 1981, but its composition shifted away from rented facilities and impermanent silos to permanent warehouses. Warehouse space more than doubled, from 658 thousand quintals to 1.6 million, and rented storage fell from 508 thousand quintales to 13 thousand. ENABAS facilities have been singled out for destruction by contra forces and, during 1985, three were destroyed in the Estelí area.[24]

The use of physical variables, rather than monetary measures, to examine ENABAS's growth permits the calculation of some productivity measures that are free of the distorting effects of inflation on some standard financial measures. First, as shown in table 5-1, productivity per worker increased 11 percent betweem 1982 and 1983, from 2.3 tons handled to 2.55 tons handled. Thereafter, it remained stable, even in the face of dropping sales. Second, warehouse throughput more than doubled, going from 54 percent of installed capacity in 1981 to 135 percent by 1984. It declined with 1985's lower sales.

Table 5-2 provides data on basic goods bought and sold by ENABAS. These comprise essential grains such as maize, beans[25], and rice for human consumption; sorghum for animal feed; and other basic consumer essentials such as sugar, salt, oil, and soap. The first part of the decade was marked by rising trends in local purchases and in sales of most products; the 1984-1985 period saw a trend reversal and drops in ENABAS's buying and selling operations, including a halt in imports of two key items, maize and sorghum. The sale of nongrain basics fell sharply, from more that 400 thousand quintales of sugar in 1984 to only 11 in 1985 and from more than 223 thousand boxes of soap in 1984 to zero sales in 1985, following a de facto transfer of most of those operations to ENABAS regional offices.[26]

Table 5-3 reproduces major categories from ENABAS's yearly income statements. During the 1980-1985 period, sales rose more than eightfold, measured in current terms, from more than 600 million Córdobas to 4.8 billion in 1985. The cost of goods sold usually exceeded sales, resulting in negative gross profits, except in 1981, which showed a low profit level, and 1985, which marked a clean break with previous government subsidy and pricing policies. Looking at some of the cost categories, although losses in cleaning and storage rose sharply, two other elements, financial and transport costs, fell in current terms.

The government's subsidy to ENABAS appears in two parts: the first comprises much of the differential between producer and consumer prices; the second remains as an accounting loss, which is offset in the balance sheet by increased government equity. From 1982 to 1984, the ENABAS accounting loss averaged approximately 1.5 percent of GDP and 20 percent of the government deficit on current account.

Table 5-1
ENABAS Operations, 1980-1985

		1980	1981	1982	1983	1984	1985
Basic grains purchases*		4,241.3	4,711.0	5,516.7	7,468.4	7,102.3	5,756.3
	Local*	1879.9	3,312.8	4,369.9	4,840.6	5,296.0	4,383.5
	Imports*	2,255.6	1,315.6	943.3	2,317.1	722.7	545.0
	Donations*	105.8	82.6	203.5	310.7	1,083.6	827.8
Basic grains sales*		2,675.4	2,783.3	4,740.0	6,074.7	6,310.3	5,463.6
Active labor force		n.a.	n.a.	2,058	2,385	n.a.	2,170
	Storage capacity*	n.a.	5,129.9	5,178.9	4,925.1	4,692.9	4,838.3
	Silos	n.a.	3,705.2	3,202.0	3,323.0	3,264.1	3,264.1
	Bodegas	n.a.	658.5	1,245.5	1,300.3	1,415.6	1,560.6
	Rental	n.a.	508.8	578.7	301.8	13.2	13.6
	Other**	n.a.	257.4	152.7	0.0	0.0	0.0
Productivity							
	Tons sold/worker	n.a.	n.a.	2.30	2.55	n.a.	2.52
	Warehouse throughput***	n.a.	54.3	91.5	123.3	134.5	112.9

Source: ENABAS, <u>Análisis global de ENABAS sobre las actividades desarrolladas durante los años</u> <u>1980-1982; Informe anual 1983; Informe anual 1985;</u> Anexo estadístico y financiero 1981; Anexo estadístico, 1982, 1983, 1984, 1985.
*   Thousands of quintales
** Borrowed or in temporary use
*** Percentages
n.a. Not available

Table 5-2
ENABAS Operations by Product by Year, 1981-1985

PRODUCT		1981	1982	1983	1984	1985
Maize(a)	Local purchase	781.5	733.5	905.0	1,271.6	1,202.8
	Imports	651.8	943.3	2,124.3	0.0	0.0
	Donations	0.0	160.2	149.1	631.3	564.2
	Sales(b)	1,541.3	1,737.7	3,023.3	1,755.0	1,670.8
	Losses(c)	-82.3	141.5	166.9	252.8	227.7
Beans(a)	Local purchase	277.1	505.1	622.6	443.2	192.9
	Imports	243.3	0.0	0.0	312.2	170.2
	Donations	67.4	43.3	62.4	154.2	14.8
	Sales(b)	498.3	503.8	738.7	709.2	387.7
	Losses(c)	18.2	79.7	71.5	248.6	-20.3
Rice(a,c)	Local purchase	809.6	1,892.8	2,235.3	2,152.1	1,127.7
	Imports	420.5	0.0	0.0	410.5	374.8
	Donations	15.2	0.0	99.2	298.0	320.9
	Sales(b)	1,077.1	1,412.5	1,752.2	2,158.7	1,866.2
	Losses(c)	11.6	98.0	31.4	62.5	-71.2
Sorghum(a)	Localpurchase	1,233.8	1,238.5	1,077.7	1,441.1	1,860.1
	Imports	0.0	0.0	192.8	0.0	0.0
	Sales(b)	1,147.8	1,104.3	707.8	1,798.8	1,273.9
	Losses(c)	340.4	366.0	112.8	-69.2	206.2
Sugar(a)	Local purchase	354.5	388.1	528.6	413.4	11.2
	Donation	0.0	0.0	0.0	0.0	12.7
	Sales	365.8	439.0	501.1	429.9	14.9
	Losses(c)	n.a.	-54.9	16.4	0.0	2.0
Salt(a)	Local purchase	87.8	114.0	110.2	79.8	0.3
	Sales	85.0	102.0	126.0	88.6	5.1
	Losses(c)	n.a.	2.1	-15.7	0.9	0.0
Oil(e)	Local purchase	153.3	170.0	586.6	425.7	14.7
	Imports	138.5	54.3	0.0	0.0	0.0
	Sales	138.6	248.2	530.7	461.3	28.1
	Losses(c)	n.a.	4.2	17.2	0.0	-1.8
Soap(f)	Local purchase	148.9	172.8	528.8	223.3	0.0
	Sales	139.4	175.9	521.9	335.0	610.2
	Losses(c)	n.a.	9.3	-97.7	0.0	18.7

Source: ENABAS, Anexo estadístico y financiero 1981, and Anexo estadístico, 1981-85.

(a) Thousands of quintales	(d) All grades of rice included
(b) Includes sales of subproducts and exports	(e) Thousands of tins of 5 gallons each
	(f) Thousands of boxes of 54 bars each
(c) Negative losses represent gain from inventory adjustment	n.a. Not available

Table 5-3
ENABAS Consolidated Income Statement, 1980-1985
Millions of current Córdobas)

	1980	1981	1982	1983	1984	1985
Income/expenditure category						
Net sales	606.5	902.1	1,123.9	1,366.5	1,650.9	4,840.3
Cost of goods sold	620.6	878.0	1,248.0	1,565.5	1,876.9	3,396.1
Gross profit	-606.5	-902.1	-1,123.9	-1,366.5	-1,650.9	-4,840.3
Operating costs	68.8	19.5	47.2	33.9	101.9	360.8
Losses in cleaning						
and storage	18.5	19.5	47.2	33.9	101.1	360.8
Sales and administrative						
expenditures	141.2	237.3	240.4	276.4	390.7	668.5
Financial costs	31.7	45.7	39.3	5.4	11.1	2.2
Transport costs	33.37	67.2	25.7	11.2	23.1	32.2
Subsidy	--	36.79	116.8	169.7	258.7	0.0
Accounting profit	-220.2	-181.8	-323.6	-334.2	-435.3	519.1
Loss plus subsidy						
as % of GDP	1.01	0.85	1.48	1.42	1.51	--
Loss plus subsidy						
as % of current						
budget deficit	34.81	15.82	20.03	17.52	20.53	--

Source: ENABAS annual income statements; INEC, Anuario estadístico de Nicaragua 1984.

ENABAS Finances: Indicators of Efficiency, 1980-1985

Table 5-4 presents some financial ratios based on the analysis of ENABAS income statements. All ratios involve the mathematical comparison of one or more elements in the income statement to net sales. In a private enterprise, such ratios can be used as standard management tools to determine problem areas in a company's operations and, once measures are undertaken to correct the problems, to monitor their implementation and to fine-tune their action. The situation is somewhat different with a public enterprise and especially so with ENABAS. Because variables related to the level of sales, the denominator of management ratios, and to cost elements in the numerator lie beyond management control, the ratio may signal problem areas, but implementing corrective measures often exceeds company authority. Notwithstanding such a sharp caveat, the evolution of the measures clearly shows the effects of external government policies on company finances and provides some insight into problems that could be made the thrust of concerted action.

Table 5-4
Income Statement Financial Indicators, 1980-1985
(Percentages)

FINANCIAL RATIOS	1980	1981	1982	1983	1984	1985
Ratio of cost of goods sold to sales	102.32	97.33	111.04	114.56	113.69	70.16
Ratio of sales and administrative expenses to sales	23.28	26.31	21.38	20.23	23.67	13.81
Ratio of financial expenditures to sales	5.23	5.06	3.49	0.39	0.67	0.04
Ratio of transportation expenses to sales	5.50	7.45	2.29	0.82	1.40	0.66
Ratio of cleaning and storage losses to sales	3.05	2.17	4.20	2.48	6.12	7.45

Source: Table 5-3

The ratio of the cost of goods sold to sales provides clear indications of the Nicaraguan government's policy of subsidizing both producer and consumer. By setting the producer price at a level higher than that paid by the consumer for the final product, the government hoped to spur the production of basic grains while holding the line on consumer expenditures. As a result, the ratio rose from 102 percent in 1980 to almost 115 percent in 1985. The policy reversal that ended subsidies in 1985 brought about a drop in the ratio to 70 percent, a figure more in line with that shown by similar firms in other countries.

The ratio of sales and administrative expenses to sales reflects costs of everyday company operations in selling and merchandising the final product that are not directly related to purchasing inputs. The ratio showed elements of stability from 1980 to 1984, remaining between 20 and 26 percent of sales. The rising prices associated with eliminating subsidies in 1985 lowered the ratio to less than 14 percent. The ratio is high by South American standards and criticism is often voiced by other government officials and in the Managua press that ENABAS has excessive costs.[27] Nicaraguan price controls help to explain, in part, the high ratio. ENABAS prices are held far below the equilibrium clearing level needed to match domestic production with irregular imports and domestic consumption. That equilibrium level lies somewhere between ENABAS prices and parallel private market prices. For example, in November 1985, the average price of ENABAS rice was 21 Córdobas per pound compared to an average of 76.98 Córdobas per pound for rice outside the ENABAS system. Corresponding figures for beans were 33 Córdobas per pound and 111.38 Córdobas, respectively.[28] The discrepancy places the private channel price at between 2.5 and 4.0 times the ENABAS price. Valuing ENABAS sales at twice their current levels provides a crude estimate of a truer ratio basis; and this would leave the ratio of expenses to sales at less than 7 percent. If we were to gauge the equilibrium price at higher than twice ENABAS levels it would lower the estimated ratio even more. Although the results still may appear high, I show below that ENABAS income statements actually understate the costs of company operations.

The ratio of financial expenditures to sales reveals the company's dependence on external finance and the availability of sufficient working capital to undertake normal company operations. As shown in figure 5-1, the ratio dropped sharply from levels of 5 percent or more of sales, which prevailed at the beginning of the decade, to less than 1 percent after 1983. In part, the ratio demonstrates the financial constriction effects on ENABAS of key provisions of the 1983 budget law that limited the contracting of new bank loans and suppliers' credits for any goods or services.[29] Another ratio showing a sharp drop is the ratio of transport costs to sales. Transportation remains a key element in assuring the optimal use of a widely dispersed purchasing and warehouse system where seasonal fluctuations in local supply and demand must be efficiently integrated into a smoothly operating national system. ENABAS's transportation cost as a percentage of sales dropped from more than 5 percent in 1980 and 1981 to less than 1 percent by 1985. Transportation costs are more susceptible to management efforts to improve efficiency through simple models that try match capacity with demand leading to a more optimal resource use.

Another nonstandard financial ratio, particularly applicable to ENABAS, is the ratio of grain losses (mermas) to sales. The ratio averaged approximately 3.0 until 1983, when it took a sharp upward turn. It continued to rise, reaching almost 7.5 percent of sales in 1985, as shown with its associated trend in figure 5-2. All grain marketing boards suffer postpurchase losses that occur as grain bought with a high moisture content loses water and weight in the drying process. Grains also undergo a thorough cleaning, losing weight as the accompanying dirt, small stones, dust, and twigs are removed. ENABAS loss percentages are higher for the first harvest that occurs in the rainy season, as the grains purchased have a higher-than-normal moisture content and the rain constrains the farmers' ability to clean them properly.

Figure 5-1
ENABAS: Cost Efficiency,1980-1985

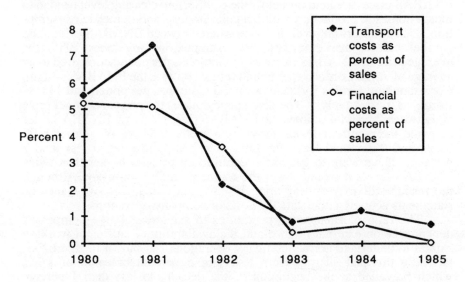

Figure 5-2
ENABAS: Storage Losses as Percentage of Sales, 1980-1985

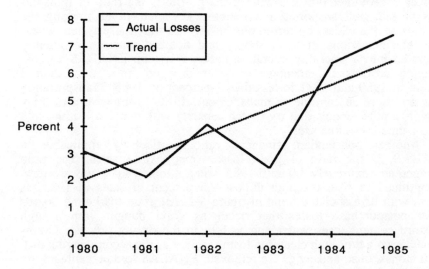

A study for the Ministry of Agricultural Development and Agrarian Reform, MIDINRA, and the National Food Program, PAN, reported average weight losses of 22.6 percent for maize, 20 percent for beans, and 16 percent for sorghum in the first harvest, compared with figures of 15, 12, and 11 percent, respectively, for grains purchased from the second or subsequent harvests.[30] Postharvest grain losses are inversely correlated with the importance of imports and donations in total grain purchases, since grains undergo drying and cleaning before shipping. Consequently, the drop in imports after 1983 partially explains the increasing rate of losses.

ENABAS Finances: Balance Sheets, 1980-1985

Table 5-5 summarizes information, measured in current Córdobas, from the ENABAS balance sheets from 1980 to 1985. Inflationary effects are discussed below. Current assets grew seventeenfold from 1980 to 1985, rising from 409 million Córdobas to 6.8 billion. Current liabilities grew at a slightly faster rate but, as assets always exceeded liabilities, the company remained solvent. Accounts receivable from ENABAS's regional operations constitute the largest single component of current assets and their accounts receivable constitute the single largest category of accounts payable. The exceedingly high figures, more than 85 percent of all accounts receivable in 1983 and 1984, indicate room for improvement in internal company accounting practices and the need for better inventory control.[31]

Fixed capital stock grew at modest rates, reflecting both the low capital intensity of ENABAS operations (fixed assets largely consist of storage and related equipment and transport vehicles) and the access to new facilities either via donations or at preferential exchange rates. The company's net worth rose only sevenfold after 1980, as the ever-increasing government equity was offset by rapidly rising accumulated losses until 1985.[32]

ENABAS Finances: Indicators of Solvency, 1980-1985

Standard financial ratios derived from the balance sheet provide a keen glimpse into a company's financial health. The current ratio compares its current assets to current liabilities and is, perhaps, the most widely used indicator of short-term company liquidity. Long experience with private firms has resulted in a standard rule of thumb that a company is in good financial health if its current ratio remains between 2.0 and 3.0. The financial crunch of the late 1970s resulted in a lowering of the minimal acceptable limit to 1.5.

No comparable rule-of-thumb figures have been derived for public enterprises, although many analysts continue to apply both, irrespective of the ownership structure of capital. Public ownership normally entails an implicit guarantee that even if a company becomes insolvent, it will not go bankrupt, leaving the creditors with debt, and many countries codify the implicit guarantee into a specific legal provision forbidding bankruptcy for public enterprises, irrespective of financial condition. ENABAS's current ratio reached its maximum value of 1.31 in 1980 and thereafter it remained, except for 1983, at or below 1.2. This low figure always remained under the acceptable limit. In other terms, although the company always maintained sufficient short-term assets to pay off its short-term liabilities, its reserves only barely kept it solvent.

Table 5-5
ENABAS Consolidated Balance Sheet, 1980-1985
(Millions of current Córdobas)

Asset/Liability Category	1980	1981	1982	1983	1984	1985
Current assets	409.2	781.6	1,704.3	2,924.0	4,217.4	6,794.4
Accounts receivable	115.4	201.0	1,277.7	2,410.8	3,673.6	4,810.6
From regions	n.a.	n.a.	1,117.2	2,127.2	3,291.4	4,104.1
Inventories	171.1	310.5	337.8	420.8	412.2	1,032.3
Fixed capital stock	152.0	187.0	220.0	289.2	351.6	414.7
Depreciation	45.1	64.5	80.5	95.3	111.6	127.1
Total assets	529.2	932.1	1,885.2	3,154.4	4,518.7	7,173.2
Current liabilities	313.3	658.7	1,550.8	2,328.2	3,702.4	5,682.5
Loans and overdrafts	147.5	387.7	281.9	3.7	137.6	60.1
Accounts payable	155.2	231.6	1,212.9	2,162.1	3,324.9	4,876.7
To regions	n.a.	n.a.	1,117.2	2,063.6	3,208.7	4,420.2
Long-term debt	3.1	2.7	16.5	24.5	41.0	19.1
Net worth	212.9	270.8	297.2	821.5	775.1	1,471.5
Government equity	--	509.0	848.3	1,207.9	1,576.6	1,706.6
Accumulated profits	148.7	-396.2	-716.1	-1,037.2	-1,469.3	-903.0

Source: ENABAS annual balance sheets.

Analysts often use the quick ratio, called the acid test, for state-trading organizations. Because STOs carry high levels of inventory whose sale could depress the market in the event of a forced liquidation, the quick ratio examines solvency without accounting for inventories. It results from the ratio of current liabilities less inventories to current liabilities. The commonly accepted rule of thumb is that financial health is demonstrated by having a quick ratio that exceeds 1.0. On that basis, ENABAS did show financial health after 1983. Prior to that date, the ratio remained below the rule-of-thumb limit.

Working with balance sheets that neglect to account for inflationary effects can lead the financial analyst into error. The working capital figures shown in table 5-6 and reproduced in figure 5-3 clearly illustrate the effects of high inflation in Nicaragua during recent years. Working capital is the excess of current assets over current liabilities and measures the funds available to a firm for routine operations. The nominal data demonstrate an almost twelvefold increase in ENABAS's working capital from 1980 to 1985, with the amount of money available to the company increasing yearly. Deflating the figures by the foodstuffs component of the Consumer Price Index for Managua provides a rough measure of the changes in purchasing power of the funds available to ENABAS.

Table 5-6
ENABAS Balance Sheet Financial Indicators
(Percentages and millions of Córdobas)

INDICATORS OF FINANCIAL SOLVENCY	1980	1981	1982	1983	1984	1985
Current ratio	1.31	1.19	1.10	1.26	1.14	1.20
Quick ratio	0.76	0.72	0.88	1.08	1.03	1.01
Working capital						
(nominal)	5.91	122.91	153.46	595.77	514.93	1,111.94
(real)	95.91	95.28	92.70	252.89	154.52	96.16
Regional accounts receivable as % of total accounts receivable	n.a.	n.a.	65.55	72.75	78.04	60.40
Regional accounts payable as % of total accounts payable	n.a.	n.a.	72.04	88.63	86.66	77.79
Price deflator	100.00	129.00	165.55	235.58	333.47	1,156.35
Net investment						
(nominal)	n.a.	15.63	17.00	54.40	46.15	47.56
(real)	n.a.	12.11	10.27	23.09	13.84	4.11
Net worth (real)	212.87	209.91	179.55	348.70	232.43	127.25
Government equity						
(real)	n.a.	87.38	79.84	72.45	32.15	69.50
Debt-equity ratio	1.49	2.44	5.34	2.84	4.83	3.87

Source: Table 5-5.

According to the deflated figures for working capital, ENABAS barely maintained the level of funds in 1985 that it had in 1980, having dropped sharply from 1983 levels. ENABAS's ability to maintain a stable level of working capital contrasts sharply with experience in Peru, the only other Latin American country with a comparable network of state-trading organizations in the late 1970s. Peru's state traders experienced negative levels of working capital at various times, so that their current liabilities exceeded funds available, even after liquidating all the company's current assets. ENABAS's net investment remained at low levels throughout the period, rising from 15 million current Córdobas in 1980 to less than 50 million in 1985. Inflation accounted for most of the growth, however, as the 1985 figure was equivalent to only 4.1 million 1980 Córdobas.

Figure 5-3
ENABAS: Working Capital, 1980-1985

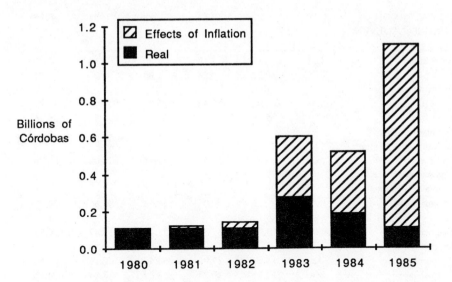

ENABAS's net worth, shown in figure 5-4 as measured in real terms, showed a pronounced downward trend until 1983, when capitalization of existing assets and government transfers provided a needed capital injection. From 1983 onward, its net worth continued to fall. Figure 5-5 shows the government share of equity in nominal terms and after the erosion caused by accumulated losses and inflation. The government's real stake in ENABAS in 1985 was lower than it had been in 1980. The debt-equity ratio provides an indication of the company's heavy indebtedness.

For private firms, a debt-equity ratio of 1.0 or less indicates that the company could pay all its creditors from paid-in capital, reserves, and retained earnings. Higher debt-equity ratios usually lead to management and investor concern that holders of company debt have an increased risk of not realizing their claims on the company. Although risk factors are presumed lower for public enterprises, there are no benchmarks, since it is expected that government guarantees, whether implicit or explicit, could be invoked in the event of the company's inability to meet claims. ENABAS ratios show high debt ratios, which exceeded 5.0 in 1982, indicating that less than 20 percent of claims could be met without external assistance.

The financial analysis clearly demonstrates two immediate priorities for ENABAS and, by extension, other Nicaraguan public enterprises. First, they need to establish accounting mechanisms to compensate for inflation. Currently, costs of capital equipment, reflected in the income statement via depreciation of historical cost figures, are dramatically understated because they neither reflect revaluations nor added depreciation, whereas windfall earnings reflected in the inflation-adjusted sales of inventory are highly overstated. In large measure, the bottom line written in black for 1985 represents false profits. Second, they need to renovate the existing accounting system to include consistent cost accounting as part of company-level performance and appraisal systems. Implementing cost accounting will enable public enterprises to monitor individual cost elements and to follow through on such wide disparities in efficiency as occurred between transport costs and losses in cleaning and storage.

An Intragovernmental, Interorganizational, Systemic Approach

Elsewhere, I have developed an intergovernmental, inter-organizational approach to considering public enterprises as part of a totally interlinked government system.[33] This part of the report applies the approach to examine ENABAS's management context and to explore the complicated set of interlinkages that bind ENABAS within the public administration system. Public enterprises in Nicaragua are commonly examined from a "top-down" or "accountability" perspective predicated on the assumption that the government created its firms as policy instruments to meet specific goals and objectives. The essence of the approach involves the design of proper systems to control the firms so that company managers are obliged to try to attain the broadly and externally defined "public good."

Figure 5-4
ENABAS: Net Worth, 1980-1985

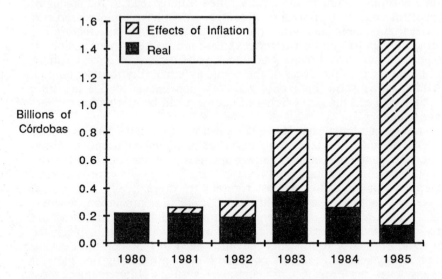

Figure 5-5
ENABAS: Government Paid-In Capital, 1980-1985

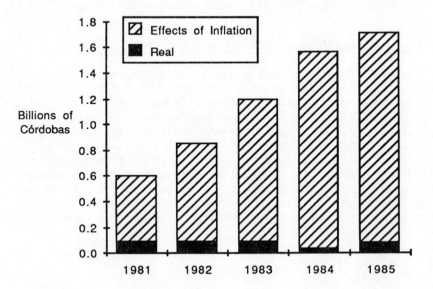

The approach has one clear failing: it neglects to account for many variables in the decision-making process that may be removed from management control either because they properly belong to the management environment for the entire state entrepreneurial system or because they result from actions of other government bodies over which the company managers have no control. A smoothly functioning entrepreneurial system can result only from the recognition that managers and their companies need a working environment that is conducive to good management practices and that frictions developing along the organizational interfaces that interlink public enterprises to other parts of the government apparatus must be identified and removed.

The Working Environment for ENABAS Action

All Nicaraguan public enterprises are situated within the context of a major transformation of the economic system whereby economic management passed from the hands of a small minority to the working classes. As the plan for economic reactivation stated in 1980:

> The growth of the APP [Area de Propiedad del Pueblo] is a completely new situation within the Nicaraguan economy. For the first time in the history of our country, *all* the people become the owners of the lands and factories that previously belonged to Somocismo. But the Area of Peoples' Property is not limited to the productive sector. The financial system has been nationalized; new state export firms have been created; the state now intervenes directly in commerce, particularly that of basic grains.[34] [Emphasis in original]

Widespread agreement about the overall context for transformation of the state entrepreneurial apparatus in favor of the people was not translated into a uniform law governing state entrepreneurial activity. Instead, each company is primarily governed by its own law of creation and the bylaws thereto. This leads to intrasystemic incoherences regarding the creation process. Sometimes companies are created or reorganized implicitly, such as occurred when ENABAS and other firms were ascribed to the Ministry of Foreign Trade by the ministerial law of creation.[35] At other times, the companies are created by individual laws, such as those for CORFIN, the Nicaraguan Financial Corporation, or COIP, the People's Industrial Corporation.[36] Still other companies are grouped, as subsidiaries, under a holding company, with no special legal identity governing their actions, as with all the firms assigned to COIP.[37] With time, specific provisions of individual laws of creation that govern individual firms' economic operations have been set aside as budgetary shortages have forced cutbacks in the scope of planned activities. Recall how the financial constriction effects of key provisions of the 1983 budget law limited ENABAS's ability to contract new bank loans and to accept suppliers' credits and thereby specifically overrode contractual liberty granted by its law of creation.[38]

Notwithstanding the lack of an overall legal framework, Nicaragua has managed to avoid one of the most pernicious effects of a similar situation in Peru, instability at top management levels.[39] In Nicaragua, directores are appointed for an indefinite term, being subject to removal principally to fulfill more pressing needs in the public administration system. The process helps foster a high degree of management commitment to the company and leads to low rotation rates among top executives.[40] Whereas a Peruvian state trader experienced yearly top management average rotation rates exceeding 50 percent from 1976 to 1980, ENABAS's rates have averaged only 10 percent per year since 1980.[41]

Government purchasing and contracting systems constitute another global aspect of the management environment in which Nicaragua has apparently fashioned a policy conducive to good management.[42] Nicaragua's system follows the similar three-part division whereby any purchases that fall below a certain lower limit can be made directly by the company; those whose cost exceeds an upper limit must be submitted to international competitive bidding.[43] The purchases costing more than the lower limit but less than the upper limit must be made via a competitive bidding procedure. The law has several provisions that assist in providing public enterprise managers with the additional autonomy necessary to run a company. First, legal limits are fixed differently for the general government than for public enterprises. The Ministry of Finance (MIFIN) sets the limits for the rest of government, and public enterprises work together with MIFIN to set specific limits for their own activities.[44] Peru made no differentiation and fixed limits so arbitrarily low that, by the end of 1981, any purchase exceeding $10,000 U.S. had to be submitted to international competitive bidding. Second, the law makes clear exception for repair of vehicles, motors, machinery, and similar equipment.[45] In Peru, damages to ships occurring in a foreign port, whose cost of repair exceeded the absurdly low upper limit, could not be undertaken until completion of the international competitive bidding process, thereby putting a ship out of service for ninety days. Third, the law makes clear exception both for routine purchases that are part of the ordinary course of business and for emergency purchases that are urgent and unforeseen.[46] In Peru, a perverse attempt to modernize the purchasing system in late 1980 included no routine or emergency escape clauses, leading to dramatic cost rises resulting from machine downtime. In sharp contrast, ENABAS relies on buhoneros, private, licensed, fly-by-night middlemen who import for a fee, to purchase critically needed spare parts.[47]

Many other parts of the management environment lay beyond the ability of either government or company executives to influence. Although they do not form part of the intragovernmental interlinked framework, they bear some mention at this point to note the difficult circumstances in which such a rich governmentally imposed environment has developed.

First, it is difficult to institute a smoothly functioning public enterprise system that fosters efficiency in a small, dependent, war-racked economy. Nicaragua has laid the bases for the system in laws that promote, rather than constrain, management autonomy. Although war, with the ensuing budgetary cutbacks for nondefense expenses, and the economic blockade, with the attendant increased difficulties in obtaining raw materials and spare parts, have resulted in increased constraints on overall management decisions, the basic, well-designed legal structure still remains.

A second contextual difficulty concerns the situation in which the government found many companies nationalized from the Somoza family and their close allies. Acting as a conduit to speed the flight of capital abroad ranked among the companies' chief objectives in 1978 and early 1979. Consequently, upon takeover, new managers entered insolvent firms whose assets had been converted into cash and whose liabilities had soared. Sanitizing financial accounts required major efforts for several years from both company managers and from ministry officials until accounts and operations had reached a semblance of normalcy.[48]

A third contextual difficulty, of particular importance for MICOIN firms, concerns consumer habits formed under the predominantly capitalist system and faced by government-owned marketing firms after 1979. Lack of coincidence between demand based on established consumption patterns and supply provided by the firms resulted in a highly charged atmosphere, often damaging to the companies' reputations. Thus, one official government report lamented the "exaggerated" increase in domestic sugar consumption after 1980[49] and Ministry of Agriculture publications indicated frustration with the high consumption of bread, cookies, beer, and soft drinks.[50] In most cases, the companies accepted the consumer context as imposing constraints on company actions. For example, ENABAS bowed to the local customs of self-diagnosis and self-treatment with popular nostrums and imported substantial quantities of "popular medicines" after April 1981.[51]

In summary, two clear lines stand out in the definition of the context for public enterprise management after 1979. First, the context was clearer than that found in many other Latin American countries. The single overall objective of running the public enterprises for the betterment of Nicaragua's people was global and amply communicated. Although there have been, and will continue to be, sharp differences over the interpretation of that objective, the ambiguities about objectives that give rise elsewhere to misunderstandings and misinterpretations of the management environment were missing in Nicaragua. Second, the legal environment managed to avoid many of the glaring mistakes found elsewhere in Latin America. The laws and their regulations were framed in consultation with company managers to better respond to their needs, instead of merely fulfilling the requirements of a broadly writ public administration system. While the exogenous system constraints still prove a heavy burden on company management, the endogenous system parameters define a favorable management environment.

Although Nicaragua has, thus far, managed to avoid the major pernicious effects of the lack of a general legal system to unify public enterprise actions, there is no guarantee that such a beneficial situation will endure. Elsewhere, it has not. For example, in Peru, during the late 1970s, high rates of rotation at the cabinet level brought about attendant high rates of rotation at top company management levels, as ministers exercised prerogatives to name board members who, naturally, placed their own candidates in positions of trust. Codifying the best of the existing situation will help ensure that the atmosphere of management stability and the thrust to efficiency remain part of the management environment.

Interinstitutional Interlinkages

Public enterprises are inserted into a fully interlinked governmental framework. Although the standard top-down power linkages (for example, a domestically oriented grain marketer such as ENABAS being placed for functional reasons under the Ministry of Internal Trade) have formed the basis for repeated analysis and change, other links, whether directly to other central government agencies or other public enterprises, or indirectly, the spinoff effects of direct relationships between two central government agencies or two other public enterprises have been neglected. The following section focuses on explaining the interlinkage framework and applying it to the recent Nicaraguan experience.[52]

Direct Bilateral Links between Central Government Institutions. Because public enterprises not only are subordinate to their controlling ministries but also are subject to rules and regulations that flow from a variety of other central government organizations, their economic, social, or financial performance depends on direct bilateral links between central government agencies. Any incompatibilities among controlling institutions or their representatives, any policy disagreements among those agencies, or any conflicts over institutional jurisdiction can have a negative impact on the public enterprises. Likewise, attempts to reduce constantly generated friction in working relationships among agencies at the level of central government can have a positive impact on company performance.

Information flows provide one clear instance of systems conflict generated at the central government level that afflicts the entire public enterprise system. Various central government agencies are charged with periodically gathering information to monitor public enterprise functioning. In Nicaragua, as in most countries, there is no effective coordination of information-gathering efforts. No single body has emerged to gather and analyze periodic public enterprise data and to channel both raw and processed data to other entities of the public administration system. For state traders, a wide variety of central government and regional government authorities gather information in addition to the companies themselves. According to a 1983 MICOIN study, these included MICOIN and all its firms, MIDINRA, the Ministry of Industry (MIND), the Energy Institute (INE), and the departmental juntas. The report lamented that, although each agency gathered data, the information did not often coincide, since each agency employed different procedures in both gathering and analysis. The net result was needless and wasteful duplication of efforts.[53] Another earlier report on Nicaragua stressed that overlapping, poorly regulated systems resulted in a deterioration of most processes at the company level by slowing down decision making and promoting conflict.[54] In rare cases, interpersonal efforts to coordinate data gathering succeeded in overcoming the barriers posed by the lack of coordinating mechanisms at the technical level.

The most serious problems posed for ENABAS arose from the interaction resulting from two conflicting and poorly coordinated price-setting mechanisms, each largely under the control of a different ministry. Conflict and lack of coordination led to enormous operating losses for ENABAS, losses that, in turn, became a subsidy. According to a study carried out by two foreign consultants, there was no subsidy policy because "their amount and distribution are not fixed by previously-taken decisions, but rather originate in the coexistence of two different price policies for the producer and for the consumer. Subsidies are, thus, the remainder or the balance of other policies."[55]

Using basic grains, ENABAS's major marketing effort, as an example, from 1981 to 1983, PAN, the Nicaraguan food program, was charged with coordinating the two sets of decisions, a role later given to the Economic Directorate in MIDINRA.[56] PAN's coordinating role was so limited that it was not even included in the list of state institutions acting on the decision to fix either producer prices or consumer prices.[57] Instead, MIDINRA's policy division formed the basic lines on revising producer prices upward to cover cost shifts. Using the extremely complicated 1983 structures illustrates the problems inherent in not applying a systemic approach. A wide variety of other government organizations intervened, without coordination, in a set of individual decisions about cost elements. Thus, rural wages were set by the Ministry of Labor (MITRAB) and the Junta for National Reconstruction (JGRN) with decisional input from MIDINRA, MIPLAN, the Ministry of Health (MINSA), the Rural Workers'-Association (ATC), and the National Union of Farmers and Ranchers (UNAG); input prices were set by the Ministry of Foreign Trade (MICE), the agricultural input state-trading organization (ENIA), an agricultural state trader (PROAGRO), the cotton marketer (ENAL), and the machinery rental firm (AGROMEC); the interest rate was set by the Central Bank (BCN) in consultation with other organizations; and land rents were set by MIDINRA.[58] Interest and decision-making parties may be grouped as (1) central government ministries and organizations; (2) crop-specific trade unions for rice, cotton, sugar, and other crops; (3) private growers' associations; and (4) mass-based trade unions, such as UNAG and ATC and the Sandinista Workers' Federation (CST). MIDINRA retained the basic power as it prepared the price proposals, setting the requested price high enough to cover the average cost of production, and submitted them to the JGRN for approval, in theory after completing all the necessary consultation and reworking.[59]

Consumer prices were set largely within MICOIN, based, in part, on ENABAS proposals to cover costs and input from COMMEMA, the Managua Municipal Market Corporation, which voiced traders' concerns.[60] MICOIN prices did not necessarily take ENABAS's costs into consideration. Instead, the pricing policy's principal objective was to assure continual access of the people to low-priced foodstuffs. The stress of political over economic efficiency and technical objectives may be related to the background and training of MICOIN officials, which is less technical, with fewer trained economists, engineers, or specialists in business administration.[61] Proposed consumer prices were also submitted to the JGRN for final approval, theoretically after MIFIN approval on the availability of funds.[62]

Maintaining the subsidies as a residual resulted in negative effects on ENABAS. The company was forced to operate at a deficit from 1980 to 1984. Providing open subsidies has been repeatedly criticized by economists and management specialists as encouraging inefficiencies at the company level by allowing any inefficiencies to be charged against the subsidy.[63] Indeed, ENABAS was repeatedly criticized for having abnormally high operating costs (see above). However, because of external price-setting mechanisms, the problem did not reside in ENABAS. Instead, it resulted from incompatibilities within the central government.

Treating subsidies as a residual, without subjecting them to minute examination and explicitly setting their levels, gave rise to other consequences. First, subsidies led to negative effects on Nicaragua's economy in the form of increasing budget deficits, increased monetary expansion, and increased inflation, all of which had wider effects on both producers and consumers.[64] Second, subsidies led to perverse effects on consumers whereby increased subsidies harmed the very low income and poorer social classes they were intended to benefit.[65] Third, subsidies led to perverse producer effects whereby producers were induced to stop producing some basic grains, instead of producing more.[66] The real purchasing power of maize- and bean-producer prices had dropped to less than 70 percent of 1980 levels and that of rice had fallen to less than 40 percent. By the end of 1984, negative effects on ENABAS, the economy, consumers, and producers had reached such high levels that Nicaraguan authorities totally reversed their position and halted subsidies.

Direct Hierarchical Relations. Direct and hierarchical relations link public enterprises with agencies of the central government that define strategy, monitor its implementation, and control other variables. The frequently discussed "accountability problem" amply deals with control-type relationships and, starting from the premise that public enterprises exist to be controlled, seeks to find the most effective manner to control them. Solutions based on the controliste approach, however, can lead to perverse consequences if the problem is systemic and key elements in the decision-making process lie beyond management control. Other top-down relationships exist, such as the information-gathering functions mentioned above, or working relationships that jointly involve ministry or central government agency and public enterprise in a project whose successful completion requires harmonious interaction.

This section concentrates on a few top-down links from MICOIN to its set of public enterprises. Jorge Barenstein, a leading public enterprise analyst, studied those links in 1981. He noted that, compared to other functional areas studied in Nicaragua at the ministerial level, there was insufficient communication between MICOIN officials and managers of the ministry's firms concerning strategic sectoral objectives. He also noted a lower concern at all levels in MICOIN with efficiency, a variable linked with increased communication. Barenstein attributed both findings to the noneconomic, nonbusiness training of many ministry officials and to the recent formation of the ministry.[67] MICOIN sources later admitted the lack of "a marketing strategy previously developed by MICOIN that details short-, medium-, and long-term policies, because it doesn't exist." Instead, they characterized overall marketing strategy as "rapid response to any pressure or crisis in the market."[68]

A deep gap existed between MICOIN officials and company executives over perceptions of relative power in the ability to make company-level decisions. MICOIN officials felt that company managers participated in only 17 percent of the decisions, but managers felt they had key input to 49 percent. The gap was most striking in marketing aspects, where company officials felt they controlled 83 percent of decisions about products and 79 percent of decisions about prices, but MICOIN officials felt that company management only provided decisive input for 30 and 18 percent, respectively.[69]

MICOIN officials have justly been concerned with achieving the proper functional organization of the ministry's portfolio, which began existence as a heterogeneous collection of companies ranging from movie theaters to supermarkets; opticians and bakeries to barbershops; sales of all items from tractors to lingerie; cafeterias, restaurants, bars, and nightclubs. A partial inventory of those firms taken in 1982 revealed fifty-seven companies, forty of which were 100 percent government-owned, and the rest with at least one-third ownership.[70] Most of these enterprises entered the public portfolio by accident in the wholesale take-overs of properties belonging to the Somoza clan and its allies without a concrete government decision ever having been taken to nationalize a barbershop, lingerie seller, or nightclub. Because accidental nationalization always entails peripheral and heterogeneous firms, instead of the standard core of public utilities found in developing countries irrespective of ideology,[71] MICOIN officials have few theoretical underpinnings to rely on when designing a portfolio management system.[72] They have taken considerable pains repeatedly to adjust the portfolio under functional grounds. The annual report on the state of the government details one of the original reorganizations that took place in 1981, whereby CORCOP, the People's Marketing Corporation, set up the previous year, was reorganized into three subsidiaries.[73]

Continual reorganization, however, can often have deleterious effects on company management by diverting attention from production or marketing and channeling it to purely administrative matters. Following yet another reshuffling of the companies in 1986, an ENABAS source described the resulting merger between ENABAS and a nonagriculture-related firm in less than enthusiastic terms. According to the source, "sufrimos la fusión."[74] Ministry officials feel, however, that the new reorganization is not an ad hoc addition, but a better correspondence to their defined strategies with the available companies being used as adequate instruments to carry out policy.[75] The need for MICOIN to develop permanent and systematic consultative mechanisms with its companies to mark out reorganizational guidelines and safeguards is readily apparent.

Indirect Hierarchical Relations. Positive or negative externalities to a public enterprise may arise from indirect hierarchical relationships between another public enterprise and a central government agency. Nicaragua has managed the externalities well, avoiding some negative effects found elsewhere. The relations between the public treasury and the public banking system for the payment of subsidies often generate problems. In Peru, food subsidy payments remained in arrears for up to ten years and petroleum subsidies only paid after inflation had eroded their value by 65 percent. In sharp contrast, the Nicaraguan treasury paid its obligations on time. The balance sheet analysis does not show major arrears on government account and ENABAS officials unanimously agreed that treasury paid when presented with the bills.

Direct Bilateral Relations between Two Public Enterprises. The fourth type of relation considered in this section concerns two public enterprises. By far the most common relation is a purely commercial one, that of buyer and seller. There may be others, such as partners in project development or partners in a mixed venture. I consider only a few cases in Nicaragua to demonstrate that the area merits increased study as a means of improving efficiency within a systemic framework that cannot be achieved in the traditional top-down perspective.

ENABAS officials reported difficulties in commercial transactions with industrial public enterprises that prefer to sell their output elsewhere instead of via the government's designated intermediaries. The problem is not a new one and arises because cash-strapped industrial firms seek to boost revenues to cover needed expenses. Even for 1982,

MICOIN sources had noted leakages to nonsecure market channels. Varying amounts of goods sold to final consumers at official prices ranged from 95 percent of output for salt, 60 percent for matches, 25 percent for washing soap, and only 2 percent for toilet paper.[76]

Farmers have shown increasing reluctance to sell their output to ENABAS in part because of the practice whereby ENABAS acts as a designated agent of the financial sector. By issuing the check in the name of the regional branch banks from which the farmer has taken the loan, ENABAS can increase overall loan recuperation rates for the public banks. However, because regional limits on funding those accounts mean that farmers have to return repeatedly until they can cash the check[77] and because the banks deduct all loan expenses, even those accruing after the farmer has tried to deposit the check only to find insufficient funds in the account, farmers have looked increasingly to the private sector to place their output.[78] Private traders further boost their relative advantage by paying in cash and selling consumer goods, practices that ENABAS does not follow.[79]

Another interenterprise problem concerns MICOIN firms. The heterogeneous nature of the ministry's portfolio gave rise to firms that competed for scarce resources. For example, in 1983, MICOIN had three importing companies. These bore no relationship to MICE, the Ministry of Foreign Trade, nor to ENIMPORT, a specialized importer.[80] Reducing such functional duplication was an objective of successive ministerial reorganizations.

The National Slaughterhouse Company of the Ministry of Agrarian Reform, ENAMARA, had a bloody battle over territory with a national network of municipal slaughterhouses. The municipal slaughterhouses were better supplied and sold meat at lower-than-official prices. The ENAMARA network had fewer supplies and sold 80 percent of its beef at higher than official prices.[81] ENAMARA tried to eliminate the competition by doing away with the municipal slaughterhouses in 1983. The national farmers' union, UNAG, protested strongly that the ENAMARA facilities were difficult to reach and that the transport cost component of beef would rise sharply.

Conclusions

The case study of ENABAS provides useful insights into the dynamics of state-trading organization expansion in developing countries. Moreover, it provides mixed results when compared to similar cases elsewhere.

With the desire to emphasize sharp policy breaks with previous regimes, revolutionary governments often lay excessive claim to the creation of public enterprises, as occurred in Peru after 1968. ENABAS fits the pattern well. Its roots far antedate its current corporate form and the 1979 break constituted a change of name and shifts in the objectives. New dynamics and a new mission for an existing organization do not constitute creation, however, and ENABAS inherited considerable physical and managerial infrastructure from its predecessor organizations.

ENABAS's performance after 1979 was mixed. Some indicators of productivity rose while others fell. Some financial indicators rose while others fell. The mixed performance highlights the need to better the cost accounting system and to integrate it into an overall management information framework.

ENABAS suffers from one of the many financial problems ailing the nonnatural resource producers in the Third World: lack of proper financial basis. In the Nicaraguan context, insufficient finance is exacerbated by high inflation and the inability of the public enterprises to maintain their assets. The income statement analysis highlights the need to institute inflationary corrections for the accounting system.

ENABAS also suffers from a conceptual difficulty that affects many state traders in basic grains, namely, the inability to recognize and properly cost its major products. ENABAS's core objective, according to the legal documents governing its behavior, is marketing. Its other actions, primarily centered around subsidizing the consumption patterns of the urban workers, are services that ENABAS provides without recognition and without adequate compensation. The so-called subsidy actually constitutes partial payment for these services; capital transfers supposedly cover the rest. These are neither subsidies nor capital transfers, but constitute payment to ENABAS for company services. As with the government's other major current or capital expenditures, decisions need to be taken after comparing the benefits of expenditures with their costs. Such decisions lie beyond ENABAS's competence, but they should be based on a clear understanding of the true nature of ENABAS's services.

ENABAS operates, as do Nicaragua's other public enterprises, in an ambiguous context. Although the context includes some legal guidelines, others are lacking. The ambiguity points to the need to study the legal situation of the portfolio and to codify the best contextual elements.

Within an interlinkage framework, uncertainty and incoherence are not universal. Although they do mark many direct bilateral relationships, such as those between MIDINRA and MICOIN that affect ENABAS or between ENABAS and other public enterprises, and because they occur at times in direct hierarchical relationships between ENABAS and its controllers/monitors at the level of central government, they do not mark indirect hierarchical relationships. Moreover, they do not always occur in the direct hierarchical links. The existing uncertainties and incoherences point to the need for a systemic approach to the portfolio, an approach that lies beyond the control of company management.

Overall, ENABAS has problems, as do most public enterprises, but it functions surprisingly well, having managed to overcome some of the growing pains associated with expansion within a turbulent environment.

Endnotes to Chapter 5

1. Centro de Investigaciones y Estudios de la Reforma Agraria (CIERA), Informe final del Proyecto Estrategia Alimentaria-- CIERA/-PAN/CIDA, Directorio de Políticas Alimentarias, vol. 3 (Managua, 1984), p. 33.

2. State trading has often been defined as the existence of some authority to regulate or determine prices or quantities of goods traded internationally. See P. J. Lloyd, "State Trading and the Theory of International Trade," in M. M. Kostecki, ed., State Trading in International Markets (New York: St. Martin's Press, 1982), pp. 118-120; and M. M. Kostecki, "State Trading by the Advanced and Developing Countries: The Background," in ibid., pp. 6-7.

3. Interview, Reynaldo López, ENABAS, July 16, 1986.

4. J. J. Lugo Marenco, "Exposición de motivos," a letter written to accompany Decreto No. 536, "Ley Creadora del Instituto Nacional de Comercio Exterior e Interior," Managua, June 30, 1960.

5. Decreto No. 536, Article 30, Paragraph a.

6. Lugo Marenco, "Exposición de motivos," p. 2.

7. Decreto No. 536, Article 1.

8. Ibid., Article 3. An IADB-sponsored study emphasized the reversed priorities by stressing internal over external issues. See Instituto Centroamericano de Administración Pública, "Las empresas públicas y otros organismos descentralizados en la República de Nicaragua" (San José, Costa Rica, 1978), p. 57.

9. Decreto no. 536, Article 5, Paragraphs h, i, j.

10. Guillermo Bendaña García and Danilo A. Guevara Tórrez, "La circulación de los granos básicos," paper presented at the First Congress on Distribution in Nicaragua "Pedro Araús Palacios" (Managua, October 1985), p. 20; and Solon Barraclough, "A Preliminary Analysis of the Nicaragua Food System," Food Systems and Society Series, Food Systems Monograph (Geneva: United Nations Research Institute for Social Development, 1982), p. 29.

11. A recent International Monetary Fund (IMF) report on Nicaragua confuses reorganizing an existing firm with creating a new public enterprise. The mistake is common and frequently occurs when a flurry of decrees reorganize most of the country's state entrepreneurial activity, as also occurred in Peru after 1968. See "Evolución económica reciente" (Washington: IMF Report SM/85/58 [S], February 1985), p. 25.

12. Bendaña and Guevara, "La circulación," p. 20.

13. Frederic Dévé and Philippe Grenier, Precios y subsidios de los granos básicos en Nicaragua (Managua: Ministerio de Desarrollo Agropecuario y Reforma Agraria [MIDINRA] & Programa Alimentario

Nicaraguense [PAN], 1984), p. 49.

14. MICOIN, Sistemas de comercialización, Vol. I, Aspectos globales (Managua, 1983), p. F-4.
15. Ibid., p. D-5.
16. Decreto No. 82, Article 9, Paragraph 6.
17. Decreto No. 82, Article 6.
18. Gobierno de Reconstrucción Nacional, Secretaría de la Junta, Dirección de Información y Gestión Estatal, "Las finalidades y funciones de las entidades del área de propiedad del pueblo" (Managua, March 30, 1980).
19. Six firms, in addition to ENABAS, formed a powerful set of foreign trade instruments. The other firms included Empresa Nicaragüense de Algodón (ENAL); Empresa Nicaragüense del Café (ENCAFE); Empresa Nicaragüense del Azúcar (ENAZUCAR); Empresa Nicaragüense de Productos del Mar (ENMAR); and Empresa Nicaragüense de Insumos Agropecuarios (ENIA). Decreto No. 82, Article 5.
20. Decreto No. 484.
21. CIERA, Distribución y consumo popular de alimentos en Managua (Managua, 1983), p. 58.
22. Alex F. McCalla and Andrew Schmitz, "State Trading in Grain," in M. M. Kostecki, ed., State Trading in International Markets (New York: St. Martin's Press, 1982), p. 65.
23. Decreto No. 824, Article 3, Paragraph f.
24. Interview, Ruth Ramírez, ENABAS, July 15, 1986.
25. Beans are included with basic grains and not separately treated as pulses.
26. ENABAS, Informe anual 1985 (Managua,1986), pp. 13-14.
27. CIERA, Informe final del Proyecto Estrategia Alimentaria, vol. 2 (Managua, 1984), p. 59. See also Dévé and Grenier, Precios y subsidios, p. 22.
28. Instituto Nacional de Estadística y Censos (INEC), Indice de precios al consumidor, diciembre 1985 (Managua, 1986), p. 18.
29. Decreto No. 1156, Ley de Presupuesto 1983, Article 5. The provisions of the budget law specifically overrode the contractual liberty granted to the company in its law of creation.
30. Dévé and Grenier, Precios y subsidios, Appendix 4, p. 26.
31. See table 6.
32. The IMF economic report on Nicaragua notes only the accumulated losses, without regard to the compensating government transfers. By comparing losses accrued from 1981 to 1983 that were taken from the balance sheet with the 1983 GDP figures, instead of relying on income statement or flow-of-funds figures, the report paints ENABAS in a more negative light than it deserves. See IMF, "Evolución económica reciente," p. 27.
33. Beyond Management Control: A Systems Approach to Public Enterprises, Technical Papers Series, no. 48 (Austin, TX: Institute of Latin American Studies, Office for Public Sector Studies, 1985), published in Spanish as "Más allá del control gerencial: Un enfoque

sistémico a las empresas públicas," in Alfred H. Saulniers et al., Las empresas públicas en el Perú (Lima: Centro Peruano de Investigación Aplicada, 1985), pp. 11-59.
34. Ministerio de Planificación (MIPLAN), Plan de reactivación económica en beneficio del pueblo (Managua, 1980), p. 19.
35. Decreto No. 82, Article 5.
36. CORFIN was created by Decreto No. 463, and COIP by Decreto No. 597.
37. Decreto No. 597, Article 6, Paragraph a.
38. Decreto No. 1156, Ley de Presupuesto 1983, Article 5.
39. Saulniers, "Más allá," pp. 23-26.
40. Nicaraguan authorities became aware of a severe shortfall between demand for skilled public sector executives and their supply in the post-Somoza environment. See Instituto Nicaragüense de Administración Pública (INAP), Centro de Instrucción para la Dirección Estatal, "Los problemas de las empresas públicas en un proceso revolucionario" (Managua, 1981), p. 7.
41. Interview, Danilo A. Guevara Tórrez, ENABAS, July 16, 1985.
42. Two highly critical case studies analyze the previous, highly bureaucratic system. See Gobierno de Reconstrucción Nacional, Secretaría General de la Junta, Dirección de Información y Gestión Estatal, "Los efectos del burocratismo sobre la producción: El caso del mango burocrático" (Managua, 1981); and idem, "Los efectos del burocratismo sobre los proyectos de infraestructura: El caso de los respuestos sin respuesta" (Managua, 1981).
43. Decreto No. 809, "Ley de contrataciones administrativas del estado, entes descentralizados o autónomos y municipalidades."
44. Ibid., Article 16.
45. Ibid., Article 14, Paragraph 4.
46. Ibid., Article 16, Paragraph 6, Subparagraphs d and f.
47. ENABAS, Informe anual 1985, p. 19.
48. Gobierno de Reconstrucción Nacional, "Informe de la Junta de Gobierno de Reconstrucción Nacional de Nicaragua presentado al Consejo de Estado el 4 de Mayo de 1982 'Dia de la Dignidad Nacional'" (Managua, 1982), p. 37.
49. Ibid., pp. 56-57. Sugar consumption was estimated at 51 kilos per person per year compared to a Ministry of Health recommendation of 28.5 kilos. See "Dificultades de la política de subsidios," Lunes Socio-Económico de Barricada, pp. 117-118.
50. CIERA, Informe final, vol. 2 (Managua, 1984), p. iii.
51. ENABAS, Informe anual 1981, Anexo estadístico y financiero (Managua, n.d.), p. 30. So popular were the nostrums that ENABAS sales reached 445 million Córdobas in the first month of imports, slightly less than half the value of ENABAS sales of soap throughout the country.
52. For a fuller explanation of the interinstitutional interlinkage framework, see Saulniers, "Más allá," pp. 30-53.

53. MICOIN, Sistemas de comercialización, vol. 6, Análisis de la situación del marco institucional en comercio interior y recomendaciones para la elaboración de una estrategia de consolidación de economía mixta en el sector, p. 84.

54. INAP, "Los problemas," pp. 7-8.

55. Dévé and Grenier, Precios y subsidios, p. 11. The authors principally speak to the provision of direct subsidies via the price-setting mechanism for foodstuffs. They examine, but do not estimate, all indirect subsidies that abounded in Nicaragua. For example, imported agricultural inputs benefited from a preferential exchange rate, and domestically produced ones were directly subsidized so that it was usually cheaper to replace than to repair machinery. See Secretaría de Planificación y Presupuesto, Plan económico 1985 (Managua, 1985), p. 9. A blizzard of agricultural credit was provided at negative rates with an implicit subsidy for 1981 calculated at 467 million Córdobas; see CIERA, Informe final, vol. 3, p. 67. And large segments of the agricultural debt were condoned: ibid., p. 45. See Clive Gray, "Towards a Conceptual Framework for Macroeconomic Evaluation of Public Enterprise Performance in Mixed Economies" (Washington: International Monetary Fund DM/83/57, 1983), for a fuller analysis of the macroeconomic impact of direct and indirect subsidies and an explanation of difficulties in their measurement.

56. MICOIN, Sistemas de comercialización, vol. 6, p. 51.

57. Ibid., p. 38, for producer prices, and p. 52, for consumer prices.

58. CIERA, Informe final, vol. 3, pp. 62-63.

59. See MICOIN, Sistemas de comercialización, vol. 6, pp. 38-80, for a detailed analysis of the dynamic interactions between all potential parties to the MICOIN-related price setting, regulatory, and control decisions taken within levels of the public administration system.

60. MICOIN sources expressed dismay over being unable to find a legal basis for COMMEMA participation in the price-setting decision: ibid., p. 53.

61. Jorge Barenstein, Algunos señalamientos sobre la gestión de las empresas del estado en Nicaragua (Managua: INAP, 1981), p. 30.

62. Ibid., p. 83.

63. All ENABAS officials interviewed unanimously declared that open-ended subsidies had not given rise to additional sources of inefficiency.

64. CIERA, Informe final, vol. 2, p. 57; and Secretaría de Planificación y Presupuesto, Plan económico 1985 (Managua, 1985), p. 6.

65. Dévé and Grenier, Precios y subsidios, p. 116. In a study of Managua, 40 percent of lower-income respondents felt that the food situation had worsened after 1979 (see CIERA, Distribución y consumo, p. 67). Although a MICOIN study claimed that the combination of price and subsidy policy weakened the cost of living increases for the poorer social classes (MICOIN, Sistemas de comercialización, vol. 1, p. C-19), consumer price index information reveals an effect so weak that the food component of the CPI rises faster

for lower-income earners than it does for upper-income groups. In 1985, the rises were 388.79 percent and 270.96 percent, respectively (see INEC, Indice de precios al consumidor, pp. 16-17). My own calculations, based on CIERA data, show that only three food groups would not have had perverse effects whereby more of the subsidy was received by upper-income groups: corn, corn tortillas, and manioc. All items have negative income elasticities of demand.

66. By 1982, farmers were so disenchanted with the pricing policy that a MICOIN study found more than 80 percent of all farmers and more than 90 percent of small farmers did not want to continue farming maize (MICOIN, Sistemas de comercialización, vol.2, Aspectos generales, p. F-35). Dévé and Grenier concluded that setting prices to provide a margin of only 10 to 20 percent above the national average financeable production costs that excluded key labor elements of shelling, transporting, and selling grains "condemns the small and medium farmers to conditions of precarious income" (Precios y subsidios, pp. 62, 127). Small and medium farmers produce more than three-fourths of Nicaragua's maize. Large farms, too, stopped producing, as it was cheaper to buy maize from ENABAS than it was to produce locally for workers' consumption (CIERA, Informe final, vol. 2, p. 57). Producer prices remained neglected, however, and a usually well-informed source emphasized, even at the end of 1983, that economic recovery leading to the attainment of earlier production levels and access to inputs remained essential to boosting maize and bean production ("Situación actual de la producción de granos básicos," Lunes Socio-Económico de Barricada, 1984).

67. Barenstein, Algunos señalamientos, p. 30.
68. MICOIN, Sistemas de comercialización, vol. 1, p. A-2.
69. Barenstein, Algunos señalamientos, pp. 39-40.
70. MICOIN, Sistemas de comercialización, vol. 6, pp. 99-100.
71. For an economic analysis of core company creation motives, see Leroy P. Jones and Edward S. Mason, "Role of Economic Factors in Determining the Size and Structure of the Public Enterprise Sector in Less-Developed Countries with Mixed Economies," in Leroy P. Jones et al., eds., Public Enterprise in Less-Developed Countries (New York: Cambridge University Press, 1982), pp. 17-48.
72. Few published references exist to accidental nationalization. On Italy's IRI, see N. S. Carey Jones, Sam M. Patankar, and M. J. Boodhoo, Politics, Public Enterprise and the Industrial Development Agency: Industrialization Policies and Practices (London: Croom Helm, 1974), p. 23; and Stuart Holland, "The National Context," in Stuart Holland, ed., The State as Entrepreneur: New Dimensions for Public Enterprise: The IRI State Shareholding Formula (London: Weidenfeld and Nicolson, 1972), pp. 57-59.
73. Gobierno de Reconstrucción Nacional, "Informe," pp. 60-63.
74. Interview, anonymous, 1986.
75. Interview, Ramón Castro, July 7, 1986.

76. MICOIN, Sistemas de comercialización, vol. 1, p. C-24.
77. Ibid., vol. 2, p. F-52.
78. Interview, Danilo A. Guevara Tórrez, ENABAS, July 16, 1986.
79. James Austin, Johnathan Fox and Walter Krueger, "The Role of the State in the Nicaraguan Food System," World Development 13, no.1 (1985): p. 126.
80. MICOIN, Sistemas de comercialización, vol. 6, p. 86.
81. Ibid., vol. 3, p. I-1-I-2.

Chapter 6

A Framework for Evaluating the Efficiency of Health Centers in Nicaragua

by

Chandler Stolp

**With the assistance of
Janine Hooker**

Introduction[1]

A dramatic improvement in health and health care services has been achieved in Nicaragua since the Somoza government was toppled in July of 1979. Along with the successes in literacy and education, these accomplishments constitute one of the main showcases of the Sandinista Revolution. This chapter first examines some of the changes that have taken place in the delivery of public health care under the Sandinista government, focusing on the productivity of health centers (centros de salud), the facilities that account for approximately two-thirds of the primary health encounters in the country. Contrasts and comparisons are occasionally made with the structure of health care delivery in El Salvador, a country with a similar recent history of civil strife. After discussing the significance of efficiency analysis for health planners and administrators in development settings, the chapter applies a set of recently developed techniques for estimating empirical production functions ("data envelopment analysis" [análisis de envoltura de datos]; DEA) and presents an illustrative (and provisional) report on the relative efficiency of health centers in the Managua region (Nicaragua's administrative Region III).

Changes in Health Care Delivery in the Post-Somoza Era

There are three major dimensions to the restructuring of health delivery that has taken place in Nicaragua since the insurrection. The first concerns the centralization and rationalization of the twenty-three autonomous institutions that made up the prerevolutionary health system.

The second relates to the "popular health councils," an innovative system of grass-roots participation in health planning and, more important, health education and training. These councils are coordinated at every level with the more traditional top-down hierarchical administration of the Ministry of Health, composed of the central administration, regional administrations, hospitals, health centers, and health posts. The third striking achievement in health delivery since 1979 is the internationally acclaimed success of a series of popular health campaigns (jornadas populares de salud) against polio, DPT, dengue fever, malaria, and unsanitary living conditions. Much has been written on each of these,[2] so only a brief sketch is provided here.

A Unified System of Health Care Delivery. Within a mere three weeks of the overthrow of Somoza on July 19, 1979, the new Sandinista government promulgated laws that reorganized the terribly inefficient prerevolutionary health care system into the Sistema Nacional Unico de Salud (SNUS), a unified system of health care under the direct super-vision of the minister of health. Until that time, public health in Nicaragua had been managed by almost two dozen autonomous institutions. Many of the twenty-three pre-Sandinista units had parallels in most Latin American countries, where the structure of public health is also frag-mented typically (although rarely to the degree found in Somoza's Nicaragua) into systems for workers, for rural areas, for the indigent, for the military, and for other groups. The largest of these health systems in prerevolutionary Nicaragua included the Social Security Institute (INSS), the Ministry of Public Health (MSP), the National Public Welfare Board (JNAPS), and the Military Hospital System.

Popular Health Councils. As the newly integrated Ministry of Health (MINSA) was being organized, the government began developing what occasionally appears to be a completely parallel organizational structure, the consejos populares de salud. These popular health councils are organized on the community, regional, and the national levels and provide for direct input from the mass organizations and from individual members of the local community in health planning, health education, health training, and popular health campaigns. At the local level, the two structures are almost indistinguishable; at the higher levels of health planning there is some concern about lack of coordination and conflicting agendas between the two structures,[3] despite the fact that the participa-tion of community organizations in health planning at all levels of SNUS is guaranteed in its principles of organization. The causes offered for the conflict between the popular health councils and MINSA are nume-rous. Among them is the observation that the "bottom-up" structure of the popular health councils is guided more by popular revolutionary principles and that the (at least formal) "top-down" structure of MINSA acts as the voice of the professional concerns and interests of physicians. There is a characteristically "Latin American" corporatist-syndicalist flavor to the form of participatory democracy found in the popular health councils. They are made up of representatives from various grass-roots popular organizations representing key sectors of contemporary Nicaraguan life: civil defense organizations (e.g., Sandinista community civil defense committees), economic organizations (e.g., unions), family organizations (e.g., neighborhood committees of mothers, community youth, and children's organizations), and educational groups (e.g., teachers' organizations), among others. Members of the community participate as citizens and as members of various economic, family, civil defense, or educational interest groups. Through Anglo-American eyes, this corporatist structure is foreign and smacks of early twentieth-century European fascism, a fact that may obscure any appreciation North of the Rio Grande of the grass-roots participatory nature of these populist Nicaraguan institutions.

Popular Health Campaigns. The third aspect of Nicaragua's revolution in health delivery relates to the campaigns that have been waged against polio, malaria, dengue fever, and unsanitary living conditions. The planning and execution of these vaccination and clean-up exercises generated significant organizational conflict between MINSA and the popular health councils. Despite these problems, however, the campaigns have generally been quite successful in meeting both their health goals (the incidence of malaria in 1982 was half that of the year before) and their political goals (a substantial proportion of the population was treated and as much as 10 percent of the population was active in the campaign).

Preliminary Comparisons with El Salvador. Although many problems in health service delivery are shared by developing countries throughout the world, some are peculiar to Central America, with its continuing legacy of conflict and undeclared wars. Even brief comparisons of the state of public health care in Nicaragua and in El Salvador impress one in at least three ways. First, the underlying problems are quite similar in both countries and can effectively be held constant in any comparative analysis. Second, a comparison of the two countries demonstrates what little difference the hundreds of millions of dollars of annual U.S. assistance to El Salvador seems to have made. Third, the comparison highlights the remarkable strides that Nicaragua has achieved in health care since 1979 (even though there has traditionally been substantially greater room for improvement in Nicaragua than in El Salvador).

Whereas Nicaragua has made great progress in unifying and rationalizing its system of health delivery in the context of a mixed economy, El Salvador maintains a unified health system in name only. The actually fragmented system of health care institutions in El Salvador includes a social security health system (for industrial workers -- coverage does not extend to family members) that covers approximately 14 percent of the population, a system for the armed forces, a system for the national telecommunications workers, and several minor systems, along with private sector health care. There is then also the public health ministry, whose primary mission is to attend to populations not covered by other systems. Although less grotesquely uncoordinated than Nicaragua's prerevolutionary system of twenty-three public health systems, the balkanization of El Salvador's health system undoubtedly contributes to substantial inefficiency. Questions of efficiency aside, Donahue speculated that the presence of so many competing health systems in prerevolutionary Nicaragua lent itself conveniently to the political patronage and vertical political control that generally served as the basis for Somoza's power.[4]

In any event, it would be a mistake to interpret the existence of a multitude of health agencies as evidence of anything akin to economic competition in health care, with all of the salutary effects such competition is supposed to provide. Barriers to entry and exit, frequent local monopolistic structures, and other insulation from price competition conspire to make systems such as that found in El Salvador substantially less than efficient. Despite the plethora of health institutions, the individual consumer is effectively locked into a particular public system with the option of turning to the private sector if his or her economic status permits it or if the gravity of the situation requires it.

Despite international efforts to foment popular participation in public health in El Salvador, citizen involvement is more narrowly circumscribed in that country than it is in Nicaragua. One faint parallel in El Salvador to Nicaragua's popular health councils is the system of patronatos, or hospital health boards. There is, however, a philanthropic or paternalistic flavor to the patronatos that is missing entirely in Nicaragua. Since the early 1960s, each hospital in El Salvador has been required by law to maintain a patronato health board comprising the director of the hospital and important patrons from the community. The primary goal of these organizations is to serve as a channel for private donations (philanthropic donations as well as donations collateral to health services received) to their respective hospitals. The importance of these donor funds in financing hospital care in the country is significant and increasing, especially as inflexible price controls over products and services in public health have led to fiscal crisis in health care.

War and conflict continue to plague both countries and to create conditions that have sharply constrained the level of funding for health care. Despite the austerity, Nicaragua has managed to more than double its real expenditures on health care since 1977; in real per capita terms this translates to an increase of approximately 50 percent.[5] In the same period of time, Fiedler estimates that per capita expenditure of the Public Health Ministry in El Salvador has declined 28 percent in real terms since 1977.[6] Naturally, comparisons like these are difficult to make in light of the significant differences in public financial management, price levels, the level of external assistance, institutional structures, the low base level of health delivery in prerevolutionary Nicaragua, and so on. Despite these caveats, however, it is undeniable that Nicaragua has made tremendous strides in improving the state of health in the country and has continued to experiment creatively with new methods of delivering primary and secondary care.

Whereas both countries officially maintain systems guaranteeing "free health care to all," the definition of "free" is a loose one, and the differences between the two systems seem to be significant. There are genuine real costs associated with medical attention in Nicaragua; these include travel time, queuing, other opportunity costs, and the scarcity of medicines. The real costs of health care in El Salvador are structurally much the same, although the impact is softened by the generally higher standard of living and the wider availability of basic medicines. Salvadorans, however, also pay nominal user fees (in practice based on a sliding scale) for many services and are requested to make additional "voluntary" contributions to the patronatos.

These differences in the actual costs of health care reveal underlying differences in pricing philosophy. There is some discussion among health policy makers in El Salvador about converting major portions of health delivery in that country into managed prepaid care systems much like HMOs in the United States.[7] There is also some talk of a less-likely alternative, namely, completely privatizing curative health care.[8] Nothing could be more remote from Nicaraguans' minds. Despite occasional friction between the popular health councils and MINSA,[9] the philosophy of health care delivery in that country is profoundly rooted in populist and socialist ideals.

The Administration of Health Centers

Each of the three general aspects of Nicaragua's health revolution- - functional unification, popular participation, and health campaigns-- has served as the focus of popular and international interest. A significant component of health delivery that has been relatively ignored in the literature is the management of health centers (centros de salud), the backbone of the Health Ministry's primary health care system, its main instrument of outreach into the community, and the focus of the empirical part of this study.

The neglect is understandable in that health care centers in Nicaragua are structurally not very different from health care centers in any other Latin American country. Institutionally, health care delivery is organized hierarchically within SNUS/MINSA. Health care delivery at the national level is, for the most part, restricted to strategic planning, although there is a national Hospital de Especialidades and a central epidemiological clinic under the direct supervision of MINSA. The military hospital system is also directed at the national level, although apparently only loosely coordinated with MINSA. Regional health divisions of MINSA maintain one or more hospitals in each of the country's six administrative regions and three "special zones" (for the sparsely populated Atlantic coast). Hospitals account for slightly more than one-third of all medical encounters in Nicaragua.

Although not unique to Nicaragua, the pyramidal administrative structure of hospitals, health centers, and health posts seems not at all unlike the administrative structure of Spanish colonial missions, each with its respective asisténcias, each asisténcia in turn managing its own capillas (chapels). Hospital regions in Nicaragua are divided into a half dozen to two dozen "health areas," each with its own health center (centro de salud) covering a population of from twenty thousand to thirty thousand. Health centers are the workhorses of the institutionalized professional health care delivery system. Together with their constituent health posts, the nation's one hundred health centers account for almost two-thirds of all medical encounters in the country. A typical health center in an urban area is staffed with five to ten physicians, a similar number of registered nurses, and fifty to eighty "other personnel," including nursing assistants and administrative staff. Fewer than 10 percent of the health centers are equipped with beds; those that are usually have no more than three.

Each health center administers a set of local health posts responsible for areas of approximately three thousand persons. Health care posts are usually attended by one physician (often a recent graduate performing his or her year of national service) and four or five nurses or auxiliaries.

In principle and in practice, the administrative hierarchy of institutional health care matches the level of attention offered and sought. All other things being equal, the seriousness of an illness, injury, or complaint determines the type of medical facility a patient seeks out. This self-selection and the pattern of referrals that are made from health posts to centers and from centers to hospitals establish what might be termed the "baseline" for the supply and demand for health services.

This baseline of utilization is, however, subject to a variety of other forces. Patients, as we noted earlier, must consider the real costs of traveling to health care facilities, costs that are significantly higher in the war zones than, say, in Managua. There may also be costs associated with foregone wages and with queuing at the health care facilities. A further, and increasingly critical, factor distorting the baseline pattern of patient choice is the availability of medicines.

Although it is difficult to measure adequately the quantity and quality of pharmaceutical stocks in all the government's health care facilities, medicines seem to be supplied to facilities in the following way: military hospitals are reputed to have the best stocks of pharmaceuticals, followed by key urban hospitals, other hospitals, key health centers, private institutions and other health centers, and, finally, health posts. If the Nicaraguan economy continues to weaken and if medicines continue to become scarcer, secondary care facilities will continue to be inefficiently overutilized for what essentially amounts to meeting primary ambulatory care needs, needs that should be met in the health centers and health posts but that are being diverted to hospitals due to the comparative advantage they enjoy in maintaining more complete pharmaceutical stocks.

A final factor that tends to distort baseline patterns of demand is the changing set of popular perceptions of quality of health care. In Managua, for example, ostensibly groundless rumors that a particular hospital is the "best" hospital in the city cause critical overutilization of that institution while others of competitive quality remain relatively underutilized.

The Significance of Efficiency Analysis in Health Planning

Popular debate concerning costs and pricing policy in health care in the developing world generally revolves around questions of equity ("What is a fair amount to charge a person from this economic class for this type of medical service?") rather than efficiency. Yet, as any economist will attest, to ignore the efficiency implications of policy choices is to cripple those policies, including those driven by considerations of equity, in the long run.

One fundamental problem with health care costs and pricing policies in Nicaragua, El Salvador, and elsewhere is that, on the one hand, we are speaking of what economists refer to as "public goods"; on the other hand, we are dealing with what are essentially "nonmarket settings," environments that inherently cannot support salubrious private competition. The crux of the matter is that in order to allocate scarce resources efficiently, it is necessary to "send the right (price) signals" to consumers and to all affected factor (input) and commodity (output) markets; modern neoclassical economic theory tells us that perfectly competitive markets can accomplish this. In order to understand the dilemma facing health planners in settings like Nicaragua and El Salvador, it is worth digressing for a moment to elaborate on the concepts of "public goods" and "nonmarket settings."

Public Goods. Economics textbooks devote much discussion to developing the principles of perfect competition in private markets for private goods. A person can purchase a private good (and, if the market is competitive, purchase that good at minimum cost) and consume that good without affecting other people's welfare positively or negatively (no externalities). The literature has a more difficult time treating a much more complex topic, that of "public goods" and "merit goods" like health care. A public good is a commodity that it is impossible to exclude others from enjoying. An example is national defense; for one citizen to enjoy a certain level of defense from the nation's enemies, all citizens must be given the same level of protection (and those with higher utility for this level of protection should be willing to pay a higher price to gain this level of defense). Merit goods are commodities that ought to be provided for their own sake; to assert that public health is a merit good is to suggest that it is a basic right and that there should be some guarantee that a certain level will be maintained (whether by the government or by the private sector), almost without regard to cost.

The quintessential economic problem with public goods and merit goods is how to finance them. Individuals have every incentive not to pay their full share of the benefits they enjoy from any public good ("since I can enjoy benefits for free, I'll let someone else pay the bill"); consequently, public goods by their very nature will be underfunded without some form of direct government provision or supporting intervention (such as a protected monopoly). Markets for public goods, in economists' terms, tend to "fail." Although public goods are typically provided by the government, the issue of whether a good is a public good or a private good is, in principle, independent of the method chosen to provide it. Telephone service in the United States, for example, qualifies as a public good but has always been provided by private firms protected under special license.

Nonmarket Settings. Just as economic theory is clearest on issues relating to private goods as opposed to public goods, it is also much more forthcoming on the logic of competitive market settings than it is on that of restricted or price-distorted market settings, such as those that pervade small dependent economies like Nicaragua's and El Salvador's. It seems to pretend that most markets are perfectly competitive. Textbooks do little more than inform readers of how to determine some of the directions in which certain price distortions will lead to misallocation of resources -- the inefficient underutilization or overutilization of factors or the underproduction or overproduction of goods.

Price distortions in Nicaragua take many forms and exist for many reasons. As a small country (approximately 3.2 million inhabitants -- roughly the size of the metropolitan area of Houston, Texas) with a traditionally open economy facing a significant economic embargo by the U.S. government, Nicaragua, without the economic base enjoyed by other countries, must bid with scarce foreign exchange for goods in external markets. Consequently, many basic commodities are priced out of line with other commodities (glass containers, to take but one example, are often substantially more expensive than the cost of their component ingredients). Second, industries that could emerge as competitive in large, open economies often evolve into monopolies in small economies, with all of the classical price distortions that attend monopolistic or oligopolistic markets (breweries and classical local monopolies like cement and heavy building materials come immediately to mind). Third, as an economy on a wartime footing, many resources that might ordinarily go to the consumer sector are funneled to the armed forces for national defense, a state of affairs that promotes further upward pressures on the prices of these commodities. Finally, as a mixed economy with a policy of explicit controls on the supplies and prices of key commodities (e.g., meat, milk, beans, pharmaceuticals), it is natural to expect the price signals that are administratively promulgated to be out of joint with black-market, international, or other prevailing price systems.

Pricing and Efficiency in Health Care. The important point of this discussion of public goods and nonmarket settings is that prices fail to send the signals that are in theory conveyed in competitive markets for private goods, signals that guarantee the efficient, minimum-cost allocation of resources within the system. There is an entire spectrum of public policy philosophies concerning the "best" corrective action to take under market failure.

A "laissez faire" philosophy of nonintervention in markets susceptible to allocative distortion would merely ratify prevailing price/income distortions and ignore entirely issues of equity (e.g., who deserves or does not deserve to suffer the consequences of unrestrained market forces). In settings where equity and other nonefficiency considerations frequently guide resource allocation, a policy of laissez faire can be a convenient instrument of vested power interests.

If the outcomes of laissez faire policies prove too unsavory, a more forgiving "free-market" philosophy might argue that the government should intervene to transform nonmarket settings into artificial private market settings. One of the goals of government, in this view, is to guarantee private competitive markets. This is a philosophy that holds (ironically?) that the existence of private markets per se is a public good in the sense that the entire public enjoys the efficiencies associated with a perfectly competitive market, and no one citizen can be excluded from enjoying what other citizens enjoy in this regard. Under this philosophy, noncompetitive markets would be broken up and state monopolies (or quasi monopolies) like public health would be privatized to emulate perfect competition--all in the name of guaranteeing that competitive price signals operate to allocate resources efficiently.

A third philosophy strikes out from the position that some markets are inherently imperfect and that some commodities are inherently public goods. According to this view, it is necessary for government to guarantee that the commodities involved are allocated efficiently or equitably. In some cases the government can act as a guarantor of market efficiency; in other cases it can provide the goods and services itself.

Each of these perspectives on market failure has its own practical implications. A confounding factor, however, arises when you consider that there is both a public-good and a private-good aspect to the provision of health care to the public. On the one hand, an individual's consumption of health care services is a matter of his or her own well-being; in principle, the patient should bear the costs of these private benefits. On the other hand, there are significant "positive externalities" (therefore, a public good aspect) to an individual's seeking medical care.

From a narrow perspective, the very fact that a neighbor has successfully been cured of an infectious disease improves my well-being by reducing the risk that I will be infected. From a broader perspective, economic development can take off only once a critical level of public health is achieved. Although the causal links are vague, there is general agreement that a certain level of public health and sanitation is a prerequisite to successful economic growth. Further complicating the situation is the difficulty of identifying, let alone measuring, the private and social benefits and costs associated with public health. All of these considerations lead to the conclusion that there is no unambiguous way to classify health care in the vocabulary of public and private goods; nor is there an unambiguously "best" way to organize public health care delivery.

Nicaragua and El Salvador: A Contrast in Public Health Policy

What is interesting about the cases of Nicaragua and El Salvador in their pursuit of public health care is that their approaches to health care as a public or private good and as properly offered in a market or nonmarket setting are in such stark contrast. Without passing judgment on the emerging policies each of these countries seems to be pursuing, or on the underlying philosophies that govern these policies, it is a fact that current public policy in El Salvador seems to be directed toward transforming a fundamentally public good (or quasi-public good) like public health care into a quasi-private good and transforming the inherently imperfect market setting in which public health is inscribed into an artificially private market setting. User fees, private prepaid care, and total privatization are all issues that enter, to greater or lesser degrees, into public debate in that country.

Nicaragua, on the other hand, has explicitly departed on a course that declares public health to be a public good and a merit good, one for which the state (through SNUS/MINSA) and the people (through the popular health councils) share responsibility. The principles of organization of the new national unified health system (SNUS) declare that:

1)   health is an unambiguous right of every citizen; it is also a responsibility of the state as well as of popular organizations;

2)   health services should be available to the entire population, regardless of geographic, economic, and cultural status;

3)   health service delivery should take an integrated approach that not only focuses on individual health or illness, but recognizes its relationship to the individual's living and work environment;

4)   health care should be delivered in a professional, multiteam effort;

5)   health activities should be planned;

6)   community organizations should participate in all SNUS health activities.[10]

Each of these declarations is subject to multiple interpretations. Many of the principles could apply to any public health organization in the entire world as well as they could to Nicaragua. There are, nevertheless, several notable elements that deserve highlighting: the central role of popular participation and popular organizations; health care for all (something that was restricted geographically, economically, and socially under Somoza); and coordinated planning. In the case of Nicaragua, all of these dimensions speak to a conception of public health as a public good to be provided collectively.

What are the consequences for efficiency of the different paths these two countries have embarked on?   From a strictly economic standpoint, the only justification for privatizing a public good and privatizing an imperfect market is to gain the advantages of efficiency that undistorted price signals can provide.   Equity considerations aside for a moment, to the extent that price signals begin to reflect the true resource costs, this approach should be able to capture and harness the power of the proverbial "invisible hand." The relevant question is how feasible is it to create this kind of an artificial environment in a small, dependent economy with a health care sector that is part of an entire system of distorted markets and with a severely distorted income distribution and yet still adhere to basic principles of "health care for all"? To manage the information necessary to effect this state of affairs would be no less daunting than what would be required to manage a totally centralized health care system.

In terms of information management, Nicaragua finds itself in a similar situation. Without the efficiencies of perfect price signals, other methods have to be devised to convey the information necessary to allocate health care resources efficiently.   The "data envelopment analysis" approach presented in the following sections of this chapter is offered as one method to guide administrators in allocating personnel and setting goals in an environment devoid of perfect price signals and markets.

How do prices and profits serve as signals? Introductory economics textbooks are generally organized around the principle of prices, costs, and profits as signals.   The broader topic is beyond the scope of this study.   To illustrate, however, a manager of several bread shops in a competitive market can "read" the market to determine what wages to pay workers and what prices to charge consumers. Profits from the various shops would serve as "attention-directing devices" in the sense that a shop that was earning substantially lower profits than other shops (or even generating losses) would deserve some investigation: costs may be too high, work habits may be inefficient, prices may be too low, demand may be insufficient, the product mix may not be in tune with local market conditions, and so on. There are other reasons besides the public good and imperfect market arguments for explaining why the bread shop example does not hold for health care, but these too are beyond the scope of this chapter.

The central point here is that the direction both of these countries are taking in health care delivery forces them to confront the issue of efficiency, specifically, how to determine adequately the efficiency of various operations in a manner that would help administrators allocate scarce resources to meet the most pressing needs in the most effective way possible. Prices, "profits," resource costs, and the like all help managers make these decisions effectively when dealing with private goods in a perfectly competitive economy. When the world does not look like this, other methods need to be explored in order to manage the information necessary for effective resource allocation.

Broad Issues in the Efficiency of Public Health Care Delivery

Before coming to grips with substitutes for adequate price signals, let us frame the concept of "efficiency" in public health more concretely, especially as it relates to the operation of health centers. Most of the dimensions to efficiency outlined below are beyond the scope of this study. They are presented here merely as directions for further thought.

The Allocation of Personnel. Ignoring the demand side for a moment, determining the optimal division of labor within health care facilities is difficult without some notion of the productivity of each kind of labor (MDs, specialists, nurses, auxiliaries, and so on) and without some feel for how these various forms of labor productively complement or substitute for each other. Health ministries typically establish guidelines for the ratio of nurses to physicians in health centers. Without detailed empirical information on the productivity of individual health centers, it is likely that these guidelines hamper the overall efficiency of the system (even if the overall average ratio is "optimal"). Productivity is also affected by the availability of basic equipment; a heart specialist, for example, cannot go about his or her business unless the health center has made a certain investment in the tools required for this type of specialty. There are many junctures in health care production where factors simply cannot substitute for other factors (a physician without antibiotics, for example, is going to be substantially less effective in curative care).

It is also important to recognize that we are speaking here (and throughout the balance of this chapter) of technical efficiency, not cost efficiency. In austere budget environments, it may be more practical to seek to allocate personnel in a manner that minimizes costs rather than move in the direction of improved technical efficiency. We see this in some form throughout the developing world, where there are significant pressures to rely less on the expensive services of physicians and substitute the less-expensive services of nurses.

Managing Pressures to Overemploy. To what extent are health ministries throughout the developing world becoming "employment agencies" in addition to carrying the burden of providing affordable health care? Political patronage in rural hospitals in many parts of the Caribbean Basin and Central America frequently reaches down even to the level of janitors. This is only a very small part of the reason the government sector accounts for such a large proportion of employment in these economies, however. Saddled with sluggish economies and vast underemployment, many countries feel great pressures to mix the global objective of delivering efficient and affordable health care with the national objective of providing meaningful employment for its citizens. It is not at all irrational to seek to support the underemployed; it is important, however, that health planners be able to understand and appreciate the costs that these mixed objectives entail. The difficulty of measuring outputs and productivity in service sectors like health makes it too easy to bloat the Public Health Ministry inefficiently.

Efficiency in the Allocation of Pharmaceuticals and Equipment. Scarce foreign exchange is needed to purchase medicines from overseas. The scarcity causes intense nonprice competition within developing countries for access to basic pharmaceuticals. Common efficiency issues include problems in identifying and obtaining a viable mix of basic medicines, determining need, allocating medicines across the country, and managing foreign donations. All of these problems (and more) are found in contemporary Nicaragua. As mentioned earlier, there seems to be a hierarchy of access to medicines, with military hospitals able to maintain the largest and best stocks, down through the system to rural clinics in nonwar zones, where people may go without basic medicines.

Efficiency in Facility Location. Imperfect markets without price signals make it difficult to determine how to locate health care facilities optimally. In addition to interpreting community and political demand, a basic set of issues that health officials have to face in locating facilities is identifying and sorting out the multiple goals that enter into the decision, for example, meeting existing and latent levels of demand, meeting the patterns of demand, minimizing duplication of services with other facilities, maximizing the population covered, minimizing patient travel time within the area, minimizing construction costs, and finding the appropriate level of service (hospital, health center, or health post). Each of these goals conflicts with one or more of the remaining goals; the most difficult task is to make the appropriate tradeoffs intelligently (all in an environment devoid of meaningful price signals).[11]

Efficiency in Budgetary Decision Making. Efficiently allocating scarce budgetary resources across programs, agencies, departments, and ministries is, at every level, an elusive exercise. Due to the difficulties of identifying and placing monetary values on the outputs of the service sector (a sector that includes government), it is not clear that anyone could recognize an "efficient" or "optimal" budgetary allocation even if one were suddenly to emerge by magic.

There are two great threads in the literature on budgeting; the first could be described as the "rationalist" (for lack of a better term), and the second as the "incrementalist." Rationalist budgeting attempts to impose efficient decision rules on the budgeting process, despite the elusiveness of optimality, whereas incrementalist budgeting, recognizing the ultimate futility of classical efficiency in budgeting, emphasizes the procedural rationality of basing this year's allocation on last year's allocation or outcome. Rationalist budgeting would have decision makers weigh the marginal benefits against the marginal costs of every program (and both against the marginal benefits and costs of increasing the overall budget) every cycle of the budget season, something that would require administrators' full-time attention for the entire fiscal year. By focusing on procedural rationality rather than on economic efficiency, incrementalist budgeting leaves the budgeting process open to political manipulation and the negotiated political process that so often characterizes bureaucratic decision making. At its worst, this causes resource allocation to become a sterile, economically inefficient, even corrupt, process. In the case of health care, it can lead to service delivery that is out of joint with existing patterns of demand and only slowly capable of meeting changing patterns of demand.

An additional factor in budgetary decision making that contributes to diffusion of control over resource allocation is the tremendous difference between initial appropriations and final end-of-year spending. Uncertainties in the fiscal and economic environment (along with solidly entrenched procedures of politics by negotiation) typically force developing countries to allocate budgetary resources in a continuing process; initial appropriations are supplemented throughout the fiscal year as "unforeseen needs" arise and as economic uncertainties evolve into certainties.[12] Consequently, the important role of the budget as a planning instrument is eroded. Financial planning horizons shrink as budgetary uncertainties grow. In order to deal with these uncertainties, it is logical that ministries and agencies will encumber existing funds (to demonstrate "need" and to increase their budgetary base for the next incremental exercise). It is likely that the encumbrances that are the product of this logic are only loosely connected with economically efficient resource allocation.

Although the existence of incremental budgeting is not sufficient reason to suspect that a resource allocation system is grossly out of line with actual needs, there is some evidence that the system in El Salvador is, in fact, losing touch with rapidly changing patterns of demand and technological change. Fiedler charges that current budgetary procedures as they affect the health sector in that country contribute to a "status quo oriented and largely inert" process that gives rise to gross misallocation of resources.[13] There are probably many reasons aside from the fundamental nature of the budgetary process in that country that contribute to this state of affairs, the most significant of which, perhaps, is the lack of coordinated planning. Despite Nicaragua's hardships, there seems to be a substantial degree of coordinated planning, all of which is inscribed in a tight budgetary process that has elements of both incremental and rationalist budgeting philosophy. One lesson that seems to emerge both here and elsewhere in the budgeting literature is that, without coordinated planning, an incremental budgetary process can devolve into a process of inefficiently allocating scarce resources.

Budgetary efficiency can also be compromised by a highly centralized system of budget control. Payroll, procurement, and almost all other disbursements, along with much of the information associated with these disbursements in Nicaragua's Ministry of Health, pass through (and, in the case of information, often remain) in a separate government ministry. As I mention below, MINSA apparently is not even able to maintain (except in very aggregate form) information on the numbers and salaries of its own staff in the health centers.

The Consumer's Decision to Utilize Health Care Facilities. A final aspect of general efficiency in health care delivery in settings like Central America concerns the individual citizen's decision to utilize health care facilities. To what degree is health care truly "free" or truly available to all? For one thing, there are many hidden costs, from the individual's point of view, that never appear in the official accounts. As I have mentioned before, these include travel costs, costs associated with queuing for services, and costs for medicines that are unavailable at the health center or hospital.

Related to this point, to what extent does the system of "free" health care create unnecessary overutilization of services, in the sense of drawing people who can afford private care and of attracting people who do not require serious attention or any attention at all? Basic economic theory tells us that, given the choice between a cheap commodity or service and a more expensive one, the rational consumer will choose the less-expensive option, all other things (especially the quality of the commodity or service) being equal. Many aspects of health care are "price elastic"; every percentage decline in price is associated with a more than proportional increase in utilization (with respect both to other goods and to close substitutes). Assuming the quality of health care is the same in the private sector in Nicaragua as it is in the public sector (there is some perception that private attention is of higher quality, and there is the fact that the quality of medicines is generally lower in the private sector), it would therefore not be surprising to find health care consumers in Nicaragua choosing less-expensive public care over more-expensive private care. Health planners in Nicaragua might wish to understand what other factors besides "price," the perceptions and realities of service quality, personal wealth, and the availability of medicines contribute to this decision conerning public or private care. Private health care should have an important role to play in meeting the objectives of SNUS.

Just as the relative price of public health care is an important factor in determining the extent to which people choose private over public care, so it affects individuals' decisions to purchase health care versus other goods and services. As a consequence of health care's being "free," there is a natural tendency for people to overconsume it relative to other commodities. It is important that health care planners appreciate the extent to which some people may be overutilizing services (visiting the health center for every minor complaint, ranging from a headache to imaginary illnesses) at the expense of those truly in need of attention. Health care resources are too scarce to be utilized inefficiently in this manner.

A final point relating to the real price of health care is that as the economy deteriorates and incomes decline, there is likely to be a greater tendency for people to prefer public to private health care. (In the language of economics, public health care is more income elastic than private care.) This is a matter that MINSA should be exploring; its consequences on the mixed economy of service provision as well as on the costs of public health care may be significant.

Measuring the Efficiency of Health Care Facilities

Efficiency Measures as Attention-Directing Devices. Developing and utilizing "efficiency" or "productivity" measures certainly cannot solve all of the problems associated with optimal resource allocation, but it can serve an important role in directing managers' attention to areas demanding special concern. Administratively monitoring the detailed day-to-day operations of each one of a large number of health care facilities is a time-consuming and cognitively taxing task. Management in this kind of an environment tends to be "interrupt-driven"; that is, attention is paid only when a given situation is dramatically out of line relative to average performance. Of course, there are many kinds of interrupts: emergency requests for budget increases, special requests for medicines, special requests for personnel, and so forth. Here, however, we are speaking of overall performance reaching either "unacceptable limits" or "exceeding expectations." A situation in which a particular health care facility, for example, is overspending the next-most-profligate facility by a substantial margin is a matter for administrative concern. Managers should direct their attention to understanding the forces that are contributing to this state of affairs and seek to control them. Likewise, if a facility is dramatically outperforming all other facilities, there should be pressures to identify the contributing factors so that lessons can be brought to bear on other situations.

A broad range of methods are typically used to assess the efficiency, productivity, and performance of health care facilities, each of which can serve to direct administrators' attention to critical situations. These range from ratio analysis, to econometric analysis, to time-motion studies.

Ratio analysis consists of expressing one factor as a proportion of another factor. Examples include performance ratios such as the "number of consultations per physician" and the "physician-to-nurse ratio," and financial ratios, like "current assets to current liabilities" and "maximum annual debt to net operating revenue." Performance ratios are often used within health institutions in the United States as cues for allocating resources, whereas financial ratios are used internally and for external review as indicators of financial health and of capacity to service debts.

An econometric analysis of health care facility efficiency is a statistical exercise that generally consists of directly estimating a hospital production function (a mathematical expression relating the various inputs of hospital service to an output such as patient days) or indirectly estimating a cost function (relating costs to output quantities and input prices). Econometric exercises provide managers with summary information on the returns to scale of the operations, of marginal rates of output transformation, and, by comparing the overall estimated performance to an individual facility's performance, some indication of the relative efficiency of individual facilities. There are several problems with econometric methods for efficiency analysis. These include substantial and costly data requirements, and few records for much of the data needed for this kind of theoretical analysis. Even more damning is the difficulty for managers of translating the abstract theoretical information derived from the models into meaningful operational terms.

Time-motion studies are classical management techniques used to determine productivity benchmarks for various activities. Developed early in this century in the context of assembly line work and associated with Frederick Taylor, time-motion studies are concerned with the measuring of human productivity under almost laboratory conditions. Norms are established, for example, for the amount of time it "should" take for a health promoter to administer one dose of a certain vaccine to a patient efficiently. At their ugliest, time-motion studies reduce to precisely the kinds of dehumanizing management control techniques that were so prominent in the social criticism (including that of Karl Marx) of the nineteenth century. Quite apart from any scientific value these studies might have and apart from the significant costs of executing them, time-motion studies would be impractical in most politically sensitive regions of the world.

Without some external notion of what constitutes "efficient" performance, there is no such thing as a measure of absolute efficiency. Of all these methods for assessing organizational performance, only the time-motion approach comes close to establishing detailed norms of behavior, standards to which the personnel involved ought to adhere. To be normative or prescriptive, ratio analysis must be accompanied with prespecified norms like "a facility is not operating up to standard if the maximum annual debt service to operating revenue ratio is outside the 6%-8% range." An important step in financing health care for hospitals in the United States, for example, is obtaining a bond rating from accredited institutions like Standard and Poors. Standard and Poors typically applies a battery of norms to a long series of financial and other ratios to determine the creditworthiness of a hospital seeking to float a bond to finance expansion or other capital investment.[14] Without such prespecified norms -- however arbitrarily determined -- ratio analysis and econometric analysis provide the manager with little more than indications of relative performance, notions of how far off a particular administrative unit is from average performance as established by the econometric model or the set of ratios calculated.

An Overview of Data Envelopment Analysis

There does exist, however, a set of techniques for empirically estimating production functions and more general "production correspondences." Production correspondences allow us to calculate indexes of relative efficiency for multiple-input, multiple-output organizations like health centers. Furthermore, these techniques lend themselves easily to analysis on microcomputers costing (in 1986) less than $1200 and directly address some of the very basic issues of efficiency I have argued ought to play a role in health care management in development settings. Data envelopment analysis (DEA) is a family of mathematical programming techniques that has been established and refined over the past ten years by a number of scholars.[15]

DEA is essentially concerned with taking existing data on multiple inputs (factors of production like the number of physician-hours) and multiple outputs (products of health care such as the number of births "produced," and the number of infants encountered) for a set of health care facilities and estimating the "efficiency frontier." Facilities falling below this frontier are, by these measures, not achieving the level of productivity enjoyed by other facilities; facilities on the frontier actually define it and are given a rating of 100 percent relative efficiency. In one sense, DEA is simply an extension of ratio analysis. Whereas an individual productivity ratio can only handle single-output/single-input situations, DEA employs techniques of mathematical programming to calculate summary productivity ratios for multiple-output/multiple-input situations.

Researchers have made use of DEA analysis in a broad range of applications. Because it does not require information on prices, DEA has been especially attractive to researchers interested in the productivity of public sector organizations.[16]

The Kinds of Information DEA Can Provide. In the context of this study, the DEA approach to efficiency analysis can perhaps be best appreciated in terms of five basic classes of information it can offer administrators of health care facilities:

1) An index of relative efficiency estimated for each facility, expressed as a percentage ranging from 0 percent (inefficient) to 100 percent (on the relative efficiency frontier);

2) An indication of the sources of inefficiency for each health care facility in terms of the specified inputs and outputs that characterize the "production correspondences" or "technology" for the form of health service delivery being analyzed;

3) A "referent set" or "peer group" of (relatively) efficient facilities identified for each facility;

4) An indication of the optimal scale of operations; and

5) Comparisons of the relative efficiency of various sets of facilities at different points in time, across geographical region, or by other classifications (e.g., comparing the efficiency of rural facilities against urban facilities).

In this study I shall focus on the first three of these as they relate to health centers in Nicaragua's Region III (Managua and environs). Although more complicated to calculate than simple productivity ratios, the DEA index of relative efficiency is a flexible and informative tool for directing attention to facilities that are either unusually productive or unusually unproductive. One by-product of the procedure used to estimate these efficiency ratios is the identification of the supposed sources of inefficiency for those facilities found to be less than 100 percent. For example, if a given facility has a relative efficiency rating of 90 percent, DEA will identify inputs (such as nursing) whose productivity improvement would bring the facility up to 100 percent relative efficiency. It will also identify those outputs that facility administrators must simultaneously pay attention to in order to reach the 100% level of productivity.

One advantage that DEA possesses over more abstract econometric analysis is that it can provide managers with operationally meaningful information ("transfer two physicians from Hospital X to Hospital -Y") rather than with abstract theoretical information (such as "marginal rates of product transformation"). The referent set of peer group facilities for a given health center, say, identifies efficient facilities that share a similar technology with the given health center in the sense that all boast similar input mixes (e.g., physician-to-nurse ratios) and case load mixes (e.g., similar proportions of birthing services, postnatal care). In terms of bureaucratic politics, the identification of referent sets for health care facilities makes it easier to provide administrators with examples of kindred institutions that are able to achieve higher productivity.

The question of optimal scale of operation, although important in many resource allocation decisions (e.g., the determination of the most efficient type of facility -- hospital, health center, health post -- in a location decision), will not be addressed in this study. Health sector applications that utilize information on scale that can be provided through data envelopment analysis are discussed in the concluding section.

Much of this information is derived from DEA as a consequence of the fact that it is based on a set of simple linear programming models, one model for each facility whose productivity is being evaluated. A short technical digression will place some of the information offered by DEA into a more coherent (although more technical) perspective. From a mathematical programming point of view, the index of relative efficiency for a given facility turns out to be a simple transformation of the optimal value of the objective function associated with the DEA linear program for the facility being evaluated. Identifying inputs that may be contributing to inefficiency and outputs that need to be increased is merely a matter of evaluating the slack terms in the respective models. Finally, identifying the referent set of similarly situated efficient facilities is merely a matter of recognizing the basis for the optimal solution to each linear programming model and translating it into the appropriate terms.

All of these points will be developed and made more explicit in subsequent sections. From a technical perspective, all that needs to be appreciated at this point is that DEA involves little more than pulling together the information that falls out of running a series of linear programs, one program for each facility.

Four Perspectives from Which to Appreciate DEA. Unfortunately, the higher-level mathematics or operations research that is required to understand and master the literature on DEA makes it difficult for practitioners to appreciate the virtues of this versatile tool of management science. In this section I attempt to unravel the mysteries of DEA sequentially by developing four key perspectives:

1)　Algebraically, the index of relative efficiency is an elaboration of output-to-input ratio measures of productivity;

2)　Graphically, the index is the minimum slope on an XY plot of output(s) against input(s);

3) From an economic or econometric perspective, a DEA exercise is similar to estimating an envelope production function or estimating the envelope facets of the "isoquant" for a production function;

4) From a mathematical programming perspective, DEA conceptually reduces to a matter of estimating minimum generalized output-to-input ratios subject to a set of constraints guaranteeing that no one facility has more than 100 percent efficiency.

DEA can thus be considered essentially an extension of ordinary ratio analysis. A typical ratio treated in ratio analysis would be the number of consultations in a facility per physician (or per physician-hour if figures on physician-hours are available). To a systems analyst, this is equivalent to imagining an abstract process that takes physicians as its input and generates consultations as its output. This simple conception of health service delivery as a "black box" is precisely what underlies the economist's notion of a production function. The most important advantage that DEA has over ratio analysis is that the latter corresponds to a black box with a single input and a single output, whereas DEA is general enough to model situations with multiple inputs and multiple outputs.

The algebraic concept of an output-to-input ratio translates geometrically to the slope of a ray from the origin to a point on an X-Y plane, the X-axis corresponding to the level of input, the Y-axis to the level of output, and the point to the (input, output) coordinates associated with a given facility (see figure 6-1). After arraying each facility in this Cartesian plane, it is easy to identify that facility corresponding to the largest slope (therefore the largest output-to-input ratio). This is the most efficient facility, relatively speaking, if we assume that the underlying technology is linear, that is, that production is governed by a constant ratio of output to input for all relevant levels of input. To the extent that this is true, the ray from the origin that passes through this "highest" point represents a production frontier; it is the margin along which most efficient production is achieved relative to the set of facilities being analyzed. The efficiency frontier, in other words, is an "envelope" that covers the data points on the graph. According to DEA, facilities lying below this envelope represent relatively inefficient organizations that could achieve efficiency by reducing inputs (moving to the left until they hit the frontier) or increasing output (moving up until they hit the frontier).

That the frontier passes through the origin indicates that there is zero production with zero level of inputs. The constant slope of this frontier, like the constant ratio implicit in ratio analysis, corresponds to the economist's concept of "constant returns to scale": increasing an input by a single unit will increase output by a constant amount regardless of the level of production. Although constant returns to scale may seem to be a restrictive assumption to make in the context of health care, Sherman provides a great deal of evidence that many kinds of production in the health sector are governed by constant returns to scale over broad ranges of inputs and outputs.[17] Although I shall not develop the point here, it is possible to extend DEA to the case of variable (piecewise linear) returns to scale.[18]

Figure 6-1
The Index of Relative Efficiency: One Input, One Output

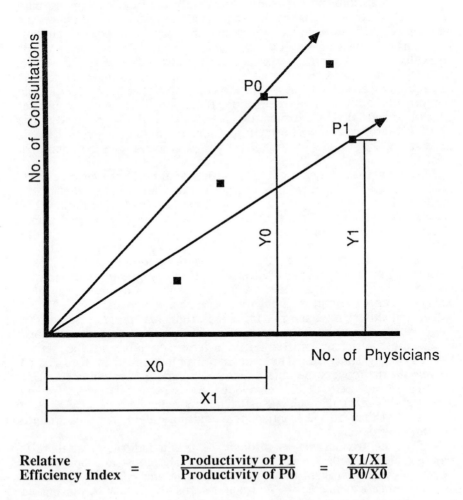

$$\text{Relative Efficiency Index} = \frac{\text{Productivity of P1}}{\text{Productivity of P0}} = \frac{Y1/X1}{P0/X0}$$

Economists frequently display production relationships like this in the form of isoquants like those in figure 6-2 for the two-input single-output example. Each axis corresponds to a factor of production (or input), and input combinations lying on an isoquant are combinations that produce the same level of output. Another way of looking at the isoquant is as a "level contour" (like those found on topological maps). The "piecewise linear" structure of the isoquants in figure 6-2 is caused by the shape of the facets that envelope the outermost points in the three-dimensional space in the same way the ray enveloped the data in figure 6-1.[19]

Figure 6-2

Production Points and Facets of Efficiency along the Isoquant

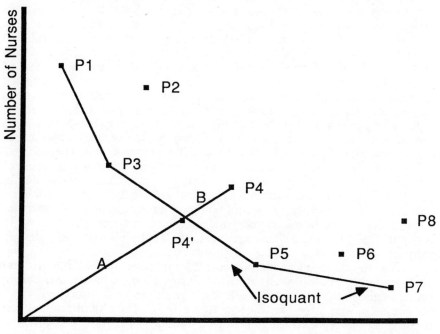

Index of Efficiency for Facility P4 = A / (A+B)

Figure 6-2 helps us highlight what is meant geometrically by the "set of referent facilities." Referent facilities are the efficient facilities lying on the production frontier or isoquant "closest" (in a complex sense) to the point under consideration. Point P4 represents a facility that produces the same level of output as all the other points on the diagram, but by lying within the isoquant it is clear that one could produce the same level of output using the same input mix at point P4'. Hence, P4' is an efficient reference point for P4. Since P3 and P4 define the efficient facet (and efficient point P4') for P4, they serve as efficient models of resource allocation that employ the same technology as P4.

It is from the mathematical programming perspective that one can appreciate how DEA extends the multiple-input, single-output case to the multiple-input, multiple-output case more accurately characteristic of production in sectors like health. Mathematically, "functions" cannot have multiple inputs; consequently, in considering this more general case we drop the term "production function" and substitute for it "production correspondence." Figure 6-3 shows the fundamental mathematical programming formulation for a DEA with one output and three inputs. The objective function represents the ratio of the output to a linear combination of the inputs for the facility whose efficiency is being analyzed (Y values correspond to outputs, Xij values to the amount of input i in facility j, the u and v are unknown values to be estimated through the optimization). By maximizing the output-to-input ratio subject to a series of constraints that force all such ratios (including the ratio to be maximized) to be less than or equal to one, the optimization routine will find values of u and v that guarantee that the optimal efficiency value Z for this facility will lie between zero (because all values are constrained to be nonnegative) and one.Repeating the estimation process for all facilities only changes the specification of the objective function; this series of optimizations yields a set of efficiency indexes for each facility. It would be tempting to interpret the estimated u and v values in terms of marginal products, but this turns out to be conceptually difficult, as DEA extends to the multiple-input, multiple-output case.

The fundamental mathematical programming formulation for the multiple-input, multiple-output case simply extends the numerator by incorporating multiple outputs and their coefficients (subscripted with r for output r, and j for facility j in figure 6-4). Each of the ratios can, in turn, be interpreted as generalized output-to-input ratios; the only difference is that the numerator and denominator are optimal linear combinations of the multiple outputs and multiple inputs, respectively. Optimality here refers to the fact that the estimated u and v values are those values that guarantee that the efficiency value for the facility being analyzed is as large as it can possibly be in light of the performance of all other facilities.

Figure 6-3
Data Envelopment Analysis (DEA): Conceptual Formulation
(Case of One Output, Three Inputs)

$$\text{Maximize } Z = \frac{u Y_0}{v_1 X_{10} + v_2 X_{20} + v_3 X_{30}}$$

subject to

$$\frac{u Y_0}{v_1 X_{10} + v_2 X_{20} + v_3 X_{30}} \leq 1$$

$$\frac{u Y_1}{v_1 X_{11} + v_2 X_{21} + v_3 X_{31}} \leq 1$$

$$\vdots$$

$$\frac{u Y_n}{v_1 X_{1n} + v_2 X_{2n} + v_3 X_{3n}} \leq 1$$

$$u, v_1, v_2, v_3 > 0$$

where:

Y_j = The level of output for facility j
X_{ij} = The level of input i in facility j

Practical Considerations. Our discussion of the mathematical programming formulation of data envelopment analysis would stop here were it not for several important points. First, the nonlinear mathematical programming formulation in figure 6-4 is not easily solved even on large mainframe computers. Second, the solution to this set of mathematical programs (one for each facility) does not provide any of the important pieces of information we promised regarding the sources of inefficiency and relevant referent sets.

Figure 6-4
Data Envelopment Analysis (DEA): The General Formulation
(Multiple Outputs and Inputs)

Maximize $Z = \dfrac{\sum u_r Y_{r0}}{\sum v_i X_{i0}}$

subject to

$$\dfrac{\sum u_r Y_{rj}}{\sum v_i X_{ij}} \leq 1 \qquad\qquad j = 0, ..., n$$

$$u_r, v_i > 0 \qquad\qquad r = 1, ..., s; \quad i = 1, ..., m$$

where:

Y_j = The level of output for facility j
X_{ij} = The level of input i in facility j
n = The number of facilities
s = The number of outputs for each facility
m = The number of inputs for each facility

Computer software for solving nonlinear optimization problems like these is substantially less efficient and more cumbersome than more common linear programming software packages. The problem here is that the DEA formulation in figure 6-4 is inherently nonlinear in terms of the variables being solved for (the u and v values); the objective function and each of the constraints is a (nonlinear) ratio of linear expressions. Fortunately, Charnes and Cooper provide a method for re-expressing the fundamental nonlinear formulation in equivalent linear form.[20] There is an entire family of equivalent linear formulations, one of which appears in figure 6-5. This linearization of the model in figure 6-4 is essentially derived by constraining the denominator in the nonlinear figure 6-4 formulation to sum to one (this condition becomes an additional constraint in the linear formulation of figure 6-5).

Figure 6-5

Data Envelopment Analysis (DEA): A Linear Formulation (Multiple Outputs and Inputs)

Maximize $Z = \sum u_r Y_{r0}$

    subject to

$$\sum v_i X_{ij} = 1$$

$$\sum u_r Y_{rj} - \sum v_i X_{ij} \leq 0 \qquad\qquad j = 0, ..., n$$

$$u_r, v_i > e \qquad\qquad r = 1, ..., s; \quad i = 1, ..., m$$

where:

    Y_j = The level of output for facility j
    X_{ij} = The level of input i in facility j
    n   = The number of facilities
    s   = The number of outputs for each facility
    m   = The number of inputs for each facility
    e   = An arbitrarily small value (such as 0.00001)

It is not difficult to see that this normalization does not change the optimal value of the objective function, although it does change the optimal values of the u and v terms (at the cost of abusing notation across figures, we continue to use the terms "u" and "v" for conceptual clarity). The newly introduced epsilon terms represent "very small values" (in the study below, they are set to 0.00001) and guarantee that the system has a solution.

There is a technical algebraic method by which one can translate this linear formulation into an equivalent "dual formulation." This turns out to have distinct advantages over the original "primal" linear formulation. The formulation in figure 6-6 is a dual equivalent to the formulation in figure 6-5.[21] One important difference is that the optimal value of the objective function in the dual formulation is precisely the inverse of that estimated in the primal formulation. There are two sets of constraints in this dual formulation. The first set represents a constraint for each of the outputs in the model and includes a term for each facility (plus an extra for the facility being analyzed). There will be as many of these constraints as there are outputs specified in the formulation. The second set of constraints consists of equations for each of the inputs in the formulation; again, there will be as many terms as there are facilities being examined (plus one). The S terms in this formulation are "slack variables" and represent the amount by which each constraint falls short of the constant values on the right-hand side. It is through these terms that we will be able to identify which factors of production have slack and which outputs need to be increased in order to bring the facility being analyzed up to the efficiency frontier.

A Perspective on DEA Methodology. Data envelopment analysis provides a method for assessing the relative efficiency of a set of facilities producing multiple services with multiple factors of production. Important things to bear in mind when evaluating a DEA exercise include the following:

1)   As a method for estimating "production correspondences," DEA imposes the assumption that there is a "common technology" generating the instances observed. Anybody familiar with the realities of health service delivery recognizes that, depending on the operational definition of the abstract concept "technology," there are significant differences in the direction and methods used in the health care sector.

2)   Since DEA is a technique for estimating empirical production correspondences, it is designed to focus on technological efficiency and not on efficiency in the sense of minimum cost.

Figure 6-6
Data Envelopment Analysis (DEA): A Dual Formulation
(Multiple Outputs and Inputs)

Maximize $h = Q + e(\sum Splus_r + \sum Sminus_i)$

   subject to

$$Y_{r0} Q - \sum Y_{rj} L_j + Splus_r = 0 \qquad r = 1, ..., s$$

$$\sum X_{ij} L_j + Sminus_i = X_{i0} \qquad i = 1, ..., m$$

$$L_j, Splus_r, Sminus_i > 0 \qquad j = 1, ..., n; \ r = 1, ..., s;$$

where:

Y_j = The level of output for facility j
X_{ij} = The level of input i in facility j
n   = The number of facilities
s   = The number of outputs for each facility
m = The number of inputs for each facility
e   = An arbitrarily small value (such as 0.00001)
Q = An unknown quantity to be solved for (essentially the inverse of the efficiency rating for the facility being analyzed)
L_j = Unknown coefficient being solved for (lambda)
$Splus_r, Sminus_i$ = Slack variables; one for each of the outputs and inputs, respectively

3) In the context of conducting a DEA of health facilities, it is extremely difficult to incorporate the element of "quality of care"; unless explicitly part of the analysis, DEA says nothing about the quality of care (a DEA-efficient facility may be substantially inferior to a DEA-inefficient institution that is delivering high-quality care).

4) Since DEA involves estimating an "envelope" of production relations, it is sensitive to bad data points; if bad data cause a facility to lie spuriously on the efficiency frontier, other (perhaps efficient) facilities will mistakenly be adjudged inefficient.

5) The assumption of returns to scale must be examined carefully; otherwise, very small facilities and very large facilities will be compared together when in fact the underlying "technologies," or modes of translating inputs into outputs,   may   be entirely uncomparable.

6) DEA is a "supply side" approach to the study of efficiency; by itself, it makes no attempt to control for changing patterns of demand that might be affecting the patient load and patient mix. DEA should be supplemented with a careful study of patterns of market area demand.

A DEA of Health Centers in Nicaragua's Region III

Health centers in Nicaragua lend themselves rather neatly to data envelopment analysis. Unlike hospitals, the inputs and outputs across various centers are more or less homogeneous. And unlike health posts, there is enough variety in personnel mix and case load to offer a richer analysis (health posts may have only one MD, and frequently have none). As discussed in the first section, health centers do not vary much in terms of the composition of personnel and in terms of the kinds of patient encounters. These considerations also make it easier for us to make the assumption that health centers are characterized by constant returns to scale production.[22]

This study focuses on the eighteen health centers in Nicaragua's Region III, the administrative area surrounding greater Managua. Basic information on the health centers of Region III appears in table 6-1. Linear programming specifications like the one in figure 6-6 are estimated for each facility. A microcomputer using the LINDO linear regression package was employed for the estimation.[23] The computer output was analyzed to determine which factors of production for each facility had been identified as being underutilized (hence unproductive) and along which outputs each facility could seek improvement in productivity.

Table 6-1
Health Centers in Region III: Input and Output Data

Health Center # / Name	Gen. Prac.	Special- ists	Nurses	Others	# of Consultations		
					<1	1-4	Others
1 Silvia Ferrufino	6	5	8	110	1413	2957	20944
2 Hér. y Márt. Nica.	8	2	5	86	1942	3405	17266
3 Carlos Rugama	7	2	8	60	1328	2563	6631
4 Francisco Buitrago	8	2	7	104	3576	6598	18336
5 Pedro Altamirano	5	4	9	112	1865	3249	14001
6 Altagracia	5	4	5	51	1204	2254	9534
7 Edgar Lang	6	4	7	82	1458	2832	9695
8 Sócrates Flores	7	5	4	98	1084	2499	12939
9 Hér. y Márt. 19 Jul	12	1	10	107	1735	2523	16523
10 Ciudad Sandino	7	3	7	96	593	1148	10925
11 Mateares	3	0	2	40	571	1126	4343
12 Vla. Carlos Fonseca	2	0	1	31	257	611	2386
13 Julio Buitrago	0	0	2	66	687	1389	5807
14 San Rafael del Sur	4	0	4	39	764	1204	7291
15 Crucero	2	0	3	31	465	569	3556
16 Flores Tipitapa	3	0	6	99	1086	1469	11477
17 San Francisco Libre	1	0	2	29	261	387	1559
18 Ticuantepe	1	0	2	77	120	181	877

The central point of this exercise is to demonstrate the utility of DEA as a tool for directing administrators' attention to areas of possible concern or interest in the delivery of health care and not to extend the methodological frontiers of DEA. A conclusive analysis of health center efficiency would require more careful attention to model specification, more thorough data analysis, and more detailed investigation of the special circumstances faced by each center.

Identification of Inputs and Outputs.   There is a fundamental problem in identifying and evaluating the inputs and outputs of health care. Inputs might include the hours spent by various classes of health care specialists (by experience and area of expertise), some measure of the stock of drugs and medicines used, and some indication of additional equipment used in delivering health services. In principle, each of these can be measured. But useful as they may be in explaining the technology of health service delivery, complete and correct data in most settings are impossible to obtain.

Identifying and measuring outputs is a substantially more difficult conceptual and practical problem for the researcher than identifying and measuring inputs. Ideally, the ultimate output of health care services isimproved health, something that can appear in the form of curing an illness, healing an injury, the prevention of disease, health education, and so on. Defining and measuring improved health along these dimensions is, of course, almost impossible. It also goes against the grain of what we have argued is one of the virtues of DEA, namely, the ability for central administrators to utilize the kind of data they typically keep on hand to create summary measures of relative efficiency.

Although MINSA headquarters in Managua maintains detailed records on the number of consultations in all one hundred health centers in the country, it does not have records on the numbers or kinds of personnel working in these centers (gross annual figures for health care centers in the aggregate are, of course, available). Although a surprising state of affairs from an outsider's perspective, the situation is explained by the fact that personnel are paid and managed by separate bureaucracies. Only by visiting each of MINSA's regional headquarters could a researcher expect to collect data matching personnel with facility, and even then the form in which the data are acquired and recorded differs across regions. Finally, there are a number of conceptual and practical problems associated with measuring the stock of drugs and equipment available to personnel working at the various health centers.

As a consequence of all of these data availability considerations, the basic production correspondence settled on for this study consisted of four inputs and three outputs. The inputs analyzed here consisted of: the number of generalist physicians in each health center, the number of specialized physicians, the number of nurses (including auxiliaries), and the number of "other personnel" (mostly administrative staff and social workers). The outputs of the health centers that were analyzed consisted of the number of consultations by age of patient: those less than one year old, those from one to four years old, and all other patients.

Neither the outputs nor the inputs here capture any notion of the quality or experience of health care personnel or the quality of attention received by patients. The set of outputs is clearly the weaker of the two segments of the database.

A database that is one step more refined would break outputs down into specific classes of medical intervention (for example, gynecology, obstetrics, trauma). As it stands, the analysis conducted here is insensitive to the different patterns of case mix that might exist across health care centers. Again, records at this level of detail for health centers were not available.

In terms of the input measures, it is important to point out that it is not possible to estimate more than the number of various classes of personnel employed any month, even though some of these may only be part-time employees. A better measure of personnel effort would be person-hours (for example, so many physician-hours per month, nurse--hours per month). Civil service pay scales are such that salaries by type of personnel could serve as a proxy for person-hours of a certain class of skilled personnel. Although this would allow us to control in some way for experience, using price-based data in nonmarket settings like this would violate the spirit of DEA. Moreover, all of these kinds of data would have to be gathered from sources outside MINSA (something that time did not permit us to do).

We collected input data on staff size for the month of December 1985 and output data for the entire final quarter (October through December) of 1985, since monthly data on consultations are not readily available. The analysis, therefore, implicitly assumes that patterns of staffing for the entire final quarter were the same as they were in the final month of that quarter. A more detailed study would analyze the homogeneity of staffing for all months and would compare an annual data envelopment analysis with a quarterly analysis.

Summary of Results. Eighteen linear programs were entered and run on a portable Compaq II microcomputer using the LINDO linear programming package. Table 6-2 represents a typical LINDO input file for a DEA run, in this case the one corresponding to Health Center #7 (Centro de Salud Edgar Lang). (The specification is that of figure 6-6; the X and Y values can be compared with the information in table 6-1.) Table 6-3 displays the LINDO output for this same run. The optimal objective function value ($Z = 1.53609100$) is the inverse of the relative efficiency index ($1/1.53609100 = 65$ percent efficient). The optimal values for the variables S1P through S4M represent the slacks associated with the various inputs and outputs.

Table 6-2
"LINDO" Command File for Executing the Analysis of the
"Edgar Lang" Health Center

!   **Objective Function**
MAX Z0 + 0.00001 S1P + 0.00001 S2P + 0.00001 S3P
   + 0.00001 S1M + 0.00001 S2M + 0.00001 S3M
   + 0.00001 S4M ST

!   **Output Contraint: "Consultations < 1 year olds"**
-1.413 L1 -1.942 L2 -1.328 L3 -3.576 L4 -1.865 L5 -1.204 L6
   -1.458 L7-1.084 L8 -1.735 L9 -0.593 L10 -0.571 L11 -0.257 L12
   -0.687 L13 -0.764 L14 -0.465 L15 -1.086 L16 -0.261 L17 -0.120
L18
   +1.458 Z0 + S1P = 0

!   **Output Constraint: "Consultations 1-4 year olds"**
-2.957 L1 -3.405 L2 -2.563 L3 -6.598 L4 -3.249 L5 -2.254 L6
   -2.832 L7 -2.499 L8 -2.523 L9 -1.148 L10 -1.126 L11 -0.611 L12
   -1.289 L13 -1.204 L14 -0.569 L15 -1.469 L16 -0.387 L17 -0.181 L18
   +2.832 Z0 + S2P = 0

!   **Output Constraints: "Other Consultations"**
-20.944 L1 -17.266 L2 -6.631 L3 -18.336 L4 -14.001 L5 -9.534 L6
   -9.695 L7 -12.939 L8 -16.523 L9 -10.925 L10 -4.343 L11 -2.386 L12
   -5.807 L13 -7.291 L14 -3.556 L15 -11.477 L16 -1.559 L17 -0.877 L18
   +9.695 Z0 + S3P = 0

!   **Input Constraint: "General Practitioners"**
6 L1 +8 L2 +7 L3 +8 L4 +5 L5 +5 L6 +6 L7 +7 L8 +12 L9 +7 L10 +
   3 L11 +2 L12 +0 L13 +4 L14 +2 L15 +3 L16 +1 L17 +1 L18 + S1M = 6

!   **Input Constraint: "Specialists"**
5 L1 +2 L2 +2 L3 +2 L4 +4 L5 +4 L6 +4 L7 +5 L8 +1 L9 +3 L10 +
   S2M = 4

!   **Input Constraint: "Nurses"**
8 L1 +5 L2 +8 L3 +7 L4 +9 L5 +5 L6 +7 L7 +4 L8 +10 L9 +7 L10 +
   2 L11 +1 L12 +2 L13 +4 L14 +3 L15 +6 L16 +2 L17 +2 L18 +S3M = 7

!   **Input Constraint: "Other Personnel"**
110 L1 +86 L2 +60 L3 +104 L4 +112 L5 +51 L6 +82 L7 +98 L8
   +107 L9 +96 L10 +40 L11 +31 L12 +66 L13 +39 L14 +31 L15 +99 L16
   +29 L17 +77 L18 + S4M = 82
END

Table 6-3
LINDO Printout for the Analysis of "Edgar Lang" Health Center
(with commentary)

LP Optimum Found at Step   13

Objective Function Value
1) 1.53609100   <=== optimal value of the objective function; the inverse of the efficiency index

Variable	Value	Reduced Cost	
Z0	1.536057	.000000	
S1P	.093588	.000000	
S2P	.000000	.059204	
S3P	.000000	.085838	optimal values
S1M	.000000	.042694	of the slack
S2M	1.902995	.000000	variables and their
S3M	1.442961	.000000	associated "shadow
S4M	.000000	.015597	pieces"
L1	.170573	.000000	
L2	.081018	.000000	
L3	.000000	.514403	
L4	.541052	.000000	
L5	.000000	.567255	
L6	.000000	.057606	values
L7	.000000	.536091	indicating
L8	.000000	.569716	the peer
L9	.000000	.614612	centers (those
L10	.000000	.791412	with non-zero
L11	.000000	.312887	values for L
L12	.000000	.328214	
L13	.000000	.455218	
L14	.000000	.082305	
L15	.000000	.230277	
L16	.000000	.600975	
L17	.000000	.338566	
L18	.000000	1.158439	

Row	Slack or Surplus	Dual Prices
2)	.000000	.000010
3)	.000000	.059214
4)	.000000	.085848
5)	.000000	.042704
6)	.000000	.000010
7)	.000000	.000010
8)	.000000	.015607

Total execution time: 3 seconds

Each constraint in table 6-2 contains a slack variable; that the value for the slack variable S1P in table 6-3 is 0.093588 says that there is some slack in the constraint associated with "number of consultations < 1 year old." This indicates that the Centro de Salud Edgar Lang is "under-producing" infant care. The value for slack variable S2M (1.902995) indicates that there is also slack in the fifth constraint, medical specialists.

Having slack in one of the factors of production for this health center is quite significant managerially. It tells managers that Centro de Salud Edgar Lang could move to the efficiency frontier if two (1.902995) medical specialists were transferred to another health center, specifically to one with no slack in medical specialists. Having no slack in a factor of production not only means that this factor is pushing the health center toward the efficiency frontier, it also indicates that this factor is pushed to its limits and could probably use additional personnel. Having slack in a facility should be interpreted as offering MINSA the opportunity to reallocate resources in a way that will improve overall productivity.

The DEA results for the Centro de Salud Edgar Lang are summarized in table 6-4 in terms that are more meaningful to managers. The reference facet (or reference set) for Edgar Lang consists of health centers 1, 2, and 4. This information is obtained from the optimal values associated with the "L" coefficients in the LINDO output of table 6-3. Notice that all "L" values are equal to zero except for L1, L2, and L4, the coefficients associated with health centers 1, 2, and 4.[24]

Table 6-4
Data Envelopment Analysis for the "Edgar Lang" Health Center

Relative Eficiency Index: 65%

Efficient Peer Group: Health Centers nos., 1, 2, 4

	Observed Value	Value if Efficient	Level of Slack
OUTPUTS:			
Consultations, age <1	1458	1552	94
Consultations, age 1-4	2832	2832	0
Other Consultations	9695	9695	0
INPUTS:			
General Practioners	6	6	0
Specialists	4	2	2
Nurses	7	6	1
Other Personnel	82	82	0

Results are summarized for all of Region III's health centers in table 6-5. The table shows the efficient referent sets and the relative efficiency index for each health center. Of the six efficient referent centers, the first three (Silvia Ferrufino, Héroes y Mártires de Nicaragua, and Francisco Buitrago) are also among the largest (see table 6-1). The fact that they serve as referents for the first ten health centers may be due to economic efficiencies of scale that they enjoy. To the extent that there may in fact be scale economies here casts a shadow on our assumption of constant returns to scale and calls for a reassessment of assumptions (and respecification of the linear programs) to accommodate this possibility. However, notice that the first ten centers for which these three centers serve as referents are also (with the possible exception of Carlos Rugama and the exception of the efficient San Rafael del Sur) among the largest health centers in the region. In other words, the largest centers are serving as referents for the larger centers; had they also served as referents for tiny centers, the possibility of scale mismatch would be more credible.

The last eight health centers, most of which are located in small municipios and pueblos outside of Managua, tend to cluster around centers 4, 13, and 14 as referents. Centers 13 and 14 (Julio Buitrago and San Rafael del Sur) with seventy-two and forty-seven personnel, respectively, are medium-to-small institutions. Centro de Salud Sócrates Flores Tipitapa, with its large staff of "other personnel" (ninety-nine of them) almost achieves 100 percent efficiency (relative efficiency = 99 percent) and may effectively be considered an efficient center itself.

Most striking, perhaps, is the observation that rural health centers located in pueblos like Ticuantepe and Ciudad Sandino tend to fare rather poorly in terms of their relative efficiency (although Centro de Salud Crucero, also in a pueblo, does rather well at 93 percent efficiency). It is likely that this poor performance is driven by the different patterns of demand and different real costs of seeking medical attention found in these relatively rural parts of Region III. A more thorough study would have to be made to refine the DEA and separate out these other effects.

Notice that DEA has created a rough clustering of health centers rather naturally in terms of their degree of urbanness and scale. The generally larger urban centers are judged against the performance of centers 1, 2, and 4; the generally smaller centers in the other municipios and in the pueblos are compared to efficient centers of their own kind. In simple ratio analysis, each facility's productivity would be compared against the most productive; unless this is done with some foresight, the comparison would be made without regard to possible differences in the technology of health care delivery in rural versus urban or large versus small settings.

Table 6-5
Data Envelopment Analysis
Summary of Preliminary Findings for Region III

Health Center # / Name	OPTIMAL INDEX (%)	REFERENT SET					
		1	2	4	11	13	14
1 Silvia Ferrufino	100	X	X	X			
2 Hér. y Márt. Nica.	100	X		X		X	
3 Carlos Rugama	87			X			
4 Francisco Buitrago	100		X	X			
5 Pedro Altamirano	83			X			
6 Altagracia	96		X	X			
7 Edgar Lang	65	X	X	X			
8 Sócrates Flores	94		X				
9 Hér. y Márt. 19 Jul	80		X				X
10 Ciudad Sandino	59	X	X			X	X
11 Mateares	100			X	X		
12 Vla. Carlos Fonseca	79				X	X	
13 Julio Buitrago	100	X	X	X		X	X
14 San Rafael del Sur	100	X	X	X		X	X
15 Crucero	93			X		X	X
16 Flores Tipitapa	99	X				X	X
17 San Francisco Libre	67			X		X	X
18 Ticuantepe	17			X		X	

Table 6-6
Summary of Slack Values:
New Proposed Goals (Ooutput Slacks S1P-S3P)
and Opportunites for Reallocative Resources (Input Slacks S1M-S4M)

Health Center # / Name	CONSULTATIONS			PERSONNEL			
	<1 (S1P)	1-4 (S2P)	Others (S3P)	Gens (S1M)	Spec. (S2M)	Nurses (S3M)	Others (S4M)
1 Silvia Ferrufino							
2 Hér. y Márt. Nica.							
3 Carlos Rugama	91		73	2.4	0.8	4.0	
4 Francisco Buitrago							
5 Pedro Altamirano		35			1.7	2.7	
6 Altagracia	60			0.5	2.9	1.9	
7 Edgar Lang	94				1.9	1.4	
8 Sócrates Flores	396	56			3.4		29.2
9 Hér. y Márt.19 Jul.	62	53		1.4		0.9	
10 Ciudad Sandino	606	1053					
11 Mateares							
12 Vla. Carlos Fonseca	69		323	1.8			
13 Julio Buitrago							
14 San Rafael del Sur							
15 Crucero		212	821			0.7	
16 Flores Tipitapa	201	780				0.9	
17 San Fran.		96	118			0.4	
18 Ticuantepe		253	786	1.0			11.0

Table 6-6 summarizes the level of slack personnel in inefficient facilities available for transfer to other facilities. The numbers are only suggestive, since it is impossible to transfer "1.4" nurses; you either transfer one or you transfer two. (Data expressed in terms of nursing hours, of course, would not suffer as much from this "lumpiness" of integer data.) The table also indicates which outputs are short of their efficient equivalents. This information can be used to set operational goals for inefficient facilities.

Discussion and Directions for Future Research

All of these results are intended merely to illustrate the potential value of data envelopment analysis for managers of health facilities; they are not by any stretch of the imagination intended to be the last word in health center efficiency in Region III. Data problems, the inability to specify more refined models, the inclusion of facilities with zero factor utilization, the short time horizon of the data, and the fact that the research team had no time to visit any of the health centers involved to enrich the analysis make it impossible to interpret these DEA results as anything more than an illustrative exercise. In addition to correcting some of these shortcomings, future research in this area should devote substantial time to careful data analysis and to the study of patterns of demand. Although difficult to conduct in a thorough manner in the kind of setting found in present-day Nicaragua, a demand study is essential in order to be able to separate out the effects of different patterns of demand on the ability of health centers to deliver health care services efficiently. The current study implicitly assumes that fluctuations in demand across seasons of the year and over years are more or less constant and that latent demand is not articulated by the presence or absence of efficiency in health centers.

Perhaps more significant than this is that the study here in no way controls for the presence of the popular health councils in providing health education and delivering certain types of health care services. Ignoring the unique institutional structure Nicaragua has established in health care can only distort the results presented here. Again, a more refined study would have to examine the impact these factors have on the efficiency of health centers. It may be that some indicator of the "production of health education" has to be incorporated into the analyses.

On a more technical plane, it should be pointed out that there are several instances of alternate optima in the solutions summarized in this section of the chapter. Although we ignored them for this presentation, a serious analysis of health center efficiency would conduct a battery of sensitivity analyses to determine how firm or sensitive these results are to small perturbations in the information. The uncertainty surrounding the quality of the data and the obvious problems with model specification surely present ample opportunity for the optima estimated to be quite wrong.

On a political plane, managers should understand that just because DEA analysis is a fairly sophisticated computer-based technique does not mean that the results are "true" or "false." Again, DEA is intended to be used as an attention-directing device, not a substitute for intelligent decision making. The bureaucratic politics of decision making in organizations makes accusing the administration of a health center of "being inefficient" an extremely sensitive matter, and one that should be handled delicately and professionally in light of the limitations of these techniques.

This kind of analysis could be extended in an important way by studying the differences in relative efficiency between rural and urban health centers, and among regional centers across the entire country. A study of rural/urban differences could help administrators better understand the possible structural differences that exist between rural and urban health care at this level of medical attention. The study could then serve as a baseline for an analysis of differences in the effectiveness of health centers in war zones compared to similar centers in nonwar zones. To the extent that other intervening factors could be controlled for, this analysis could result in a comparatively firm estimate of the real efficiency costs in health services borne by MINSA and the Nicaraguan population as a whole in the face of the contra war.

Endnotes for Chapter 6.

1. The study of urban health facilities was funded in part by the Mike Hogg Foundation. I am particularly grateful to the Nicaraguan Ministry of Health (MINSA) for generously supplying me with a place to work, for opening its archives to me, and for freeing up time for one of its most capable research staff members, Janine Hooker, to work with me on the empirical part of this project.

2. See Thomas Bossert, "Health Care in Revolutionary Nicaragua," in Thomas W. Walker, ed., Nicaragua in Revolution (New York: Praeger, 1982); John M. Donahue, "The Politics of Health Care in Nicaragua before and after the Revolution of 1979," Human Organization 42, no. 3 (Fall 1983): 264-272; idem, "Studying the Transition to Socialism in the Nicaraguan Health System," Medical Anthropology Quarterly 15, no. 3 (1984): 70-71; idem, The Nicaraguan Revolution in Health (South Hadley, MA: Bergin and Garvey, 1986); Joseph L. Ripp, "Revolution in Health Care in Nicaragua," Medical Anthropology Quarterly 15, no. 3 (1984): 68-74; Richard Garfield, "Nicaragua's Health," New York Times (February 2,1984); Harvey Williams, "An Uncertain Prognosis: Some Factors May Limit Progress in the Nicaraguan Health Care System," Medical Anthropology Quarterly 15, no. 3 (1984): 72-73; and Paula A. Braverman and Milton I. Roemer,

"Health Personnel Training in the Nicaraguan Health Sector," International Journal of Health Services 15, no. 4 (1985).

3. Donahue, The Nicaraguan Revolution in Health.
4. Ibid., p. 13.
5. Oscar Orellana, "Nicaragua: estudio del sector salud" (Managua: Organización Panamericana de Salud, 1985); and my own calculations.
6. John L. Fiedler, An Economic Analysis of Segments of the Public Health Sector of El Salvador (Silver Spring, MD: Birch and Davis Associates, 1986), p. III-8.
7. Personal communications; see also ibid.
8. Fiedler, An Economic Analysis.
9. Donahue, The Nicaraguan Revolution in Health.
10. Ministerio de Salud (MINSA), Principios y políticas del gobierno de Nicaragua, el sistema nacional único de salud: tres años de revolución 1979-1982 (Managua: MINSA, 1982).
11. Significant work in the formal application of mathematical programming to facility problems can be found in Richard L. Church and David J. Eaton, "Hierchical Location Analysis Utilizing Covering Objectives," in A. Ghosh and G. Rushton, eds., Spatial Analysis and Location-Analysis Models (New York: Van Nostrand Reinhold, 1986); and David J. Eaton et al., "Determining Ambulance Deployment in Santo Domingo, Dominican Republic," Journal of the Operational Research Society 37, no. 2 (February 1986): 113-126.
12. Aaron Wildavsky, Budgeting: A Comparative Theory of Budgetary Processes (New York: Little Brown, 1975).
13. Fiedler, An Economic Analysis, p. iii.
14. Standard and Poors, "Health Care Financing," in Standard and Poor's Municipal Credit Overview (New York: Standard and Poors, 1984).
15. Edward L. Rhodes, "Data Envelopment Analysis and Related Approaches for Measuring the Efficiency of Decision Making Units with an Application to Program Follow Through in U.S. Education," PhD diss., School of Urban and Public Affairs, Carnegie-Mellon University, 1978; A. Charnes, W. W. Cooper, and E. Rhodes, "Short Communication: Measuring the Efficiency of Decision Making Units," European Journal of Operational Research, no. 339 (1979); R. D. Banker, A. Charnes, and W. W. Cooper, "Some Models for Estimating Technical and Scale Inefficiencies in Data Envelopment Analysis," Management Science 30, no. 9 (September 1984): 1078-1092; and Rajiv D. Banker, "Studies in Cost Allocation and Efficiency Evaluation," Phd diss., Graduate School of Business Administration, Harvard University, 1984.
16. The earliest work on DEA, Rhodes, "Data Envelopment Analysis" (1978), was concerned with assessing the effectiveness of a primary school enrichment program. For examples of how DEA has been applied in examining the comparative efficiency of various public schools, see Authella M. Bessent and E. Wailand Bessent, "Determining the Comparative Efficiency of Schools through Data Envelopment

Analysis," Educational Administration Quarterly 16, no. 2 (Spring 1980): 57-75; A. Bessent et al., "An Application of Mathematical Programming to Assess Productivity in the Houston Independent School District," Management Science 28, no. 12 (December 1982): 1355-1367; and A. Bessent, W. Bessent, and A. Charles, "Evaluation of Educational Program Proposals by Means of DEA," Educational Administration Quarterly 19, no. 2 (Spring 1983): 82-107. In the health field, Sherman applies DEA to the study of medical-surgical units in a set of hospitals in the northeast United States (see H. David Sherman, "Measurement of Hospital Technical Efficiency: A Comparative Evaluation of Data Envelopment Analysis and Other Efficiency Measurement Techniques for Measuring and Locating Inefficiency in Health Care Organizations," PhD diss., Graduate School of Business Administration, Harvard University, 1981). Charnes et al., evaluate the performance of two dozen U.S. army health care facilities (see A. Charnes et al., "Efficiency Analysis of Uses of Medical Care Resources in the U.S. Army Health Services Command," Research Report CCS 526, Center for Cybernetic Studies, University of Texas at Austin, 1985). Banker, Conrad, and Strauss compare DEA with an econometric analysis of hospitals in North Carolina (see R. D. Banker, R. F. Conrad, and R. P. Strauss, "A Comparative Application of Data Envelopment Analysis and Translog Methods: An Illustrative Study of Hospital Production," Management Science 32, no. 1 [January 1986]: 30-44). Other applications include analyses of U.S. Air Force combat units (see C. T. Clark, "Evaluating the Efficiency of Air Force Combat Units," Graduate School of Business Technical Report EPC002, University of Texas at Austin, 1982); and public utilities in Texas (see Dennis Thomas, PhD diss., Graduate School of Business Administration, University of Texas at Austin, 1985).

17. Sherman, "Measurement of Hospital Technical Efficiency."
18. Charnes, Cooper, and Rhodes, "Short Communicaton."
19. Isoquants are theoretically constrained to be negatively sloped and convex to the origin; a positive slope somewhere along the isoquant would imply that the same level of production could be achieved by reducing the level of all inputs. Since this would be inefficient, it contradicts the definition of an isoquant as the locus of efficient points. (The question of convexity is more complex and beyond the scope of this chapter.)
20. A. Charnes and W. W. Cooper, "Programming with Linear Fractional Functionals," Naval Research Quarterly 9, nos. 3 and 4 (1962): 181-186; idem, "An Explicit General Solution in Linear Fractional Programming," Naval Research Quarterly 20, no. 3 (1973): 449-467.
21. A. Charnes, W. W. Cooper, and E. Rhodes, "Measuring the Efficiency of Decision Making Units," European Journal of Operational Research 2 (1978): 429-444.

22. See Sherman, "Measurement of Hospital Technical Efficiency," for further evidence that constant returns to scale is a reasonable assumption for broad ranges of inputs and outputs in health care.

23. Linus Schrage, <u>Linear, Integer, and Quadratic Programming with LINDO</u> (Palo Alto, CA: The Scientific Press, 1984).

24. To appreciate the reason for this requires an understanding of the dual procedures to this formulation, something that is beyond the scope of this study.

Chapter 7

Labor Organization and Participation in the Mixed Economy: The Case of Sugar Production

by

Scott Whiteford
and
Terry Hoops

With the assistance of
Alfonso DuBois
and
Martha Juárez

Introduction[1]

The triumph of the Nicaraguan Revolution was followed by a profound reorganization of social relations of production and political power. Mass organizations, which had been instrumental in the Revolution, were linked in new ways to the political and economic process. Debates about the emerging structures were heated because they dealt with the reordering of national society. Fundamental decisions about the allocation and distribution of power were made by national leaders committed to the idea of popular participation.

The economic strategy developed by the new government was based on a mixed economy and a national social structure that would include both capitalist and "popular" business and marketing structures. The commitment to a mixed economy raised critical theoretical and practical questions about the nature of the state and who controls it. The temporal dimension was equally problematical because it was unclear whether the new state system would be transitional or a structurally permanent arrangement.

Central to this debate was the role of the mixed economy in postrevolutionary Nicaragua. The shift in power created by the Revolution and the transformation of the relations of production presented obstacles to the private sector. At the same time, the decision to keep that sector viable raised potential internal contradictions to the emerging political and economic system and had implications for genuine participation by workers.

In this chapter, we explore some of the issues in labor organization and the participatory process by examining the new organizational forms and what they mean to workers. We chose to examine private and public enterprises within the sugar industry because it includes both an agricultural and an industrial component. The comparison allowed us to explore critical aspects of the logic, the contradictions, and the social implications of the mixed economy and how it influenced the nature of popular participation. We attempt to document the complexity of the transformational process and to delineate key variables that influence the process.

The mass organizations have been regarded as the foundation blocks of the postrevolutionary governing process. The key organizations are the neighborhood-based Sandinista Defense Committees (CDS), the Farm Workers Association (ATC), the Sandinista Labor Federation (CST), and the National Association of Women (AMNLAE). These organizations were automatically granted seventeen of the forty-seven seats in the original Council of State. In addition, the organizations were given positions in the newly created departmental-level and national-level Programmatic Coordinating Committees.

In theory, mass organizations in the revolutionary society were to fulfill various functions: to raise group consciousness and organize participation in the solution of collective problems, to defend the Revolution, to articulate their members' needs and demands to the government, to provide a forum for discussion, to support the process of economic reactivation, to improve the standard of living of the members, and to contribute to the elimination of unjust social, economic, and ideological structures.[2]   Further, they were expected to participate in the political process by being able to communicate grass-roots concerns and criticisms to the top levels of government and the FSLN. Proposals and policy issues from the top were to be taken to the local level for discussion and evaluation that would, in turn, have an impact on implementation.

It was expected that the mass organizations would communicate effectively among themselves to reduce conflict and duplication. Mass organizations were also charged with educating both urban and rural people in the process of democratic participation.[3]   They were to participate in the political process by democratic means, although execution of policy was to be centralized. Leaders of the organizations were to be elected, and leadership was to be collective. Evaluation and self-criticism were fundamental dimensions of the process.[4]

The implementation of these structures and policies has been difficult for many reasons. The process was new, people lacked experience in participatory democracy, and many lacked a sense of efficiency. Despite the problems, the participation of the mass organizations in the political process made a major impact during the initial years of the Revolution and continued to be a cornerstone of the new government in 1986.

In this chapter we focus on one organization, the Sandinista Workers' Federation (CST), working in one situation, the sugar industry. As of 1986, the union was the largest in the country and had played a major role in political and economic restructuring. It was affiliated with the FSLN and was an active component of the revolutionary process.[5]

Before the Revolution, less than 6 percent of labor was unionized. The CST and the ATC were major forces in mobilizing labor. The ATC mobilized the rural workers while the CST organized the unions in the city.[6] By 1984, according to Stahler-Sholk, the CST and the ATC together represented around 75 per cent of organized labor, with the CST claiming 100,000 members.[7] The ATC's original focus was the coffee and cotton farms. Workers on the sugar farms and sugar mills (ingenios) were incorporated into the CST after negotiations with the ATC. They decided that sugar production posed unique problems because of the importance of the factory work force in the production process. It was critical that the union forge an alliance between industrial workers and field workers. As a result, the two unions decided to have the CST organize the sugar sector.

The dominant position of the CST unions on the sugar plantations did not go unchallenged. In 1980 there were major clashes between worker groups on several ingenios (as the combined farms and mills are generally known throughout Latin America). The Frente Obrera (FO), a labor organization associated with the Socialist Party, led strikes for higher wages while the CST pushed for a program of improved working and living conditions ("social wages"). The clashes between the two unions in the form of violent strikes led by the Frente Obrera took place on both private and state ingenios. Generally, the CST was supportive of the government and endorsed the government's programs for social wages, salary austerity, and higher productivity. The Sandinista government strongly supported the CST position.

The conflict highlights some of the problems in defining participation. In revolutionary Nicaragua, one position contended that structures must be established to facilitate participation and that these may be established by the state and by national organizations. The state should involve workers in the production and administration processes. According to this view, participation should be both political and economic. In addition, the state must create the conditions for participation not only in the structuring of state enterprises, but also in the raising of the workers' consciousness. The revolutionary state and the unions have parallel and overlapping goals. The tensions and contradictions that arise between them are circumstantial and conditional.[8]

A contrasting view argued that a true participatory movement would have to come from the workers themselves. The workers must take the initiative, according to this view, since the level at which initiation takes place signifies the distinction between a single change in administrative structures and a transformation of the relations of production and the full maturation of the "reivindicación" of the working class. From this perspective, there is an inherent conflict between the state and institutionalized revolution and workers' participatory movements. To those who held this view, the Nicaraguan state during the initial years was in a transitional stage, one which would eventually allow full worker control.[9]

Sugar has traditionally been a critical commodity in Nicaragua because it generates foreign revenue and provides an important source of calories in the diet. Thus, sugar is directly influenced by fluctuations in the world market and international political agreements as well as by shifts in internal consumption patterns. These factors affect government development strategies and programs, which, in turn, influence the allocation of scarce resources such as agricultural credit, loans for mill or field equipment, and, ultimately, labor. At the local level, these factors have an impact on the organization of production, employment patterns, and the structure of participation.

The process is not unidirectional, however, because worker or producer mobilization at the local level can be politically significant and can force the government to adopt programs for political rather than strictly economic reasons. Equally important, powerful local-level interests can also influence patterns of credit or resource allocation.

One of the objectives of our study was to define how these processes operate in Nicaragua, some seven years after the insurrection, and to describe the role of labor in their operation. In other parts of Latin America, the power of labor has usually been minimal. Argentine sugar workers have relatively little power, even over their own work conditions, despite being unionized.[10] In Mexico the seasonal workers are seldom members of unions, but the small cane growers are organized into the Confederación Nacional de Campesinos (CNC), which is directly affiliated with the ruling Partido Revolucionario Institucional (PRI). Yet for years the Mexican government forced peasants who lived near the sugar mills to grow cane and to sell it at very low prices. Often the mills were privately owned, but sugar prices were kept low for domestic consumption. This, in turn, helped the expansion of transnational corporations such as Coca Cola, Gerber, Kellogg, and the makers of Wonderbread, which, in turn, increased their consumption of sugar, incorporating it into processed food. The low prices for sugar in Mexico forced decapitalization of the sugar mills and ultimately led to the importation of sugar during the early 1980s. Neither field nor factory labor had much impact on management or government policy.

Sugar and Development in Nicaragua

Both coffee and cotton have played key roles in the development and expansion of capitalism in Nicaragua, but sugar has also played an important role since the colonial period. Sugar production has been characterized by the concentration of power and administrative control within the industrial sector.[11] Inherent in the configuration is an industrial complex that requires both large investments of capital and a skilled labor force. As a result, production has been hierarchically organized; and labor, including factory and field workers, seasonal cane cutters, truckers, and cane growers, has been segmented. Thus labor was often difficult to organize; and unions on sugar plantations were often weak.

At the time of the Revolution in 1979, sugar was Nicaragua's third most important export. Until the major shift in the world sugar market in 1983, the Nicaraguan government "considered sugar the most efficient generator of foreign exchange" and made the efficient development of ingenios a priority.[12] Sugar production for domestic consumption was deemed equally important because more than half of the total national production was consumed within the country.[13] In fact the percentage of the national production consumed domestically was higher in Nicaragua than in most of the sugar-producing countries of Latin America.

During the 1950s, there were more than twenty ingenios in Nicaragua, most of which were relatively small. The Somoza family and the Pellas-Lacayo group dominated sugar production in prerevolutionary Nicaragua, with the Pellas-Lacayo group controlling about 70 percent of the national production. The Ingenio San Antonio, owned by the Pellas-Lacayo group dominated production and exports. Ingenio San Antonio maintained a distinct advantage in several competitive areas: it had the only factory in the country that could produce refined sugar; it also produced the best-quality rum, a rum that could be sold abroad as well as marketed internally. The group increased its holdings by buying two ingenios, which are today Ingenio Germán Pomares and Ingenio Javier Guerra.

Somoza, in an effort to gain political and economic leverage in sugar production, purchased what was then called Ingenio Montelimar (now Ingenio Julio Buitrago). With the expansion of the American sugar market in the 1960s, when the United States stopped buying Cuban sugar, Somoza purchased Ingenio Dolores (today Benjamín Zeledón) and Ingenio Santa Rita (now Camilo Ortega). The latter was broken up and its machinery sent to Cubra Hill to create a new ingenio. The sugarcane formerly processed at Santa Rita was sent to Montelimar.

This domination allowed the Pellas-Lacayo group to maintain control of sugar production in an uneasy alliance with Somoza. Nevertheless, the two competed vigorously for the internal market.

The Nicaraguan sugar industry was profoundly affected by the Revolution. The three ingenios owned by Somoza were nationalized and converted into integrated into the public sector (área de propiedad del pueblo, or APP). The state also took possession of two other ingenios that had accumulated unmanageable debts and had gone bankrupt: Ingenio Monte Rosa, which was renamed Germán Pomares, and Ingenio Amalia, renamed Javier Guerra.

The sugar industry became, after 1979. a classic example of the mixed economy, with private and public enterprises competing for the market. Just prior to the Revolution, Ingenio San Antonio (of the Pellas-Lacayo group) processed 46.5 percent of the cane in the country. By the 1981-82 harvest, this percentage had risen to 52.6 percent. It was not until 1985-86 that all of the state <u>ingenios</u> together processed more cane than Ingenio San Antonio by itself. And throughout this period, independent (private) cane growers grew cane and sold it to both private and state mills.[14]

The new government established agencies to facilitate the production, processing, and distribution of sugarcane. ENAZUCAR was created as an autonomous company of Ministry of Internal Commerce (MICE) to handle the export sale of sugar. The government also established a local entity, CANCA, to manage the sale of sugar internally. The state played the key role in establishing internal prices. In the past, they had been pegged to the world market, but after the Revolution, they were established below world market prices.[15]

Sugar exports have been uneven since the Revolution. In 1981 the price on the world market began to fall and continued to do so through the end of 1986. The shift in price was a result of the expanding use of artificial sweeteners, the production of corn sugar, and the increased production of many developing countries. The market for Nicaraguan sugar has also varied. Sugar from the 1983-84 harvest was exported only to the United States and Algeria. In 1984-85 Nicaragua sold sugar to these two nations and to West Germany, Sri Lanka, and Pakistan. None of these countries bought sugar from Nicaragua in 1985-86. Instead, Cuba (which sold its sugar to the Soviet Union for a profit), France, England, Holland, and the Soviet Union purchased Nicaraguan sugar. Total exports of sugar fell from a high of 2,743,990 tons in 1982-83 to 1,634,799 tons in 1985-86. Equally important, sugar prices in 1985-86 were only a third of what they had been in 1980-81. As a result, sugar fell from being the export crop that generated the most foreign exchange for its investment to one in which the government was subsidizing exports.

The changes in the international market left the Nicaraguan government in a difficult situation. There was a need for foreign currency, and the export of sugar could generate such earnings. On the other hand, much of the equipment for processing sugar must be imported, and this required foreign exchange. If the sugar mills become too antiquated, the price of Nicaraguan sugar will become even less competitive. To withdraw support from sugar production in 1986 would have created serious economic problems in regions where sugar was raised and processed. It would also have made the country more dependent on external sources of calories.

At the same time that the government was confronting this dilemma, it also made a commitment to build one of the most modern and mechanized sugar complexes in the world. With the financial and technical aid of the Cuban government, Nicaragua added a new state enterprise to produce sugar. The decision to build the new complex was the subject of heated debate and multiple studies. After it is working at full capacity, questions will certainly be raised concerning closing some of the the smaller and less efficient sugar mills in the country.

Production and Labor Relations on Two State Ingenios

In this section, we compare two state agroindustrial complexes that were owned by the Somoza family before the Revolution. Both are located on the Pacific coast and both raise and process sugarcane. Before the Revolution, work conditions on both ingenios were harsh. After the Revolution both experienced a decline in production and were reorganized. Efficiency on both farms has improved substantially since 1979, but they differ in the role labor has played in defining priorities and defending the rights of workers.

Before 1979 workers on the ingenios were prohibited from forming unions or mobilizing in any way. During the 1970s, neither ingenio was a center of labor mobilization against Somoza, although a small number of workers repeatedly tried to organize. Before the revolutionary period, dissident workers on both ingenios were fired and forced from company housing. Housing was crowded and poor, work hours were long, and the pay was very low. With the Revolution, the government confiscated the plantations from the Somoza family and converted them into the Empresa Agroindustrial de Reforma Agraria Julio Buitrago Urroz (which we shall call simply "Ingenio Julio Buitrago") and the Empresa Agroindustrial de Reforma Agraria Benjamín Zeledón (Ingenio Benjamín Zeladón).

Ingenio Julio Buitrago. This state farm is located in Masachapa, roughly 45 kilometers south of Managua. During the harvest season, more than three hundred men work in the sugar mill in rotating shifts. During the nonharvest period only half this number are employed. In addition to the factory workers, six hundred men have permanent employment on the ingenio. During the harvest season, the ingenio hires four hundred additional men to help with the cutting of the cane. The seasonal workers are recruited from small neighboring communities where many have subsistence plots.

In the 1985-86 season, Julio Buitrago recorded the highest yields of any sugar complex in the country: 60.38 tons of cane per manzana (see table 7-1). This was a significant increase from 1980-81 when the complex produced 46.72 tons per manzana. Equally impressive, the sugar content of the cane increased from 173.77 pounds per ton in 1980-81, to 211.56 pounds per ton in 1985-86.[16]

It is located in a region with little rainfall; thus water is a major factor inhibiting production. As a result, the total area planted with sugarcane has been gradually reduced from a high of 5,726.0 manzanas in 1980-81 to 4,977.03 manzanas in 1985-86. Most of the irrigation water is taken from local streams that it controls.

The agricultural complex is divided into eleven State Production Units (UPEs), which are the primary units of local production. These units form the base of union organization and production. There is work specialization within the units, and teams are organized to handle irrigation, cultivation, and herbicide application.

Table 7-1
A Comparison of Agro-industrial Parameters
Among Various Sugar Enterprises, 1980-1986

INGENIOS	80/81	81/82	82/83	83/84	84/85	85/86
INGENIO BENJAMIN ZELADON						
Harvested area(a)	7,565	6,901	8,764	7,343	6,626.24	6,822.93
Agricultural yield(b)	43.26	47.75	46.41	51.81	42.40	41.10
Industrial yield(c)	188.83	190.07	200.46	196.39	195.37	212.81
Agro-industrial yield(d)	81.69	90.79	93.15	101.74	82.84	87.51
Sugar production(e)	618,008	626,512	816,343	747,085	548,922	597,094
Cane production(f)	327,270	329,610	407,224	380,413	280,969	380,571
INGENIO JULIO BUITRAGO						
Harvested area(a)	5,726	5,374	5,394	5,209	5,092.54	4,977.03
Agricutural yield(b)	46.72	66.71	48.67	49.57	57.17	60.38
Industrial yield(c)	173.77	174.57	185.96	199.43	213.37	211.56
Agroindustrial yield(d)	81.19	116.47	90.51	98.86	121.98	127.74
Sugar production(e)	464.885	625,934	488,214	514,969	621,172	635,784
Cane production(f)	267,519	358,549	262,532	258,219	291,119	300,526
ALL STATE FARMS						
Harvested area(a)	22,119	23,711	26,984	25,894	25,694	26,615
Agricultural yield(b)	46.54	54.31	47.36	51.60	47.24	47.92
Industrial yield(c)	168.41	174.81	188.18	190.95	197.31	198.92
Agroindustrial yield(d)	78.39	94.95	89.12	98.54	93.21	95.35
Sugar production(e)	1,733,923	2,251,419	2,404,948	2,551,601	2,395,229	2,537,762
Cane production(f)	1,029,535	1,287,851	1,277,976	1,336,242	1,213,919	1,275,541
INGENIO SAN ANTONIO						
Harvested area(a)	23,198	26,233	26,249	24,988	24,923	24,484
Agricultural yield(b)	59.05	54.50	51.04	57.91	42.90	49.43
Industrial yield(c)	184.45	188.81	190.50	182.42	183.12	176.12
Agroindustrial yield(d)	108.93	102.95	97.25	105.65	78.59	87.26
Sugar production(e)	2,525,915	2,700,576	2,552,747	2,640,007	1,958,724	2,136,462
Cane produccion(f)	1,369,968	1,430,281	1,339,990	1,447,142	1,069,631	1,213,078
NATIONAL TOTALS						
Harvested area(a)	45,317	49,944	53,233	57,882	50,617.92	51,099.10
Agricultural yield(b)	52.94	54.42	49.18	54.70	45.11	48.70
Industrial yield(c)	177.57	182.18	189.37	186.52	190.66	187.82
Agroindustrial yield(d)	94.02	99.15	93.13	102.03	86.01	91.47
Sugar production(e)	4,260,838	4,951,995	4,957,695	5,191,608	4,353,953	4,674,224
Cane production(f)	2,399,503	2,718,132	2,617,966	2,783,384	2,283,550	2,488,619

Source: Dirección de Industria Azucarera, "Análisis de la zafra," 1986.

(a) Manzanas   (d) Quintales/manzana
(b) Ton/manzanas   (e) Quintales
(c) Lbs/ton   (f) Tons

Ingenio Benjamín Zeledón. This farm is farther south than Julio Buitrago, near the city of Rivas. It has more than 6,236 manzanas planted with cane that is processed in the factory. Of these, 3,156 manzanas belong to the ingenio while 3,080 are planted by independent growers known as colonos. The yields of the colonos are lower than those of the firm's own production because their land is not as good. It is important to note that 50 percent of the colonos are minifundistas who have fewer than fifty manzanas of land planted with cane, so their yields are much lower than those of the colonos who average more than one hundred manzanas of land. The ingenio gives the colonos water for irrigation, fertilizers, and low-interest credits. The fact that the ingenio must buy such a large percentage of its cane from colonos creates an important distinction between it and Ingenio Buitrago. Many of the colonos belong to UNAG, the powerful peasant union. The union has pressured the government for what its members regard as fair prices for cane.

More than 550 men were employed at Benjamín Zeledón in 1986 to cut cane; slightly more than half were seasonal workers; the rest were permanent employees. The seasonal workers tended to be local, and most were semiproletarian, working their own subsistence plots during the growing season. Like Ingenio Julio Buitrago, Ingenio Benjamín Zeledón has attempted to reduce the number of seasonal workers by hiring more permanent workers, who also cut cane during the harvest season. Seasonal labor had become increasingly difficult to find, by 1986, because, according to the local consensus, land reform had given peasants enough land on which to survive without resorting to seasonal work. Equally important, the war and the draft had created a serious shortage of labor in the countryside. As a result, all of the ingenios were attempting to mechanize the harvest to reduce their dependence on seasonal labor.

The Benjamín Zeledón sugar mill is not as modern as that of Julio Buitrago. As a result the mill was plagued by equipment failures during various harvests. In 1985-86 its 6,822.93 manzanas of cultivated land produced 380,571 tons of cane. The 1985-86 harvest was less successful than anticipated because of factors ranging from lack of parts to scarcity of seasonal workers. Production levels per manzana fell from a peak of 51.8 tons of sugar in 1982-83 to 41.1 in 1985-86. At the same time, the sugar content of harvested cane improved significantly, to a high of 212.81 pounds of sugar per ton of cane from a 1980-81 low of 188 pounds per ton.

Link to the State. These ingenios are part of the state agricultural complex that is controlled by the Ministry of Agricultural Development and Agrarian Reform (MIDINRA). MIDINRA distributed technical information about sugar production to the six state farms. Its Dirección Industrial Azucarera coordinated the private plantations. The Dirección also collects national information on production. MIDINRA has decentralized in an effort to develop greater administrative efficiency. Regional directors manage the primary production units, serving as the primary link between the production unit and the central office. The lines of command are not always clear because the central office is organized by geographic region rather than by operational lines.

All of the sugar produced is sold directly to the state sugar marketing enterprise, ENAZUCAR. Sugar destined for domestic consumption is transferred to MICOIN, which handles distribution within the country through ENABAS. The export of sugar is managed by MICE. All financial transactions are handled by the Banco Central.

Each company negotiates its loans through the Dirección Industrial Azúcarera with the Banco Central and must pay the bank back directly. The 1985-86 season was the first in which the sugar industry was not subsidized. The government was able to export sugar as well as meet internal consumption demands.

Labor Organization. All the workers in the sugar industry were members of the Central Sandinista de Trabajadores (CST), the primary union for industrial workers in Nicaragua. Although most of the agricultural workers in the country are members of the Asociación de Trabajadores del Campo (ATC), sugar workers were incorporated into the CST because of the importance of the industrial components of production and processing. All workers at the ingenios were automatically members of the union. Very few women work in industrial sugar production anywhere in the world; consequently, it is not surprising to find few women union members and no women leaders in the local unions we studied. The local union was integrated into a structure that gave it access to the highest levels of the government. National-level CST leaders had direct access to the minister of labor and the government officials in charge of labor issues. The union representatives participated directly in salary and price negotiations with representatives of the national program for systematizing wages (SNOTS). Pressure to work for union goals could also be carried out through the FSLN. Local petitions for improvements in housing, health programs, and education could all be carried to the highest levels of government if they were designated as priorities.

At the local level in the unions we studied, the basic unit of organization was the Junta Directiva (JD). Workers elected representatives to the Junta Directiva based on their units of production. Of the twenty-three members, thirteen were selected with specific positions and formed an Executive Committee. The JD had two roles, which were potentially contradictory: it was supposed to enhance the production process by facilitating the program of the company; at the same time, it was charged with resolving the social and economic problems of the workers. The JD had direct access to the regional representatives of both the CST and the FSLN.

The second major suborganizational unit was the Consejo Socio--Laboral (CSL). The CSL was designed as a local-level forum to address social issues and workers' problems. It was made up of the coordinators of the different production units of the ingenio. This included representatives from the factory, from transportation, from field labor (divided by work specialty, such as irrigation, cane cutting, and spraying), as well as from specific units. The administration of the firm sent four representatives to the CSL, including the administrator and the head of the office of Human Resources. (The Office of Human Resources was officially part of the ingenio administration and was delegated the job of labor relations.) The CSL provided the forum to discuss a range of social programs, including education and sports; but the levels of salaries, food, and housing were also examined at CSL meetings. On both ingenios seasonal workers have used the CSL to obtain access to land for planting subsistence crops.

The third institutionalized mechanism to facilitate worker participation is the Consejo Consultivo (CC). The CC provided the structure, prescribed by law, for sharing production information with labor. Each head of a division of a state company was, in theory, required to inform workers about the key issues facing his or her program, including full information about production levels, cost of production, and internal problems. Meetings were held once a month, and regional leaders of the CST and the FSLN were also invited.

Both ingenios were incorporated into an administrative structure that was designed to facilitate worker participation in management and management participation in resolving worker problems. The structure, particularly the Juntas Directivas, decentralized important aspects of this process. Decentralization increased local accountability for production as well as contributing to the resolution of social problems. At the same time, however, access to credit for the enterprise, sales, procurement of inputs, and, ultimately, administration was highly centralized.

Despite the institutional mechanisms for addressing problems, the Junta Directiva did not always resolve the problems raised by the workers. Workers at Julio Buitrago were repeatedly frustrated by results of their petitions and felt that the Junta Directiva and, specifically, its social problems council (Consejo Socio-Laboral) were unresponsive to many of their problems. When asked about these reactions, the labor leaders stated that people's expectations had been raised by the Revolution and, at times, they expected too much and asked for more than they had a right to by law. As a result of these dissatisfactions, local workers at Julio Buitrago mobilized to change the composition of the union leadership. And the 1986 union election resulted in a complete change.

Participation. Since the Revolution, significant progress has been made on the ingenios with regard to health, education, and work and housing conditions. These social wages were not as much a product of local union pressures as a result of broader political implementation of the goals of the Revolution. Nevertheless, how health and educational improvements were implemented did depend on local-level organization and leadership. The degree to which the change is either imposed from above or controlled and managed at the local level could have a profound effect on the long-run success of the program.

Increasing worker participation on the state sugar ingenios has been an elusive goal, in part because of labor's lack of previous experience with unions as well as the highly centralized nature of sugar production. As a result of these factors, many workers tended to let the government, through the union, manage major issues such as education, health, and production, despite their being able, structurally, to take a much more active role in these areas, as workers have in other sectors of the labor force.

Of equal importance was the war. Workers recognized the need to raise production without substantially increasing cost. As a result, labor was much less inclined to agitate for wage improvements, knowing the government was economically hard-pressed. Participation under these conditions became a process of asserting individual rights through authorized channels, for previously established benefits. Nevertheless, it was generally felt within the sugar industry that workers at Benjamín Zeledón were more actively engaged in both management and the pursuit of worker needs than are those of Julio Buitrago, despite many similarities between the two ingenios.

On both ingenios, individual workers had brought significant labor grievances to the Junta Directiva. The grievances had concerned issues as varied as poor housing and unequal access to Christmas toys sold at discount prices by the ingenio. The most common complaints had focused on the distribution and quality of services. For example, on Julio Buitrago, the most common issues dealt with by the Junta Directiva concerned worker treatment at the hospital, pharmacy, and company lunchroom, and concerns about the inequitable distribution of basic grains. The lack of labor participation in the management of the ingenio had not been a major issue for the workers. Few workers at that point felt they needed or were prepared for this responsibility.[17]

Salaries have always been an important issue for the Junta Directiva. They were set at the national level after considerable negotiations between the government and the labor unions. They were then presented to the workers as part of the salary and wage scale (tabla salarial), the established set of salaries for different levels of work. For many workers, the key to salary advances lay in changing their work classifications and moving into higher positions. This was a source of considerable conflict and negotiation, but often it was carried out at the individual level.

In 1986 there was a general feeling among the workers we interviewed that, given the war and its economic impact on the country, their salaries were as fair as possible. There was remarkable consensus that increased productivity was critical for the country. Economic incentives were recognized as an important part of this process. The leaders of the unions on both ingenios worked hard to establish this perspective, and they appeared to have been successful.

Several factors, however, complicated efforts to expand worker participation. First, there was considerable diversity of economic activity on an ingenio. All workers were members of the union, but there were significant pay differences. Inequality within both the totality of Nicaraguan society and the union presented a potential threat to people's perceptions of the Revolution. As long as workers perceived their social position and interests as being part of the revolutionary process, they will be willing to accept moral incentives. Workers we interviewed identified strongly with the transformation process and their role in it. They were very aware of the threat to their position presented by the contras.

Second, workers needed to continue to see improvements in their social wages. Improvements in housing, education, and health services needed to be ongoing. Because the war had limited the resources available for social programs, progress in some of these areas had been slow, especially at Julio Buitrago. There was tremendous competition across the nation for scarce resources; and, if the local union was not active or well linked to the national union, fewer resources would be allocated to social projects on the specific ingenios. Workers at Benjamín Zeledón seemed to have a much stronger sense than those at Julio Buitrago that the administration and the union had a strong commitment to worker needs.

Third, workers needed to feel they were participating in the planning and evaluation of the production process. In theory, the change of relations of production meant greater worker participation in the enterprise. On neither of the two ingenios studied, however, did workers feel that their participation in the production process had increased appreciably. The Consejos Consultativos provided a framework for information sharing in which management told labor leaders about ingenio production goals and reviewed production figures at the end of the harvest. But the agenda of these sessions was set by the administrators. Production information was shared with all workers at general assemblies. Some production planning was organized by work section, and workers were encouraged to monitor production. Workers could, and often did, make suggestions on how to improve production or work conditions. Factory workers, who controlled considerable technical information, played a particularly important role in coming up with organizational or technical solutions to production problems.

One of the inherent problems in worker participation in management has been that the ingenios are organized hierarchically. The power of administrators is based on their structural positions, and they control the information needed to run the company. The union often does not get access to the same information and, when it does, workers seldom have the technical capacity to analyze the data.

Workers did not, however, feel that they had the power to challenge management decisions nor did they want such power. The participatory process was still in the early stages and was developing during a period of foreign aggression. Few workers had technical training and most lacked the confidence to force confrontations with professional administrators. According to workers, past administrators at Julio Buitrago resisted worker input. At Benjamín Zeledón, the feeling was that management was open to worker input. Various cases were cited in which factory organization and harvesting procedures were modified in accordance with workers' suggestions were cited. In addition, workers pointed to a new pig farm and dairy, which were developed, in part, because of workers' desires to expand employment opportunities for family members.

The scarcity of technicians hurt the participatory process. Technical personnel were often classified with the administration and did not have to be members of the union. At Julio Buitrago, workers did not even share dining facilities with administrators or technicians. The new technicians then graduating from training programs were very sensitive to the social goals of the Revolution. However, when technicians made serious errors or committed crimes such as hoarding, they were seldom fired; their skills were simply too important.

If workers cannot remove incompetent administrators or technicians, the participatory process is threatened. There were cases, however, in which administrators had been removed from state farms because of pressure from unions. These cases hinted at the power of the unions and their potential to make a major contribution.

There is an inherent danger of local-level labor leaders becoming entrenched and closing the avenues of potential rank-and-file participation. At Julio Buitrago, many people felt that the union had become paternalistic and had allocated too much responsibility to the administration. This became a major issue in the 1986 elections, when a new group of leaders was elected.

It is reasonable to expect the degree of political involvement in nonwork aspects of life to influence general political awareness and participation in unions. In cases where nonwork activity is not generated by the unions, it can have a positive influence on union involvement. High levels of union participation can, in turn, generate greater consciousness and activity in other spheres of political and economic activity. At Benjamín Zeledón, the CDSs and labor organizations were very active in community and ingenio life. The CDSs on Julio Buitrago were weak and some were inactive. The important mass organization for women, AMNLAE, was also inactive at Ingenio Julio Buitrago, but it was active at Benjamín Zeledón.

The Private Sector: The Case of San Antonio

Nicaragua's revolutionary economy is mixed: 40 percent of the general economy is state-owned and run; 60 percent belongs to the private sector. Included in the state-owned sector are exporting and importing activities, banking and financing services, natural resources, and some agricultural and industrial production.[18] The majority of the productive sectors of the economy, however, are in private hands: 51 percent of industry and 75 percent of agriculture.[19] This is a unique framework for carrying out a revolutionary program; and it is criticized by political factions to both the right and the left of the Sandinista party.

The mixed economic system constitutes, in an odd way, a logical and coherent system within the revolutionary program. It is a system in which private capital can prosper, but which also contains of number of stabilizing contradictions and tensions that allow it to work politically and economically. Labor in the private sector has increased its power and expanded its negotiating strength to improve wages and work conditions. In some cases labor leaders have assumed the responsibility for gaining greater participation in management and budget planning. Many local workers' organizations consider it their obligation to contribute to the revolutionary aims of a worker-controlled and -governed economy. This entails the raising of revolutionary worker consciousness; the encouragement of militant, even armed, worker involvement; vigilance over the private estate and its production hierarchy; and political involvement at local, regional, and national levels. When the state apparatus supports worker participation at all levels, one is confronted with a historical situation in which private capital and worker participation seem to be mutually exclusive concepts.

Nevertheless, the contradiction provides a stabilizing and, to a degree, prosperous situation within which private capital can operate. The revolutionary state at this stage is committed to both worker participation and private capital for what it considers both sound and pragmatic economic reasons. The state depends on private capital as its primary resource for generating the foreign exchange critical to reactivating the economy. In part, this strategy is also necessary to put private administrative skills to use in the production process. Furthermore, the nationalistic bourgeoisie, which supported the overthrow of Somoza, played a role in the early development of the new revolutionary state and was subsequently incorporated into the national development strategy both politically and economically.[20]

On the other side of the coin, the revolutionary government remains committed to actively promoting worker participation within the national political and economic structure. It sees the role of workers as one of leadership in the process of revolutionary transformation within the country. Union initiative is strongly encouraged. Worker organizations, as well as other mass organizations, have held several seats on the Council of State and have institutional ties to a number of key government ministries and agencies. Worker participation is more than an ideological aim of the government; it has also served as a means of solving many of the problems the government faced after the Revolution. Among those problems were the paralysis of the economy and the flight of more than half the skilled industrial and agricultural technicians. The problem was exacerbated by the absorption into public administration of many of the technically skilled and "conscienticized" people who had stayed in the country. The Sandinista government saw direct worker participation as its only recourse in reactivating the economy and implemented a program of worker education and conscienticization.

Thousands of CDSs and other mass groups organized at the local level were able to provide a base for national reorganization. The revolutionary government views worker participation as a means of counterbalancing the pressures that the bourgeoisie put on government policy. Worker organizations serve as vigilantes to watch over private interests, to put pressure on private holdings and companies to produce, and to prevent decapitalization. Pressure of this type at a local level permits the national government to pursue the aims of a mixed economy and to promote worker participation openly in the private sector.

The Ingenio San Antonio. This is one of the largest private companies in Nicaragua. Its parent company, Nicaragua Sugar Estates Company, has numerous economic interests, including not only sugar, but also rum distilling, automotive importation and retailing, and banking and financing interests in Nicaragua and the United States. The ingenio is the largest in Central America and claims to be among the ten largest in the world. It produces approximately 50 percent of the sugar in Nicaragua, most of it refined. It is also by far the largest employer in the sugar industry, employing more than three thousand permanent workers and another twenty-five hundred seasonal laborers during the peak of the harvest season. The cane it processes is grown on more than twenty-five thousand manzanas, 70 percent on its own land and about 30 percent on the land of more than eighty colonos.[21] A recently developed area for cane growth, financed through the IFC, is almost completely mechanized. Other holdings are used to graze cattle and to grow food crops for workers.[22] It thus dominates a large part of the landscape near Nicaragua's second city, León, stretching from close to the port of Corinto to Chichigalpa and the Panamerican Highway.

Ingenio San Antonio is one of the most modern private enterprises in Nicaragua. It was founded in 1890 with British and Nicaraguan capital. It became wholly owned by Nicaraguans in 1935. During the long period of Somoza rule, it maintained an ambiguous relationship with the dictator. It resisted Somoza's efforts to take it over and to control the national sugar markets through its ties to powerful business and financial allies both in Nicaragua and the United States. San Antonio was the first and

only ingenio in prerevolutionary Nicaragua to have union representation.
Its union was affiliated with the Nicaraguan Workers Federation
(CTN), a labor organization that existed long before the insurrection and
which remains an active rival of the CST. The CTN was able to organize
the workers at San Antonio despite ingenio efforts to repress labor
organizing in the late 1930s.[23]   The union was able to pressure the
ingenio to build a hospital, to honor the eight-hour workday, to build
better housing for workers, and to open a night school. Conflict has
continued intermittently to the present, however.

San Antonio has an administrative structure suited to its role as a
private capitalist enterprise. The company is owned by 142 shareholders,
who vote on company policy.[24]   Most of the shareholders belong to
three well-known, financially powerful families with ties to local and
international financial institutions. This structure has permitted the
company to seek financing for expansion of production from international
financial institutions such as the IFC and the Wells Fargo Bank.[25] The
company headquarters are located in Granada, where the executive
officer, José António Pellas, resides. He is not involved in the everyday
operation of the ingenio. The administration is arranged hierarchically
and sectorally and places strong emphasis on the division of capital from
labor. It is headed by the administrator, who coordinates a committee
of seven or eight directors, each in charge of a different sector of
operation. Under each of the sectors are a number of engineers,
technicians, and specialists who respond to the director of their sector.
The technicians are strictly separated from workers. They are provided
separate and better housing, higher pay, and other privileges; thus it was
not surprising that no technicians belonged to the union.[26]

The personnel director claims that administrators and technicians
have autonomy in hiring workers, although the union challenges this claim
and states that hiring is done according to lists that it presents to the
company. Also included in the administrative sectors are secretaries and
certain service personnel, who generally shy away from union membership
as well. As expected, the technical and financial sectors of the company
are centralized and closely controlled by management and, therefore, are
two of the areas least accessible to workers. The factory takes prece-
dence in company structure as well, and its closely monitored coordination of other ingenio activities has made the mill the most efficient in
Nicaragua.[27]   In general, the administrative structure of the company has
varied little, as far we know, since the Revolution.

The ingenio produces 2,850,000 quintales of sugar a year, about 52
percent for export. Its mills approximately 8,000 tons of cane per day,
based on efficient coordination between factory and field management,
efficient use of varieties of cane in a system that allows optimum plant
maturation, and high level of irrigation. Approximately 70 percent of the
ingenio's cane is under irrigation. Despite great expansion efforts in the
late 1970s and in 1983, production levels per hectare have decreased in
recent years. This can be attributed to several factors, such as the aging

of factory and field equipment and machinery, the shortage of investment dollars to repair and update equipment, and the fall of world sugar prices. It may also be that production incentives have been lowered in the Sandinista mixed economy, since profits at some level are effectively guaranteed.[28] San Antonio is the only ingenio in Nicaragua with the capacity to produce refined sugar, adding to its value to the Sandinista state, because the state has had to rely much more heavily than before on refined sugar for export.

Link to the State. Although San Antonio is a private enterprise, the financing and marketing of its sugar goes through the same channels as the state ingenios. To receive loans for production, for repair or replacement of machinery, or for expansion, it must submit a budget to the Dirección de Azúcar and the Central Bank. The Central Bank makes its decisions about the distribution of scarce foreign revenues by considering the needs of all of the ingenios, but San Antonio receives particularly favorable treatment because much of the sugar it produces is exported, generating foreign revenues. The ingenio must submit its production plans and the estimated costs of production to MIDINRA. The sugar produced on the ingenio is sold to ENAZUCAR, which determines which portion will be exported and which will go to the internal market. San Antonio is paid for its sugar at the same rates as are other ingenios. This generally favors San Antonio because it produces sugar at a lower cost than do the state ingenios. As a private enterprise, San Antonio is also guaranteed a profit return, even when it suffers actual losses. This has been a source of conflict between the government and the union.

Labor. The majority of San Antonio's workers and their families are presently affiliated with the Sindicato Ronald Altamirano, a union affiliated with the CST, although several other unions have operated on the ingenio, primarily the Socialist-backed FO (Frente Obrera) and the ingenio-preferred CUS, of Social Democratic tendencies. Not all members of certain sectors of the labor force, especially the service workers and the administrative personnel, are affiliated with the CST. Nevertheless, the CST is the only union to represent the workers before the administration, and agreements it signs with the ingenio cover all of workers.

The central organ of the union is the junta directiva. Its ten members represent the different sectors of the production process. The field and factory sectors have more than one representative, in accordance with their importance in the ingenio; the administrative employees, general service workers, transportation employees and mechanics, and general service employees each have one representative. The junta meets with the directors of each of the sectors and departments, twenty-four engineers in all. Although the meetings serve a variety of functions, primarily they evaluate each of the production sectors and make suggestions, criticisms, and recommendations. The union leaders we interviewed stated that the meetings have not been very successful because the engineers have boycotted many of them and have often refused to resolve problems raised by the union.

Each of the work areas has a comité sindical, with seventy members. There is also a committee formed of representatives of each of the twenty-one colonias (workers' colonies). These consider the housing problems of the nine thousand inhabitants of the ingenio. The various committees are seen as primary vehicles for worker participation on the ingenio. They have received little attention from the ingenio, however, which limits their effectiveness. There is also a Consejo de Producción, consisting of both management personnel and workers, but it has had little success because of lack of management involvement. During the 1985-86 year, the Consejo met twice to evaluate the harvest; but, we were told, it is rare for it to meet even that many times a year. The union also has close ties to other mass organizations such as the CDS, AMNLAE, and Juventud Sandinista, the Sandinista youth organization.

Conflict between the union and management has erupted over a number of issues. The union feels that the ingenio fails to supervise work adequately, which is necessary, it suggests, "because of a lack of worker discipline." Mismanagement is another issue. The union accused management of abandoning the fields in 1986 by failing to assign weeding tasks early in the season, before the weeds grew large and were tougher to dig out. The union also feels that technicians are given special treatment and that the resources the ingenio derives from the government are unjustly distributed. Directors in the factory are said to arrive late and to fail to manage their sectors responsibly. The union accuses management of embezzling resources such as tractors, building materials, and profits derived from buying sugarcane from the colonos.

On the other hand, union leaders also feel that they have made a number of gains: they have succeeded in raising the consciousness of workers on the ingenio; they have obtained uniform treatment for workers in the different areas of production; and all workers now have life insurance. The union feels it has triumphed in establishing CST hegemony on the ingenio, after confronting movements to establish other unions. The union is successfully confronting the owner of the company with grievances by calling on the government to apply pressure on the ingenio.[29]   San Antonio was the first ingenio to apply the nationally-mandated SNOTS wage scale fully, and the union has strictly enforced its application.

Participation. Worker participation at San Antonio has reached levels similar to those found at typical state enterprises, although the accomplishments are in somewhat different areas because of the context of private capital in which San Antonio workers are employed. Significant advances have been made in the areas of education, health, and work conditions, although many of them represent nationwide increases in social services and other public programs, rather than the result of worker-management negotiations at the firm.

Services such as transportation to work and sanitary services are now provided at no direct cost to workers or their families. The families of workers who volunteer for military service are cared for. A store provides subsidized basic grains to workers and their families. Both seasonal and permanent workers have retirement benefits. And new housing has been built for a number of company employees.

These accomplishments are grounded on a number of factors. Not least of these is that, prior to the Revolution, there was a well-established (although moderate) union movement, which had a great deal of experience in confronting management. Thus, there was already worker consciousness, organizational skills, and awareness of the value of worker organization, all of which were immensely helpful in the organizational process after the Revolution. The widely publicized confrontation between the union and management, strengthened by the government's willingness to listen to workers' demands (since it was workers who ultimately secure the leverage the government has over private enterprises such as San Antonio), also raised the level of workers' interest and involvement. In addition, union distrust of the ingenio's management has created further interest in participation and vigilance over the company.

We found that the workers at San Antonio had gathered detailed and very well documented inside information on company finances, policy toward competing unions, efforts to divide the labor force through favoritism, and bad management practices. There was also a distrust of the government agricultural institutions (the Ministry of Agriculture and Agrarian Reform, MIDINRA, in particular), which were seen by the union to be closely allied with private management and antiunion interests.[30]

The sectoral organization of the CST also helped to promote worker participation. Its sugar sector meets on a regular basis, and it is clear that local union leaders are aware of the internal conditions of each of the other ingenios. The sectoral-level organization promotes union policies and aims for the entire sugar industry. It provides a means for union leaders not only to defend the interests of their own workers, but also to support other unions in achieving participatory aims. The sectoral-level organization is recent, and there are still inequities between ingenios, but there have been advances as well in regularizing the work situation. One area in which this has been most apparent is in the establishment of policy regarding the implementation of the SNOTS scale. It is clear that this union has served as a source of leverage, of support, and of information for the union in the private sector. It is also interesting to note that San Antonio's union has often been the initiator and the most aggressive force in the cross-union movement. Union leaders expressed concern, for example, about the slow implementation of participation in Buitrago, and the sectoral level may have had an active interventionist role in changing both the ingenio and union leadership.

Ironically, the factors that have stimulated worker participation in the private ingenio have also, in other ways, hindered the participatory process. Possibly the greatest block to the participation of workers is the antagonistic relationship between management and labor. It is noteworthy that San Antonio's management claimed to be one of the most progressive enterprises in Nicaragua long before the Revolution. Some facts bear this out. San Antonio provided social benefits for workers long before most other companies in the country even considered implementing such programs; it was the only ingenio to provide social security benefits to its workers during the Somoza period; it built and staffed, at its own expense, a hospital that served not only the people of the ingenio, but also the residents of nearby Chichigalpa with the best medical care in the area.[31] The company also provided housing for all of its workers. It subsidized basic grains for its workers, built a dining hall where single workers could eat at subsidized prices, and provided an extensive sports and recreational program, which included impressive baseball diamonds, a swimming pool, sports equipment, and other amenities. The ingenio also built several schools at its own expense. And wages were known to be higher at San Antonio than at any of the other ingenios in the country. Management today claims that Sandinista reforms have actually curtailed the benefits workers received prior to the Revolution.

Nevertheless, the relationship between labor and the administration has perhaps been more antagonistic at San Antonio than at any of the sugar estates. Between 1979 and 1982, the company was racked by a number of strikes, worker demonstrations, and other confrontations, which the government attempted to resolve quietly. The greatest source of conflict has been worker participation in areas that management considers to be its exclusive territory.

The local CST branch has accused the company of attempting to bar all efforts by workers to participate in decision making and in evaluation of production and investment levels. It accuses management of using a number of strategies to break union strength in the ingenio, including efforts to create divisions in the labor force by emphasizing hierarchical differences between workers. Management did this by clandestinely paying technical and some factory workers above-normal wage rates. The union also accuses the ingenio of promoting a moderate union that is more favorably inclined toward management policy so as to compete with the local CST for worker loyalties. Finally, it accuses the company of trying to sabotage and subvert the revolutionary process through mismanagement, decapitalization, and irresponsibility.

The conflict intensified recently when the corporation refused to provide the union with the key financial and technical information necessary for evaluating company management performance. The union clandestinely accumulated these data by recruiting from the company technical and bureaucratic staff, who provided insider documentation. The union has publicized the conflict, putting pressure on the government to resolve the issue in favor of the CST. The company, in turn, has campaigned to tarnish the union's image. It has accused the union of being an appendage of government policy aimed at lowering the standard of living of workers.   This campaign may have had some success: seasonal workers have directed their strike every year (except the last) at the union for failing to represent them actively before the company and for failing to push for higher wages and better working conditions. The union and the Ministry of Labor (MITRAB) have stepped in to resolve the conflicts.

The axis of the conflict at San Antonio is the separation and antagonism between labor and capitalist management. The corporation feels that it, as a private enterprise, has the right to make top-down decisions regarding the production process and planning, hiring, and investments.   It views the role of the union in the classical sense, as essentially protecting the interests of workers.   From this perspective, the role of the union is to bargain for better working conditions, better wages, greater job security, and other issues that are traditionally of concern to the worker.   This role does not include involvement in technical, financial, or productive matters within the administrative process.

It is interesting to note that the corporation management views the labor-management relationship in cultural terms and sees labor difficulties as being the product of the workers' lack of culture and education. In contrast, the union sees the conflict in terms of the ultimate triumph of the working class over private enterprise.   It views its role as one of vigilance over the gains of the Revolution and, ultimately, as the vanguard in taking over and transforming private enterprise.

Our interviews with workers indicate that they are not entirely clear about their attitudes toward company management. The portrayal of the company as provider of benefits and competitive wages, as the builder of sports facilities, as provider of education and transportation service, has put the company in the paternalistic role of benefactor.   The company appears to push for worker benefits as opposed to government restrictions. Payment arrangements that better the SNOTS rates in some sectors create a benevolent image of company aims. This is despite the fact that many accomplishments were actually produced after the Revolution and, arguably, through government and union pressure.

It may be that the government itself contributes to the ambiguity of worker consciousness by portraying private capital within the mixed economy as a partner in the revolutionary process. Thus, the government and corporations such as San Antonio appear as allies in the struggle to consolidate the Revolution. Understandably, an ideological coherence is lacking in this case, since relations of production have not been transformed, and workers' interests have not been revindicated. Nevertheless, there is also an understanding among workers about the revolutionary aims of the government and of the CST, and workers appear to understand the need to increase productivity for revolutionary purposes. Sacrifice in terms of wages and the subsidization of basic grains seems to be understood as well. The image workers have of management thus seems ambivalent, a product of an ever-intensifying ideological and image-making battle.

Conclusion

This chapter raises the question of whether worker participation takes place to a lesser degree in the private sector of the sugar industry than it does on state-owned ingenios. Theoretically, state ingenios should have a greater degree of worker participation because of the revolutionary nature of the state enterprise. The unions and the administration of these ingenios have similar political aims, which include the concrete goal of increasing productivity. The state provides and supports a common ideological base for both labor and management, diminishing the possibilities of conflict between them. Furthermore, the aims of the state enterprise are ultimately political rather than economic in the private sector; the goal of accumulation on state ingenios is to sustain and advance the revolutionary effort. Theoretically, at least, workers and management share a common class consciousness, although they fulfill different functions. Finally, management and workers share the objective of increasing the standard of living of workers and bettering their working conditions and opportunities.

Nevertheless, state sugar enterprises confront a variety of problems that tend to limit levels of worker participation. First, the Sandinista government has been faced with a shortage of technical personnel within the country and has often had to rely on technicians who do not share the revolutionary zeal of the mass organizations.[32] These technicians, administrators, and management personnel often attempt to promote top-down decision making in the state enterprises in which they work. Also, the lack of ideological transformation of management people promotes conditions in which the union is seen as being a simple transmitter of administrative and government policy. A lack of conscious and independent union leadership within an enterprise may contribute to this attitude. In such situations, management feels that workers, particularly seasonal and field workers, have little expertise in running the ingenio and are not capable of making production decisions.

Second, although workers on state ingenios seem to understand and support the revolutionary goals of the state, those goals are often foreign to the workers' reality. Revolutionary goals include reactivation of the economy, defense against outside aggressors, and national unity. These goals are often mentioned by the government and the mass organizations when workers are called on to make further sacrifices. Although visible betterment of conditions has certainly occurred on the state ingenios in the form of a "social wage," the lack of tangible rewards of the Revolution may be cause for disillusionment. Real wages have shrunk, skilled younger workers have entered the military service (depriving families of an income earner), rations have become increasingly smaller, and food and other essentials have become ever more scarce. The problem of workers distancing themselves from the political commitments they may have previously demonstrated, "distanciación," has grown in these situations in which there are increasing problems with the delivery of "social wage" benefits such as retirement benefits, distribution of land to grow subsistence foods, medical benefits, and improved housing. We noted a direct relationship between the level of disillusionment on the part of sugar workers and their degree of participation. In general, the more immediate the benefits of the social wage, the higher the degree of participation we saw. This may explain, in part, the different levels of participation that we observed on the state ingenios.

Third, the lack of training, of expertise, and of class consciousness has limited worker participation on the state ingenios. The unions, the CDS, and the other mass organizations have made efforts to promote consciousness and to create greater knowledge of the productive process among workers, but the more immediate needs of reactivating production often make it difficult to transform worker consciousness quickly. We noted that workers are more active on ingenios where the visibility of the Sandinista party, the union, and other mass organizations is high. The activities of these organizations contribute to increasing the workers' ideological support of the revolutionary process. In contrast, we noted that, where the party and mass organizations were less active, workers were less inclined to take their participatory role seriously.[33]

Finally, the strength of government-sponsored programs and goals may hinder the raising of levels of participation on the state enterprise, particularly in a war economy struggling to build up foreign currency reserves, short on manpower, and faced with shortages of food and other essential goods. The government has sought to inform the Nicaraguan people of the conditions the country faces, the need for higher productivity, and thus the need for stricter production and distribution programs. In its push toward these goals, it has also restricted autonomous worker activities. Union activities are limited in a number of official ways: workers do not have the right to strike or the right to insist on higher wages; and worker grievances must go through official channels and institutions. Despite this, workers at various times have forced official policy changes with strikes, demonstrations, press coverage of grievances, and other forms of pressure.

In those situations in which there was competition between unions for the same labor bases during the early stages of the Revolution, there are now higher levels of politicization and union recruitment and activity. The defense of revolutionary attainments has been actively promoted by the CDS and other mass organizations as they have organized unions and promoted worker consciousness and participation. This was the case of the Ingenio Zeledón, where very tough battles were fought among different unions for the loyalty of workers. In all the cases we studied, the CST triumphed over the other unions but not without mobilizing a large part of the labor force.

Worker participation on the private <u>ingenio</u> faces a different set of constraints. As we noted above, the primary constraint is the private capitalist ownership of the enterprise. On one hand, the restriction is structural: workers cannot form part of the management decision--making body, as they do on state enterprises. There is a contradiction between management and worker interests. The structural conflict is exacerbated by a management hierarchy that has always opposed union participation and has attempted to subvert union aims. Nevertheless, levels of worker initiative and activity are high, and workers have been able to press their demands and achieve many of their goals. Workers' levels of participation are, in part, a response to their need to defend their interests against management practices. But participation is also due to the promotion of worker class consciousness by the union. Union leaders portray the workers' struggle on the <u>ingenio</u> as an unfinished one, one whose victory will result ultimately in the transformation of the relations of production and in worker control of the <u>ingenio</u>.

Ultimately, the nature of participation on sugar-based agro-industrial complexes, private or public, depends on a number of factors discussed in this article and raises several critical questions for the future. One question is whether national agrarian policy focused on raising productivity can also meet workers' demands for greater participation. Although raising productivity and enhancing participation may be conflicting demands, it is feasible to argue that both may be achieved. Another critical issue is the nature of sugar production itself. The structure of a highly centralized technified system such as an <u>ingenio</u> presents problems concerning the participation of all workers in the production process, particularly the temporary and unskilled. How the internal hierarchies and decision making processes are transformed by the revolutionary process influences participation as well as productivity. Thus, the tension between productive structure and workers' participation will continue to be an important issue in revolutionary Nicaragua.

Endnotes to Chapter 7

1. This research, carried out in 1986, was made possible by a grant from the Ford Foundation and the generous institutional and collegial support of INIES. We deeply appreciate the creative energy and organizational skill of Michael Conroy and Francisco López, who forged the institutional linkage for the research. We would also like to thank Verónica Frenkel and Joanna Chataway, project coordinators. Alfonso DeBois generously provided invaluable information he had gathered in previous research and lent his expertise to our research process. Martha Juárez Ponce, a true colleague, made a major contribution to the research. We are

grateful to Gary Ruchwarger and Wilfredo Gutiérrez, who kindly lent us their excellent manuscripts, and to Marvin Ortega, for sharing ideas and interpretations. We want to thank all of the people on the ingenios who made the research possible. Given that this is a preliminary study, we hope it accurately reflects a significant aspect of their struggle and achievements. Finally, we want to emphasize the uniquely open aspects of Nicaraguan society. People in diverse organizations -- CST, Dirección de Azúcar, ATC, MICE, CIERA, the three ingenios studied, and other agencies were open and immensely cooperative. To them we owe our appreciation and friendship.

2. Luis Serra, "The Sandinista Mass Organizations," in Thomas W. Walker, ed., Nicaragua in Revolution (New York: Praeger, 1982), p. 97.

3. Gary Ruchwarger, People in Power: Forging a Grass Roots Democracy in Nicaragua (South Hadley, MA: Bergin and Garvey Press, 1987).

4. Serra, "The Sandinista Mass Organizations," p. 97.

5. Many of the other unions in the country are not affiliated with the FSLN. For example, the Frente Obrera (FO) is affiliated with the Partido Marxista Leninista de Nicaragua; the Confederación de Trabajadores Nicaragüenses (CTN) is affiliated with the Partido Popular Social Cristiano; and the Confederación de Unificación Socialista (CUS) is affiliated with the Partido Socialista Demócrata, which, in turn, is affiliated with the Confederación Internacional de Organizaciones del Sindicalismo Libre.

6. Marifeli Pérez-Stable, "The Working Class in the Nicaraguan Revolution," in Walker, Nicaragua in Revolution, p. 138.

7. Richard Stahler-Sholk, "Organized Labor in Nicaragua," in Sheldon L. Maram and Gerald Michael Greenfield, eds., Latin American Labor Organizations (Westport, CT: Greenwood Press, 1986), p. 10.

8. Carlos M. Vilas, "El movimiento obrero en la Revolución Sandinista," in Richard Harris and Carlos Vilas, eds., La revolución en Nicaragua: Liberación nacional, democracia popular y transformación (Mexico City: Ediciones Era, 1985).

9. Marvin Ortega, "La participación obrera en la gestión de las empresas agropecuarias del APP," in ibid.

10. Scott Whiteford, Workers from the North: Plantations, Bolivian Labor and the City in Northwest Argentina (Austin: University of Texas Press, 1981).

11. Sugar production is unique in that it combines industrial and agricultural capitalism into one operation. As Sepulveda notes, the rate of profit is higher in the industrial sector, in the transformation of sugar into an industrial product, than in the cultivation of cane (see Cristián Sepúlveda, "Acumulación y contracciones en el sistema de agroexportación azucarera de Nicaragua" [1983], manuscript). This means that the ingenio itself is dominant in the production process, although it represents fewer workers and administrative personnel than field workers, and therefore control

over production is very centralized. It also results in the "captivization" of an agrarian sector by an industrial one, including the control over large expanses of land. A "forced" fusion occurs between agricultural and industrial interests. This is evident particularly in labor, where the greatest source of labor recruitment is agricultural, and a small elite sector is industrial. The factory workers have different interests and concerns than the field workers. The centralization of production was helpful in the takeover of the ingenios by the Sandinistas, and yet this very fact has made it more difficult to create genuine participation for all the workers.

12. Forrest D. Colburn, Post-Revolutionary Nicaragua: State, Class, and the Dilemmas of Agrarian Policy (Berkeley and Los Angeles: University of California Press, 1986), p. 12.

13. Historically, the expansion of the sugar industry in Nicaragua responded to the opening up of external markets, not to the increase of internal consumption. This was primarily because external markets "subsidized" internal consumption. Under the Sandinistas the pattern was reversed: expansion has occurred due to the increase of internal demand. For this reason the government has had to rationalize internal consumption. The internal market has always represented a "loss." Thus, the government is confronted with a contradiction: it is bound by its revolutionary aims to provide at least minimal levels of sugar, a basic commodity, to the Nicaraguan population, and yet the increase of consumption has resulted in a loss of foreign revenues. The consequence of this situation has been government support of sugar production, and particularly of the private ingenio. The construction of the ingenio Victorio del Julio, financed with Cuban capital, has also been a consequence of this policy. From a technical and economic view, these are extremely debatable investment policies. Politically, they represent the tightrope the government must walk between the requirements of internal consumption and the need for foreign reserves.

14. Dirección Industrial Azucarera (DRA), Análisis de la zafra 1985-1986: empresas estatales y empresa privada (Managua: MIDINRA, 1986).

15. See Cristián Sepúlveda, "Acumulación y contradicciones en el sistema de agroexportación azucarera de Nicaragua" (1983), manuscript, for an excellent analysis of sugar pricing.

16. Figures on production are all from DRA, Análisis de la zafra, 1985-1986.

17. See Wilfredo Gutiérrez, Mario Castro, and Jimmy Chavarría, "Estudio de la participación obrera en la gestión: caso del Ingenio Julio Buitrago," for an excellent study of the meeting reports and minutes at Julio Buitrago (paper presented at the IV Congreso Nicaragüense de Ciencias Sociales, Managua, 1985). We have drawn on this study to complement our interviews.

18. We found cases in which water rights are not state-owned, but rather controlled and sold by private owners.
19. Colburn, Post-Revolutionary Nicaragua, p. 43. The owners of San Antonio are such a case. The national bourgeoisie has been represented politically and economically, but not ideologically, within the Sandinista revolution (see Sholk, "Organized Labor in Nicaragua").
20. Serra notes that mass organizations held seventeen of forty-seven seats on the Council of State; nine went to the CDS, three each to the ATC and CST, one to AMNLAE, and one to the Juventud Sandinista-19 de Julio (see Serra, "The Sandinista Mass Organizations," p. 98).
21. Sepúlveda, "Acumulación y contradicciones." The author notes that many private cotton growers in the region have switched to growing cane, which they sell to either San Antonio or Ingenio Germán Pomares. Thus cane production has increased from an estimated fifty-four colonos in 1981 (see Food and Agriculture Organization (FAO), Proyecto de análisis de la agroindustria de Nicaragua: Agroindustria azucarera prediagnóstico [Managua: FAO, 1982]). On average, San Antonio's colonos produce cane on more than two hundred manzanas each, a relatively large landholding. Other ingenio colonos average about fifty manzanas of cane, except for Ingenio Benjamín Zeledón, where minifundistas grow cane. The implication is that there are no peasants, except possibly at Zeledón, who produce cane for the ingenios. The growth of cane production has presented problems for San Antonio, as it has in Julio Buitrago, since the cane has to be hauled greater distances. This makes this cane more costly than cane grown by the ingenio, not only because of transportation costs but also because of the reduction of sugar levels in the cane transport.
22. The ingenio farms 10 manzanas of vegetable crops, 250 of rice, and 300 of maize. It also grazes dairy cattle to provide milk to the workers.
23. Early union organizers on San Antonio affiliated with Somoza, as well as with the Socialist party. The Somoza connection gave them some leverage in getting their demands met by the ingenio. Nevertheless, whenever labor unrest became too great, the National Guard was called in to repress the movement and to imprison union leaders.
24. International Finance Corporation (IFC), "Report and Recommendation of the President of the Board of Directors on a Proposed Investment in Propiedades Azucareras de Nicaragua Limitada" (Managua: IFC, 1976). 80 percent of the shares are owned by 50 percent of the shareholders. The Pellas family is by far the dominant interest in the company.
25. A large expansion project was carried out in 1977-78 through the incorporation of a new area known as Río Grande into sugar production and an accompanying expansion of milling capacities. The ingenio again attempted to expand production in 1983, primarily

through new irrigation projects, the incorporation of new colono areas, and the addition of a new Brazilian-made caldera. The ingenio traditionally had very close ties to the Bank of America in Nicaragua, which has been a primary source of financing. Its owners also had financial interests in the bank.

26. According to union accounts, the technicians deemed some of the best in the country are paid above the SNOTS wage scales. This is managed through a variety of mechanisms, including donating labor hours to technicians. It should also be noted that both union and management agree that technicians at San Antonio are with the company in part because they reject the aims of the Revolution and therefore refuse to work in the state sector. Management views this positively; the union, in contrast, seems to view the company as a haven of rejected and reactionary management personnel, unable or unwilling to work in the state sector.

27. Production rate is seventy-one quintales per manzana, higher than on any of the other ingenios.

28. The union claims that, despite actual production losses last year, the ingenio owners were able to make a profit of 200 million Córdobas. The statement was a bitter comment on the contradiction in a government policy that stresses greater productivity but guarantees profits to private enterprises, despite their inefficiency and disinterest.

29. A document expressing union grievances was prepared and sent to the National Assembly, the national CST headquarters, and MIDINRA this year after a meeting between workers and the principal owner of the company failed to resolve problems.

30. MIDINRA was criticized as having high-level personnel who are private landowners who sell cane to the ingenio. Furthermore, there was a great deal of criticism of the new ingenio, Victoria de Julio, a Cuban investment, which is highly mechanized and technified. The union general secretary stated openly that the union was blocked by workers on that ingenio, for all consider themselves técnicos.

31. Interview with the personnel manager of the ingenio, 21 August 1986. It should be noted that these historical data are not confirmed, and we found that workers and management often claimed to be the initiators of the same action or benefit. In the case of the hospital specifically, union pressure was at least part of reason the ingenio built it.

32. Marvin Ortega, director of agrarian research in CIERA, stated in an interview that Nicaragua lost over half of its technicians in all fields after the Revolution.

33. This was the explanation the general secretary of the CST union at San Antonio gave for the lack of participation on Ingenio Julio Buitrago. He stated that neither the party nor the union had played active roles on the ingenio. He also mentioned that this situation had improved recently and had resulted in changes in both union leadership and the ingenio management.

Chapter 8
The Evolution of Food and Agricultural Policies During Economic Crisis and War

by

María Verónica Frenkel

Introduction

From 1979 to 1986, Nicaragua pioneered in the development of new programs to increase the production and improve the distribution of food products from agriculture. However, in 1986, food shortages were becoming more apparent. In an attempt to shed light upon this issue, this chapter explores the food and agricultural policies that have been undertaken in Nicaragua since 1979 and their relevance to the shortages that occurred.

The difficulties that the revolutionary government has faced in formulating appropriate policies to address the issue of food security are not unique to Nicaragua. In recent years, several other South American countries and all of the Central American nations, most significantly, Costa Rica, have experienced recurring food deficits and have become importers of food, rather than exporters, as they were in the past.[1] As a result of increasing population growth, combined with the extension and elaboration of a commercial agricultural export sector, land available for food production has decreased, and the food resources of many parts of Latin America are being threatened.[2] This decline in food self-sufficiency has led to growing problems with external dependence, vulnerability to volatile foreign staples markets, and increasing costs of food imports and, most significantly, worsening poverty and malnutrition.

Many scholars have argued that the degrees of food insecurity and hunger, as well as the level of nutrition in a society, are not determined primarily by a country's total food *production* or production potential, but instead are the results of the political process that directs the *distribution* of a country's income and resources, including land, credit, investment, services, etc., whether scarce or abundant.[3] The traditional pattern of agricultural development in Latin America has tended to direct these resources away from food production for domestic consumption, primarily in the hands of the peasantry, toward the production of agro-export commodities, highly concentrated in increasingly large landholdings. Any adjustment away from this traditional pattern of agriculture in order to improve food self-sufficiency and the lives of the peasantry would require profound change in the political, economic, and social structures of the society. In Nicaragua, the Revolution of 1979 provided the opportunity for such a profound change.

In this chapter I provide a survey of various Nicaraguan government programs and policies that have affected food supply and highlight the conflicts and contradictions that determined their evolution between 1979 and 1986. After a brief discussion of the agricultural legacy of Somoza, I present an overview of the initial debates and discussion that framed the orientation of economic policy in general and food policy in particular. The third section discusses the revolutionary government's programs designed to increase the production of basic grains. These programs include land redistribution, increased allocation of credit and production inputs to the peasantry, investments in basic grains production, and higher peasant producer prices. The fourth section examines policies created to ensure the entire country access to food. These include efforts to restructure the marketing system, price subsidization policies, and policies designed to redistribute income to increase the buying power of the poor.

In 1985 the government began to transform its food policies significantly, reflecting an overall policy shift toward a "survival economy" and the prioritization of production and defense, in the face of tremendous economic hardships and the contra war. The policy changes also reflected the government's willingness to address some of the inadequacies and contradictions inherent in some of its original policies and its efforts to adapt to changing conditions. In my discussion of each policy, I shall examine such contradictions and assess the government's response to them. In the final section I shall evaluate the overall impact of such policies by examining their effects on the consumption and nutrition levels of the Nicaraguan population.

Prerevolutionary Agricultural Development

It is becoming increasingly clear that the problems of malnutrition in Central America are directly linked to the phenomenon of land scarcity. It has been argued that land scarcity in the region is not primarily the result of a high rate of population growth, but instead of increasing land concentration.[4] This concentration occurred in two major phases -- during the late 1800s and after the Great Depression of the 1930s -- each fueled by the expansion of export crops, coffee, and bananas in the first phase, and sugar, cotton, and beef in the second. During the 1870s Nicaragua, like its neighbors, began to develop an economy based on export agriculture. This initiated the progressive separation of peasants from their land. Coffee production was introduced into the Pacific coastal highlands, and an emerging coffee elite, with the consent and, in some cases, assistance of the government, brought pressure to bear on small farmers in order to consolidate the land into larger holdings.[5]

Under the Somoza dynasty (1936-1979), Nicaragua continued to follow the agro-export development model. Stagnant world demand for coffee and bananas during the Depression and World War II necessitated the search for new export crops. In the 1950s, responding to increases in the world demand and market price for cotton, and as a result of the availability of pesticides after World War II, a tremendous expansion in cotton cultivation occurred in Nicaragua, seemingly overnight. Large plantations displaced thousands of peasants from the fertile flatlands of the Pacific region.

When the price of cotton declined sharply in the mid-1960s, investments were diverted into cattle raising for the export of beef, since a market for processed meats and fast foods was developing in the United States.[6] The amount of land dedicated to pasture doubled between 1960 and 1975, and many peasants lost the land on which they could produce basic foods or were pushed off onto marginal, unproductive lands.[7] Although beef production was expanding at a rapid rate, per capita domestic consumption was declining because of the increasing amount of beef being exported. Between 1964 and 1974, per capita beef consumption dropped 12.5 percent, a painful drop for a country already suffering from protein deficiency.[8]

The large commercial producers were able to make higher profits by producing export crops than were the peasants, who were producing for the restricted internal market; thus, increasing numbers of peasants were bought off their lands. Many were also simply forced off, since the political power of the large producers made it easy to incorporate peasant lands into their operations and to restrict peasants' property rights. Despite the fact that a land reform program was launched in 1964, partially in response to encouragement from the Alliance for Progress, from 1960 to 1976 coffee production increased by 148 percent, sugarcane by 249 percent, cotton by 282 percent and beef by 268 percent. During this same period, total production of corn, beans, and sorghum increased by only about 60 percent and the average yields of these staple foods showed practically no increase at all during the 1960s and 1970s.[9] In the few instances when prime lands were planted in basic food crops, it was to produce corn and sorghum to feed cattle destined for the U.S. hamburger market.[10]

Brockett has argued that the socioeconomic structure within which government policies are implemented substantially determines their effect. In prerevolutionary Nicaragua, with many of the larger export producers being either Somoza associates or family members, state economic policy interventions were designed to encourage export production.

The prerevolutionary economic situation, which was based on export cultivation, led to changes in the socioeconomic base of the country. The government implemented policies of credit, services, and infrastructure for roads and transport, electricity, technical assistance and education, agro-industrial development, etc., with the goal of providing incentives to the large producer and of intensifying agro-export production.[11]

The concentration of credit in exports is illustrated by the statistics for 1976, which show that coffee, cotton, and sugarcane, all controlled by large landowners, received 90 percent of agricultural credit, leaving the meager remainder for basic grains production.[12] In addition, the willingness of the United States, Nicaragua's primary source of financing, to provide dollars was generally tied to an agreement to use such finances for agro-export production, rather than for social programs or domestic consumption.

Adherence to an agro-export development model resulted in a series of structural difficulties for the Nicaraguan economy. It defined Nicaragua's role in the world economy as a dependent one: it was vulnerable to international market fluctuations in the prices for its primary exports and dependent on external sources of financing for export production. Furthermore, the expansion of export production had serious repercussions for the poor. As stated by the Nicaraguan Food Program, "fluctuations in international market prices affected the amount of foreign exchange received for exports, which had serious repercussions in the workers' salary and national income, while food production for domestic consumption showed alarming deficits and dependency on food imports was increasing."[13] Estimates indicate that in 1978, 70 percent of the agricultural economically active population (EAP) earned less than needed to meet minimum subsistence requirements.[14] The United Nations Economic Commission for Latin America (UNECLA) stated that 62.5 percent of the prerevolutionary Nicaraguan population lived in a state of critical poverty and that the poorest 50 percent of the population received only 16 percent of total income.[15]

Uneven performance in staples production and the subsequent dependence on food imports also had important nutritional consequences. A 1976 USAID study indicated that 42 percent of children under the age of four suffered from first-degree malnutrition[16] and that 57 percent of the rural population suffered from some degree of malnutrition.[17] A study conducted by the Food and Agriculture Organization of the United Nations (FAO) showed that the bottom 50 percent of the income strata consumed only about one-fourth of the animal protein that was consumed by the top 5 percent, reflecting the inequalities in the distribution of wealth.[18]

In sum, although the agro-export development model may have resulted in rapid economic growth and increased Nicaragua's integration into world markets, it had also created the conditions for a broad-based alliance against the regime by having favored only a select few at the expense of the majority of Nicaragua's population. By promising radical structural reforms in the food and agricultural sectors to alter this historical social inequality, the Sandinistas were able to rely on the support of the agrarian population during and after the Revolution.

Initial Debates over Agricultural Policy

The fundamental goal of the revolutionary government was to reorient the economy to satisfy the basic needs of the majority. One member of the early Planning Ministry staff characterized the Nicaraguan "difference" as follows:

> Our strategy differs from other models of economic development whose first priority is to establish a model of accumulation. Our first objective is to satisfy the basic needs of the majority of the population. This creates a new logic, which we call the "logic of the majority," that is to say, the logic of the poor. Instead of organizing the economy from the perspective and interest of the top 5 percent, as was done during the Somoza dynasty, we are trying to organize the economy from the perspective of the majority.[19]

Before the Revolution, capital had free rein, but now the state intended to assume leadership in the new economy in order to change the political balance between landlord and peasant and between capital and labor. It was committed to redistributing resources and raising the standard of living of the poor.[20] The state expanded rapidly after the Revolution with the intention of shifting the economy away from traditional agro-exports to a more dynamic, nationally integrated development program and of encouraging rapid and sustained economic growth.[21] However, reactivation of agro-export production would be necessary for generating the foreign exchange needed for investment in the new social programs directed at poor peasants, landless workers, and urban unemployed in the form of land, credit, education, health care, and rent reductions. In addition, since a domestic capital-goods industry was for the most part nonexistent, foreign exchange generated by agro-exports would provide for essential intermediate and capital goods needed for agricultural, industrial, commercial, and infrastructural development.[22] Thus, the new government recognized that for immediate economic recovery, it would be crucial to reactivate and maintain this agro-export production, regardless of the ownership of this sector.

Within this context, the government chose a "mixed economy" approach in which various forms of property would coexist and in which the new state sector and the cooperative sectors would work with the private agricultural sector, that is, the traditional export producers. It would simultaneously maintain the "basic needs" approach. The state would regulate the allocation of resources in line with its political orientation toward satisfying the basic needs of the "popular sectors." Many in the government argued that combining the two approaches would condition government policies toward addressing basic needs, including food policies, in that, with limited resources to direct to both sectors of agriculture, the government's options for alleviating the food problem and reorienting the economy toward production for the internal market would be constrained.

Food policy options were also limited by the urgency of increasing the food supply. The liberation struggle itself had worsened an already desperate food situation. The "final offensive" in 1979 happened to coincide with the period when fields should have been prepared for planting corn, beans, and other staple foods; and food production was forecast to plummet 40 percent following the victory.[23]   In addition, government programs had increased the demand for food by increasing purchasing power through policies that resulted in more jobs, higher wages, easier access to credit for the campesinos, and lower rents for land and urban housing, as discussed below. The government's initial reaction was to import basic grains, but many argued that such a strategy could leave the country vulnerable to pressures from external agents, reflecting yet another constraint on economic policy in general and food policy specifically.

Thus, the debate began between those in the new government advocating a "food first" or self-sufficiency approach and those concerned with maintaining agro-exports to generate much-needed foreign exchange. However, when, in 1981, the Reagan administration abruptly canceled a $9.8 million loan to import wheat from the United States, it was decided that achieving food self-sufficiency would be made a top national priority.[24]   However, the new government did not eliminate the goal of maintaining agro-export production, as it recognized that many export products (cotton, sugar, beef) were vital not only for generating foreign exchange but also for providing basic raw materials or food products consumed internally.[25]

Self-sufficiency in basic grains was the cornerstone of the new national food program (PAN), which was inaugurated in 1981. As the initial PAN declaration maintained, the new strategy would be aimed at "achieving food security for the Nicaraguan people through self-sufficiency in basic grains and the creation of a distribution and commercialization system based on the interests and participation of the masses."[26] As stated in a more recent PAN document,

> Such a strategy was implemented to confront problems of hunger, malnutrition, and poverty and to assure everyone access to an adequate diet. It was designed to attack the causes of these problems in all aspects of the food system. In doing so, such a strategy implies profound structural changes, which would call for a new orientation in agriculture toward basic grains production for domestic consumption, a new marketing system to assure just distribution and redistribution of national income to increase consumption levels of the popular sectors.[27]

To confront the problems of hunger and malnutrition, the government would have to address the historical and structural economic problems in the production, distribution, and consumption sides simultaneously, despite the constraints of an export-dependent economy.

Increasing Food Production

The initial concern of the revolutionary government was to increase production; therefore, its main task was to motivate and support small farmers, traditionally the principal suppliers of the nation's staple foods. This involved dramatic changes in the production structure, through the redistribution of land in an agrarian reform, as well as new pricing and credit policies. As PAN's Five-Year Plan stated, the government was attempting to "maximize the utilization of available land for basic grain production, using incentives such as credit and guaranteed producer prices for peasant producers as well as for state and private farms."[28]

The Agrarian Reform Laws and Titling Programs.   Since the historical pattern of land concentration centered on the growth of export crops and cattle, one of the new government's first major efforts was to deconcentrate and redistribute some of this land.   Within twenty-four hours of the revolutionary takeover, Decree No. 3 confiscated all property belonging to Somoza and his closest associates, an act that gave the government control of 20 percent of the country's agricultural land[29] and 25 percent of economic production.[30]   Much of this land was reorganized as state farms due to a reluctance to disrupt the essential agro-export production, which had traditionally taken place on these lands, by dividing it and turning it over to individual farmers.[31] However, approximately one-fifth of this land was to be redistributed to small-holding or landless peasants.[32]

Although the first phase of the agrarian reform transformed social relations for a segment of the labor force by bringing a significant portion of the agro-export economy into state hands, the remainder of the landless work force and peasants were unaffected by the policy. In addition, the consolidation of the state sector had no effect on food production for domestic consumption because the state farms were primarily export-oriented enterprises.[33]   Pressure from the ATC, the Rural Workers' Association, and from peasants began to mount for jobs, state services, credit, legal titles, and access to land. The government felt constrained by its alliance to the private sector and its commitment to private property and the mixed economy. In 1980, the state began to debate the question of a new agrarian reform law, a discussion that brought out disagreements over the role of the private sector and private property, over the "path" toward socialism in the mixed economy, and about the type of production units that would be created through the reform -- individual small farms or cooperatives.[34]

A series of land invasions and growing momentum for an expanded agrarian reform program encouraged government officials to pass the New Agrarian Reform Law in August of 1981, a second, larger step in the land redistribution process. This new law allowed the government to confiscate property in the event of prolonged abandonment, nonproduction, or decapitalization, or land which was underused or idle. However, the law affected only plots that were larger than 500 <u>manzanas</u> in the Pacific coastal region and 1,000 <u>manzanas</u> in the interior region.[35] This law was consistent with the government commitment to economic recovery through the mixed economy. However, it did constitute a structural change by eliminating the previous option of private owners to withhold their property from productive use.[36] As of November 1983, over 436 farms had been expropriated under the new law. Of these, over 63 percent had failed to exploit the land efficiently. Of the land redistributed, 79 percent went to production cooperatives and the remaining 21 percent to individual titles.[37]

The government recognized that a variety of land tenure patterns, from production cooperatives to state farms, was inevitable because the historical process of social differentiation, induced by agro-export development, had created a highly heterogeneous rural social structure.[38] Due to the difficulties of incorporating the highly dispersed group of small producers of basic grains into the agrarian reform process and of providing them technical and financial assistance, the government encouraged the formation of production or service cooperatives. In September 1981 it issued Decree No. 826, the Agricultural Cooperatives Law, which provided the institutional framework for organizing and operating cooperatives and established the individual rights of members.[39]

Simultaneous with the increase in cooperative formation, the UNAG, the National Union of Farmers and Ranchers, which had also formed in 1981, was arguing in favor of allowing individual titles to be given to the small basic grains producers. Many of these producers were squatters on public domain lands who were pushing for secure title to the land that they had worked for years. Insecure land tenure had prevented many of them from making longer-term investments in basic grains production, causing them to produce solely for subsistence rather than for the domestic market. In an effort to provide incentives to encourage their production and participation in the food strategy, in 1982 the MIDINRA, the Ministry of Agricultural Development and Agrarian Reform, began a program to distribute secure land titles to these settlers. During 1983, 300,000 <u>manzanas</u> were titled through this program. Some have argued that the government's need to maintain the support of UNAG became particularly crucial during 1983-84, given the upcoming elections and increasing level of <u>contra</u> activity.[40]

In 1983 an acceleration of the agrarian reform began to transform the quality and quantity of land available to basic grains producers. Most of the land titles were in the fertile Pacific coastal region.[41] This policy was made possible by MIDINRA's efforts to shift livestock production, which traditionally occupied these fertile lands, to more appropriate, traditionally-unused lands in the central highlands and frontier regions, in order to bring the Pacific coastal areas back into basic grain cultivation.[42] However, pressures from the war in frontier areas and slaughtering of herds by the contras were major obstacles to the government's attempts to move more cattle out of the Pacific lands. Thus, the contra war increased the tensions over land used to grow export crops or for food production.

Despite the implementation of a stricter Agrarian Reform Law in 1981, the majority of land and productive capability still remained in private hands. In 1984, private producers still accounted for about two-thirds of the production of cotton, coffee, and beef; and private farmers controlled 70 percent of all agricultural land.[43] As long as private owners continued to operate efficiently, maintain investment, and obey labor, health, and other laws, they could keep their businesses forever. In spite of this, much of the private sector viewed the new laws as evidence of government hostility. Larger private commercial farmers continued to be important producers of rice, sorghum, and cottonseed for the domestic food economy, but their diminished political influence created a negative investment climate and tensions began to rise.

Difficulties with the large commercial producers were not the only conflicts generated by the agrarian reform policies. Conflict also arose over the emphasis on cooperatives as the form of production organization. Until 1985, with some exceptions, forming a cooperative had been a condition for receiving land; however, many basic grains producers were unaccustomed to this form of production, and thus were untouched by the reform.[44] Second, during the first three years of the agrarian reform, well over two-thirds of the expropriated land was taken over by the state, a fact that was used by the contras as propaganda. In addition, at the end of 1985, there were still 105,000 families with little or no land in Nicaragua. Half of these landless were concentrated in Region IV, the Pacific region, especially near Masaya. In 1985, this region also had 30,000 minifundistas with plots too small to support themselves. Furthermore, the contra war and the "empty border" policy increased the number of landless peasants and farmers. The government's ability to respond to the needs of the landless was limited by the fact that, under the 1981 Agrarian Reform Law, only 11 percent of cultivated land in the country fell into the category for potential expropriation.[45] As a result of such conditions, in May 1985 peasants in Masaya began demonstrations demanding land, and a private farm was seized. In other parts of the country, similar actions were being planned. The government had to respond.

Because of increasing pressures from the contra war and the government's need to maintain support of the individual peasants who did not wish to form cooperatives, particularly in the war zones, the Sandinistas began in 1985 to transform their agrarian reform policy significantly, in order to address some of the inadequacies of the previous policy. The 1985 Agrarian Reform Plan provided that 60 percent of the new land to be redistributed would go to cooperatives and 6 percent to individual families. However, almost half the land actually distributed was given to 5,636 individual farmers, three times as many as had received land in the period from 1981 to 1984.[46] In addition, 95 percent of the expropriated land went to cooperatives and to small and medium individual producers, and only 5 percent to the state sector, indicating another shift in the distribution pattern.[47] Another interesting trend was that 60 percent of the land distributed in 1985 came from the state sector and 40 percent from negotiated sales and expropriations.[48] Apparently, in 1985 the size of the state sector in agriculture decreased.

What appeared to be a new, third phase of the agrarian reform was formalized on January 11, 1986, when a third Agrarian Reform Law was announced. It removed the 1981 limits on land subject to expropriation and authorized the expropriation of land for "public use or social interest." The new revision made it much easier to redistribute land where it was most needed. As a result of the 1986 reform, the number of small private producers, who generally produce basic grains, increased dramatically, a development that policy-makers predicted would have a positive effect on domestic food production and would alleviate food shortages. Despite these optimistic predictions, however, other policy--makers remained uncertain as to what the actual effect would be. Although the inclination of these farmers may be to cultivate basic grains for domestic consumption, which would ease the food shortages, some officials have voiced concern that this would lead to a decline in production of export crops, which would hurt foreign exchange earnings. There was also concern that the new land distribution would increase the process of "campesinización," the tendency for peasant farmers to farm their own land year-round, leaving the large state and private export farms without seasonal laborers. In contrast, others argued that peasants might abandon basic grain production in favor of export crops once they recognized that the latter were more profitable, thereby lessening the reform's ability to eliminate food shortages. Apparently, the debate over the agrarian reform was as lively in 1986 as it had been during the initial years of the Revolution.

Price Support Policies and Intervention in Rural Markets. As Timmer has pointed out, Latin American governments have often resorted to depressing food prices to placate urban consumers, usually considered the most politically important group, and to maintain industrial profits and growth by keeping urban wages lower.[49]   Such price freezing often comes at the expense of the basic-foods producers and, thus, of long-term food productivity.[50]   During the Somoza period, the government developed INCEI, the Nicaraguan Institute for Foreign and Domestic Trade, for the specific purpose of holding down the prices of basic foods by releasing large quantities of stored grains as domestic prices began to rise.   By restraining price increases in the staples sector, the state forced the economically disadvantaged peasant producers to subsidize the rest of the economy or to join the harvest labor force in the agro-export sector in order to supplement their incomes.[51]   Therefore, the historical inequalities of the marketing system had left the peasants receiving minimum return from their produce and the urban workers barely surviving on minimal wages while the market middlemen prospered.

One of the major objectives of food pricing policy after the Revolution was to eliminate this historical disequilibrium, which had been a disincentive to food production. One of the government's crucial policy instruments to fulfill this objective was guaranteed producer prices, periodically increased, for a variety of basic food products, including basic grains, beans, milk, meat, and sugar. Producer prices would be controlled through ENABAS, the Nicaraguan Basic Foodstuffs Enterprise, an arm of the Ministry of Internal Trade.[52]   Official prices administered through ENABAS increased significantly for the 1981-82 crop year: maize up 66 percent and rice 77 percent.[53]   Between 1981 and mid-1984 the government tripled its guaranteed price for corn and raised the price for beans, Nicaragua's most important staple food, by 78 percent.   Producer prices for sorghum also doubled during this period.[54]   Producers initially proved responsive to these increases, thus validating the effectiveness of pricing policy as an incentive mechanism.   It is important to point out that the government went to great lengths to avoid placing the burden of these producer price increases on the consumer by implementing a consumer subsidy policy, to be discussed below.

There were several difficulties associated with the new pricing policy. First, government guarantees of higher prices for food to small farmers initially contributed to labor shortages in that they provided incentives to individual small farmers to produce on their own land and not be forced to work for agro-exporters.[55]   Second, although price guarantees protected the peasant producers from the traditional price fluctuations and exploitative exchange relations that had historically undermined their income, prices set for corn and other peasant products were unable to keep pace with rising rural consumer prices. Whereas the producer price for corn and beans had increased sevenfold between 1978 and 1984, the price for a pair of rubber boots had increased 28 times and that of a pair of trousers 140 times.[56]   The terms of trade between the countryside and the city were rapidly moving against the former, creating a disincentive to production, particularly of basic foods. In addition, many peasant farmers found it cheaper to buy their food at the government-subsidized consumer prices (to be discussed below) than to produce it, resulting in an even greater decline in food production.[57]

Schejtman has argued that one of the primary reasons for the contradictions in producer pricing policy has been that the Nicaraguan government often tended to treat diverse forms of production -- peasant, capitalist, cooperative, and state -- as one, and, in doing so, found it difficult to design policies specifically adapted to the logic of peasant production.[58] Pricing policy was generalized to suit a variety of agricultural sectors, despite the fact that each had a different production logic which would condition the potential effectiveness of the policy. A 1986 survey of 1,000 peasants indicated that the main demand of the peasant producers was for access to basic consumer goods at affordable prices, rather than for higher producer prices. The study also indicated that these peasants calculated the increases in producer prices only in terms of relative changes in input and consumer prices.[59] The government would have to address these considerations as well.

Another contradiction that resulted from the producer pricing policy and state intervention in rural markets was that rural marketing structures became increasingly disarticulated. Price controls displaced merchants from commercial activities in rural areas, and the state was often unable to fill the gap immediately in performing the functions that these agents had performed, thereby restricting access to the food that was being produced. In many cases, an individual merchant not only had bought the peasants' produce, but also had provided loans to the small producers and sold them production inputs and consumer goods, in many cases, on credit. State attempts to replace these functions often decentralized them among numerous state institutions. This division of functions necessitated extra trips for the peasant producer and often a loss of time in having to deal with different bureaucratic agencies. As Peter Utting notes, the time lag between the disarticulation of old structures and the consolidation of new ones to replace them reflected a much broader problem associated with the transition process in general and one that the planning process needs to deal with more effectively.[60]

In addition, due to the dispersion throughout the country of the large number of small-scale basic grains producers, the government lacked the personnel and technical capacity to control the basic grains market completely. With an expanding black market, resulting from the widening gap between supply and demand, many producers found government prices less appealing than those of the parallel or black markets, and thus the amount of basic grains that ENABAS controlled was decreasing.[61] This phenomenon reflected the difficulty of effectively administering price control policies and in retaining a certain level of market control in the context of a mixed economy where a free market, with potential speculators, influenced policy implementation.

In order to address these contradictions, in mid-1984, in the face of worrisome drops in basic grains production, primarily of corn and beans, significant producer price increases were announced for agricultural and livestock producers. In February 1985, even more dramatic increases in producer prices took effect in an effort to boost food production further; and dollar incentives to producers were introduced. However, the impact of these incentives was considered minimal.[62]

A more significant and successful government policy change occurred in the rural marketing sector when a strong effort was made to address the peasants' demands by supplying rural areas through rural supply centers (the expendios rurales and centros de abastecimiento rural, CARs), which would provide the peasant producer more immediate access to consumer goods at controlled prices.[63] In addition, during the summer of 1986, the government initiated efforts to create empresas territoriales, territorial enterprises, in an attempt to centralize the various bureaucratic functions of buying and selling to fulfill the functions essential to the peasant producers in a more simplified manner.[64] Furthermore, recognizing in 1985 the difficulty of controlling the entire market for corn and beans and capturing the produce of thousands of dispersed small producers, the government deregulated the commercialization of basic grains. By allowing "honest" private merchants to buy the producers' goods, the efficiency of the marketing system improved and provided an important incentive to basic grains producers.

Although this deregulation reduced the government's already-expanding bureaucracy, it also raised concern that peasants would sell more of their produce to the parallel market. In an attempt to deal with this problem, the government made an effort during 1986 to design agreements with peasant producers by which they would sell a certain portion of their crop to ENABAS at official prices in return for guaranteed production inputs and supplies.[65] Thus it was apparent that in 1986 the state was adjusting its rural marketing and pricing policies in an attempt to resolve some of the initial contradictions. However, problems with bottlenecks, bureaucratic inefficiency and delays, and increasing sales to the parallel market were still creating difficulties, demonstrating that much remained to be done.

Credit Allocation. It is often argued that redistribution of land, without a simultaneous redirection of investment and other resources, particularly credit, to help the small producer, is an insufficient policy for addressing the needs of the peasantry. As James Austin points out, "Access to credit is the key to other inputs."[66] In fact, many would maintain that the agrarian reforms of Bolivia, Peru and Mexico all failed because these reforms were limited strictly to land redistribution. The revolutionary government of Nicaragua took its agrarian reform a step farther. Prior to the Revolution, the private agro-export sector in Nicaragua controlled the provision of agri-production inputs, including credit, fertilizer, seed, and technological assistance. Large export producers received over 85 percent of the loans made by the financial system to the agri-sector from 1968 to 1979.[67] Staple crops produced for the internal market received less than 10 percent of agricultural credit in 1970, despite their being grown on over half the agricultural land. For the bulk of the small producers, whose primary crop was maize, credit remained virtually nonexistent before the Revolution.[68] By consolidating the Sistema Financiero Nacional (SFN) in 1979, the revolutionary state broke the power of the traditional economic groups and gained control over some of the essential tools necessary to transform the economy. By controlling the allocation of finance, determining investment priorities, and restructuring credit, the government was able to rupture the bond between the agro-export elites and the financial infrastructure, allowing for a "democratization of credit."[69]

Control of the SFN enabled the government to assume direct control over internal distribution of credit and the allocation of financial resources to both public and private sectors and to direct these resources in accordance with the new political orientation and the basic needs-/mixed economy approach. Nationalizing the banks gave the government complete control of the formal credit channels, so production loans were the principal instrument used initially to stimulate basic grains production. Therefore, the Nicaraguan government was able to target the production of basic foods as a priority area, because over 90 percent of production is by small producers.[70] Small-sized and medium-sized individual producers, as well as cooperative members previously excluded from access to credit, were now incorporated into the financial system.

Reflecting the government's new priority of foodstuff production, 313 percent more area planted in basic grains was financed during the 1980-81 cycle than in the 1977-78 cycle. Peasant producers with holdings under thirty-six manzanas or in production cooperatives accounted for 92 percent of that acreage.[71] Loans to small farmers multiplied sevenfold between 1979 and 1980,[72] and by 1981, 51 percent of corn farmers received credit as compared to 27 percent in 1978-79.[73] The total amount of credit allocated to the countryside in 1980 was $70 million.[74] Not only was credit more available, but credit terms were more flexible. In an effort to benefit the basic grains sector, small farmers were charged 13 percent; to encourage collectivization, cooperatives received the most favorable interest rate, 8 percent, much lower than the 20 percent rate of inflation.[75]

This policy of "spilling of credit into the countryside" was criticized in its early stages for its lack of focus and its inefficiency, since, because of limited access to other inputs, production did not increase proportionately.[76] Low production levels, exacerbated by the 1982 floods and drought, led to problems with repayment, as small farmers' debts reached massive proportions in 1983.[77] As a result, the government agreed to waive the debts of 38,000 small farmers, totaling 350 million Córdobas in 1983.[78] Nonetheless, despite the subsequent leveling off of lending after 1983, in 1984, small and medium independent farmers and cooperative members obtained sufficient bank credit to plant 632,900 acres of corn, beans, and other staple crops, a figure that contrasts sharply with a peak of 34,000 acres before the Revolution.[79]

With control of the financial system, the revolutionary government was also able to determine the direction of investments. Immediately following the insurrection, the quality of most land devoted to basic grains was low, since the peasant producers had been pushed from the more fertile lands by export production and since there was little irrigation or fertilization. Although efforts would be made to transfer food production to more fertile lands, the government also decided to make significant investments in irrigation and fertilizers. It developed the Plan Contingente de Granos Básicos, the Emergency Grain Plan, a capital- and technology-intensive effort to raise basic grains production on large state farms. Although partially successful, the program's high suscep- tibility to technical failure and its high import needs made it somewhat inappropriate.[80] As a result, in 1986 the state began directing their efforts at modernizing peasant production with the hope that increased irrigation would remove the small farmer's vulnerability to unfortunate weather conditions and allow for year-round production and more crop cycles.[81]

Furthermore, the historical development of agro-export production had pushed Nicaragua's peasants off the Pacific coastal plains into the interior highlands. This shifted much of the country's food cultivation to areas where roads were poor or nonexistent. Delivery of inputs for food production and transportation of the food to market was therefore difficult and costly. To alleviate this problem, the revolutionary govern- ment began diverting some of its investment to road construction to these areas. In addition, efforts were made to supply credit to the small staples producers in the form of inputs such as seeds, tools, and fer- tilizers. Furthermore, the government set up training programs for improved farming, storing, and transport techniques to increase yields and decrease losses from spoilage.[82]

According to some analysts, redirection of financial policy toward the peasant basic grains sector has been relatively effective in increasing food production. In one study by CIERA, the Agrarian Reform Research Center, a significant percentage of peasants interviewed for the study reported increases in production and attributed the increase to improved access to credit and inputs, as well as to land.[83] However, in 1986 there was increasing tension with the private sector due to these policies, aggravated further by growing economic pressures. For instance, the private agro-export producers complained that concentration of credit and investment in basic grains production left little for export production and thus inhibited their ability to produce. However, the government sub- sidized export production, as it did basic grains, by keeping interest rates for commercial growers at 17 percent, still below inflation.[84]

Furthermore, to reduce the private sector's need to risk substantial amounts of its own capital, the February 1985 stabilization plan gave credit advances covering 100 percent of cotton producers' production costs and 80 percent of the expenses for coffee and sugar cultivation.[85] Indeed, although the share of the financed area planted for domestic consumption had risen to 47 percent by 1982, as compared to 33 percent in 1977, the government still showed a willingness to continue financing export production as well.[86]   However, with increasing financial constraints and efforts to curb the fiscal deficit brought to bear by a worsening economic situation, the amount of money available for investments and credit will be limited, and, thus, the competition between both sectors will continue, at least for the near future.

Production Results.   The government's new policies initially had positive results in production in the staples sector.   The greatest success was in rice production, which increased by 93 percent between 1977 and 1982, allowing the country to achieve self-sufficiency by 1983.[87]   Concentrated primarily on large state and private farms, this increase is more a reflection of the increasing investment in irrigation and fertilizers than of the policies of the agrarian reform.   Bean production rose 50 percent during the same period;[88] and although output levels for other staple crops began to decline in the 1983-84 harvest, bean production grew steadily.[89]

However, basic grains production often failed to live up to expectations, for, as Minister of Agriculture Jaime Wheelock noted in 1983, Nicaragua was investing ten times as much in the production of basic grains as it did in the prerevolutionary period but only attaining an overall 50 percent increase in staples output.[90]   Corn production, in particular, was a disappointment because, although growth rates were positive during the 1980-81 harvest, corn still lagged far behind other staples.   Furthermore, the 1982 floods caused output to fall below pre-1977 levels.[91]   Given the importance of corn in the Nicaraguan diet, this decline presented planners with a serious disappointment.

In sum, initial increases in staples production reduced some of the deficit in basic grains production, virtually eliminating the need to import rice and beans by 1981.   The problems with corn production, however, necessitated increased corn imports in 1982, thus keeping food self-sufficiency out of reach.   Furthermore, production levels for all products declined in 1985.   The combination of the war, the foreign exchange crisis, and the disequilibrium created by some of the government's own policies was taking its toll.   At the time of this writing, it was too early to determine what effect the 1985 and 1986 policy changes would have on the 1986 production cycle.

Production of export crops increased much less than staple foods. By 1981, most exports had returned to 1977 levels, but cotton production, an important foreign exchange generator, fell dramatically in 1982, barely reaching half the 1977 levels.[92]   Government replacement of cotton with staples production and the increasing hostility of the cotton growers (due to increasing expropriations, government controls on exports and needed imports, and uncertainty about the security of their land) may have been factors leading to this decrease in production. However, contrary to the claims of the private export sector, the revolutionary government of Nicaragua has not tried to socialize the entire productive process or to eliminate private capital. On the contrary, it has offered guarantees to the private sector with respect to private property and has urged private enterprise to play an important role in the reactivation and development of the economy.[93] As Joseph Thome has argued, agrarian reform in Nicaragua has been characterized by the maintenance of a strong capitalist private sector within the political and ideological context of socialist goals.[94]

Data from MIDINRA indicate that the private sector's share of staples -- beans, rice, corn, and sorghum -- remained over 60 percent in 1982, and that of export products -- cotton, coffee, and sugar -- over 70 percent.[95] The government agreed to put up the working capital through plentiful credit, to guarantee minimum prices at which private producers could make a profit, and to absorb any sudden drop in international market prices in order to leave producers free to use their money to make further investments in production.[96] In 1981, a World Bank study found sufficient guarantees to conclude that the Nicaraguan government had constructed a "framework wherein the private sector can satisfactorily operate."[97]

To summarize, various factors influenced the development of agrarian policies in Nicaragua between 1979 and 1986, including electoral politics, the counterrevolutionary threat, structural contradictions resulting from the new policies, and the balance of payments crisis. The revolutionary government's response to these tensions was to try to increase the production of both exports and basic foods and to utilize both public and private enterprise. The evolution of the land redistribution during this period exemplified the difficulties associated with designing and implementing policies to encourage production among such a heterogeneous and dispersed rural population as exists in Nicaragua.[98] The emphasis on cooperative formation and state acquisition of expropriated lands during the first three years of the agrarian reform had to be reconsidered in the face of resulting contradictions and conflicts with these various sectors. In addition, the exigencies of an export-based economy forced policy-- makers to be sensitive to the needs of the private agro-export sector while designing and implementing policies to benefit the peasant producers. As Thome argues, the ability of the government to rethink and adjust its agrarian policies during the first seven years illustrates its ability to subsume ideological goals in favor of "political pragmatism, economic reality and result-oriented policies."[99] However, it was apparent in 1986 that the government would be forced to continue demonstrating such flexibility and ingenuity in dealing with the aforementioned tensions and contradictions and in finding the most appropriate means of balancing the needs of the two agricultural sectors.

Increasing Food Consumption through Improved Distribution

Lappé and Collins suggest that food self-sufficiency means more than eliminating food imports by increasing local production; it also means ensuring every member of society an adequate diet.[100]   Brockett agrees that expansion of food production will not necessarily lead to improved nutrition for the poorest people, since increased consumption is a function of income as well as of production.[101]   As Collins insightfully pointed out, even if Nicaragua achieved food self-sufficiency by increasing food production, it could still fail to eliminate hunger if food itself were either economically or physically out of the reach of the poor.[102]   And as the National Food Program's Five-Year Plan states, "PAN's efforts must extend beyond production. It must work with the entire food chain to assure that products will reach consumers."[103]

The Nicaraguan government has also addressed the consumption side of the food problem by developing mechanisms to ensure the population's access to adequate food supplies. These policies were designed to more equitable distribution of food and to increase the purchasing power of the poor.

Establishing Control over the Marketing of Basic Foods. Prior to the Revolution, intermediaries controlled credit, transportation, and storage facilities and thereby captured an estimated 89 percent of the price paid by the consumer.[104] The state trading agency under Somoza, INCEI, rarely purchased large quantities of national production and its infrastructural organization was ineffective and disorganized.[105]   Immediately after the overthrow of Somoza, the state decided to play a greater role in managing the commodity flows of staples in the markets through control over imports, procurement, wholesaling, and retailing, in order to guarantee that everyone in the country would have physical access to essential foods. To reach such goals, the government made ENABAS responsible for carrying out the new marketing strategy in line with the government's policy orientation toward basic needs.

First, ENABAS controlled Nicaragua's international trade in basic grains. By controlling the allocation of foreign exchange and the import-export sector, the government was able to decide which goods would continue to be imported and which would be excluded during the period of economic crisis and decreasing foreign exchange. The pattern of imports reflected the general consumption policies of the government, those oriented toward basic foods and raw materials required by the food industry.   Between 1978 and 1981, the value of basic food imports rose 450 percent, making up 13.2 percent of total imports. Among all food products imported, basic food began to receive strict priority, with its share reaching 84.4 percent of the total in 1982.[106] However, Nicaragua's trade deficit was increasing at an average annual rate of $427 million between 1980 and 1984, resulting in increasing external debt and a debt service ratio that reached 32 percent in 1981.[107] Furthermore, in an attempt to increase domestic production, the government began large investment projects, particularly in agricultural production, infrastructure, and energy. This policy move created competition for foreign exchange between food products for consumption and capital goods needed for investment. In addition, in 1981 concern was increasing over dependency on the external market, primarily the United States, for these basic food imports. As a result of these problems, food imports declined by 50 percent in 1982.[108] In 1984, with the U.S. mining of Nicaraguan ports, and Nicaragua's vulnerability to external economic pressure and blockade measures becoming more apparent, high priority was given to local food production, and imports were limited by allocation of foreign exchange to inputs and capital goods needed for domestic food production.[109]

On the domestic side, as described above, ENABAS began to buy basic grains directly from producers at official prices in an attempt to increase state regulation and control of essential consumer products. However, over time the state recognized the limits of its ability to collect from the thousands of peasants dispersed throughout the countryside and to organize distribution of basic grains due to its inexperience with storage and transport techniques. It decided it would work through the established network of private merchants instead of expanding the state bureaucracy.[110] This policy shift greatly increased the state's share of basic grains between 1980 and 1983, with its share of corn increasing from 15 percent to 23 percent, that of rice from 23 percent to 81 percent, that of beans from 23 percent to 60 percent, and that of sorghum from 67 percent to 93 percent.[111] However, as mentioned earlier, ENABAS's intervention into the market had displaced many merchants without replacing their functions, resulting in growing disarticulation between the rural and urban markets and difficulty in getting basic food to certain areas of the country where new channels had not been efficiently developed.[112] In 1985, in light of such limitations in the distribution of basic grains, the state further liberalized the marketing of beans and corn in some interior regions of the country. It decided instead to concentrate its efforts on controlling the distribution of manufactured and agro-industrial goods, whose procurement was concentrated in relatively few enterprises and thus more easily controlled.[113] Such decisions highlight the government's willingness to work with the market, not against it, and to operate within the context of a mixed economy.

At the wholesale level, the government hoped to replace the traditional wholesale facility, the Mercado Oriental, with a new state market. However, as the employer of thousands of low-income traders, mostly women, the traditional market continued to flourish. The government did have more success acting as retailer and supplying retail outlets, including the private ones, with goods at wholesale prices that would allow them a sufficient profit margin. ENABAS began by creating a network of state-run people's stores, or tiendas populares, which grew in number to seventy-two in 1982 and to over one hundred by 1984.[114] However, these were often not well-integrated into the community and were not as accessible to or as well liked by the consumers as the private stores. By 1982, it was becoming increasingly apparent that the state could not successfully control a decentralized marketing system. Therefore, ENABAS attempted to develop a working relationship with the existing private shopkeepers, the owners of the pulperías with "good reputations" in their communities, and to transform their stores into expendios populares. By 1983 there were over thirty-seven hundred such expendios, retail outlets run by their owners which provided basic items at the official controlled prices in exchange for a government guarantee of an adequate supply of goods at prices that would ensure a decent profit margin.[115] By 1984, their number had increased to six thousand.[116] Once again, in this instance the government chose to take advantage of the private sector's experience and ability by working with the market, instead of unnecessarily straining the growing bureaucracy.

The government also worked through the traditional private distribution system -- large markets with small-scale vendors -- by creating thirty-six new neighborhood markets, but as mentioned above, the Mercado Oriental still was dominant. The government also took over eleven supermarkets that prior to the Revolution served only middle-class and upper-class consumers and began using them to retail basic foods, instead of solely luxury goods. In 1986, a number of these supermarkets were converted into special supply centers for workers (CATS). In an effort to meet the needs of the productive sector, until 1985, ENABAS supplied basic foodstuffs directly to commissaries set up in workplaces with over thirty workers so that food could be included as part of the workers' "social wage." As Collins points out, one negative side effect of this policy was that, since most of the workers in these workplaces were men, women were made to feel marginalized in not being able to "handle the money."[117]

In 1982, the government's food distribution programs began to suffer from intermittent scarcities of certain foods caused by, for example, bad weather, contra attacks, production difficulties, increasing speculation and hoarding, growing demand, and poor administrative decisions. According to a MICOIN study, in 1982 ten basic products were in short supply, indicating weaknesses in the commercialization system.[118] Between 1980 and 1985, for example, per capita distribution of beans in Region III, the Managua region, declined by 39 percent, and that of corn declined by 33 percent.[119] To handle the shortage of sugar in 1982, the government initiated a rationing system that entitled each family to five pounds of sugar per month. This rationing system was expanded in 1983 to include rice, corn, beans, cooking oil, and a few other nonfood items, an act that initially subjected the government to great criticism.[120]   Although this policy of planned food distribution established family quotas that may have been insufficient to cover household requirements, it nevertheless ensured that the majority of the population would have access to a minimum quantity of some of the most important foods in the local diet at prices that were heavily subsidized until 1985.[121]

In addition, in order to boost civilian morale in the war-torn areas, the government was forced to shift away from the traditional policy of favoring Managua in the distribution of goods, and instead to favor the defense forces and outlying war regions; this shift created even more serious scarcities in Managua. In contrast to the 39 percent drop in per capita consumption of beans in Managua between 1980 and 1985, during the same period, per capita consumption of beans increased by 105 percent in Region I, and by 155 percent in Region V. Furthermore, while Managua's per capita consumption of corn decreased 33 percent during this time period, the national average had increased by 8 percent.[122] Managua, with less than a third of the national population, had been accustomed to consuming more than half the country's food prior to the Revolution;[123] thus, the redirection of government priorities was bound to be met by increasing complaints in the capital. Although giving the countryside consumption priority over the major city is a unique reversal of traditional Latin American policy, discontent in Managua over shortages and long lines may present a future political difficulty for the Revolution. The main opposition parties, the contras, and the Reagan administration have already used the scarcities, as well as inflation, as a major focus of their anti-Sandinista campaign.

As a result of the economic crisis and the increasing scarcity of products, the government made the industrial workers and agricultural producers, in other words, the productive sectors, state employees, and defense a priority. Its distribution policies began to reflect those priorities. In 1985, the workplace commissaries were replaced by Workers' Supply Centers, Centros de Abastecimiento para los Trabajadores (CATs), after an agreement between the Central Sandinista de Trabajadores (CST), the main union of factory workers, and MICOIN. Under this agreement, workers would be given privileged access to basic goods in special supermarkets in the cities in return for a promise from the workers not to resell the goods purchased from these centers. This was an effort to curb the black market sale of goods supplied at commissaries, which was becoming a serious problem.[124]   By the fall of 1986, five of Managua's eight supermarkets were converted into CATs. By removing access to these supermarkets from the nonproductive, informal, sector, the government created a disincentive for that sector in an effort to halt the worrisome increase in informal activity.

Government control of the marketing system has created some tension in the private sector. By 1983, 50 percent of staples were handled by ENABAS, with the private sector playing a decreasing role. The large-scale growers of basic goods disliked having to compete with the fixed low prices of the government.[125] In addition, certain groups of large producers who traditionally had grown enough food to feed their employees now preferred to sell their produce at the higher producer price and buy it back from ENABAS at the lower consumer price to feed their work force, unnecessarily inflating ENABAS's marketing costs.[126] It is important to note that the state also controlled the export marketing sector, representing producers in international negotiations. This resulted in price stabilization and a more predictable return for the export farmers. However, the private sector has accused the state of poor negotiating performance, due to inexperience, and of moderating profits. Although the government guaranteed prices to export producers to ensure them a profit, thus subsidizing any sudden drops in international prices, many exporters preferred to continue taking risks independently in the unstable international market.[127]

Initial Efforts at Price Controls. In order to improve the consumers' ability to purchase basic foods, the government employed three policy instruments: price controls, consumption subsidies, and employment and wage increases. As mentioned above, since the traditional Latin American poor family often spends more than 50 percent of its income on food, yet still fails to obtain adequate nutrition, any slight rise in food prices means a tightening of already constricting belts and disaster for the urban poor.[128] Therefore, the new government of Nicaragua, through MICOIN, concentrated its price control efforts on basic staples: rice, beans, maize, beef, pork, poultry, eggs, cheese, sugar, salt, cooking oil, and coffee.[129] In 1983 a study was conducted by INIES, the Nicaraguan Institute for Social and Economic Research, comparing the rise in the costs of that basic consumer goods basket of twenty-one essential items in the Central American countries between January 1982 and January 1983. According to its findings, Costa Rica registered a 102 percent increase, El Salvador, 24 percent, Guatemala, 20 percent, and Honduras, 29 percent, as compared to an 11 percent increase in Nicaragua.[130]

Controlling prices may be practically impossible in an economy where such a large number of private distributors and marketers, both small and large, operate. As a result, it was very difficult for the state to ensure compliance with the official prices set by the government. It therefore has relied on the communities themselves to organize volunteer inspectors to assist in enforcing the price controls. Hesitant initially to punish price violators harshly, the government planned to buy enough of the basic grains itself directly from the producers through ENABAS (as discussed above) and to store enough of the supply so that it could release enough onto the market at a low, stable price to undercut speculators without resorting to policing.[131] Violations of price controls, hoarding, and speculation increased dramatically after 1982 due to the pressures on the economy from the war and its negative impact on production, which helped create a profitable environment for speculators. Wild rumors of shortages often trigger a vicious circle in which speculators and those who can afford to, buy up goods to sell on the black market and create greater shortages and wilder rumors.

The problem reached crisis proportions in 1984. Amidst a widespread public outcry against such speculation and with the participation of the Sandinista Defense Committees (CDSs), the government decided to ration eight basic goods, including rice, beans, corn, oil, and sugar, under a New Law of Consumer Protection.[132] The difficulty of capturing the entire corn and beans market has already been mentioned. Furthermore, the small producers, particularly of corn, found the government's price insufficient in comparison with inflation. As a result, many peasant farmers chose to engage in other nonproductive activities.[133] In recognition of this policy conflict, the state revised its rationing program in August 1985 by dropping corn from the list of rationed goods.[134] However, the government also increased the number of basic products to be included on the guaranty card system to secure the supply for workers and introduced a series of controls on marketing activities.[135] During the spring of 1986, the government made efforts to enforce these controls by closing down a number of merchants at the Mercado Oriental who were speculating in basic foods. Despite the difficulties in implementing price controls, such a policy nevertheless ensured that essential products sold in the "secure" outlets, that is, the expendios, could be found at a low price.

Price Subsidization. It has been argued that controlling the consumer prices of basic goods, especially food, creates low producer prices, which means low income, for the peasants who produce those goods. Thus, many peasants are discouraged from growing food except for their own families, resulting in a decrease in food production.[136] Timmer similarly maintains that price control policies designed to benefit the urban consumer traditionally operate at the expense of the rural producer, but he goes on to argue in favor of a food policy that entails food consumption interventions that stimulate the poor producer through higher prices, yet still prevent a price squeeze on the urban poor.[137] I have already indicated that the Nicaraguan government's initial goal was to support the basic grains producers with price guarantees to keep up with inflation. However, the government concurrently wanted to maintain the fixed prices of the basic food items in order to aid the consumer. To achieve both ends, it needed a second policy instrument, subsidization.

As the USDA reported, subsidies for corn, beans, rice, sorghum, sugar, and milk averaged 78 percent of the total subsidies between 1980 and 1983, having tripled during that period.[138] In the case of corn, consumers paid less than two-thirds of the price guaranteed to producers in 1982.[139] In 1983, the ratio of producer to consumer prices for beans and rice, the two most important staple foods of the Nicaraguan diet, was 150.0 and 135.6, respectively, reflecting a massive absorption of cost on the part of the government.[140] As production, storage, transportation, and other logistics costs increased, the state's expenditures on food subsidies rose dramatically between 1980 and 1982, accounting for 6 percent of the national budget and over 30 percent of the fiscal deficit in 1982.[141] A study by CIERA estimated the total subsidy for 1980-1982 at over one billion Córdobas ($100 million at the official exchange rate), a huge financial burden for the state in a time of fiscal austerity.[142] Nevertheless, as Spalding concisely argues, "the commitment to increase peasant incomes, stimulate staples production, and stretch the buying power of urban marginals while retarding inflation kept the program growing throughout the 1979-1982 period."[143] By 1984 food subsidies represented 45 percent of total government budgetary transfers and 6.3 percent of government expenditure.[144] However, due to the impact of external aggression on the economy, the pressures on government spending, a large fiscal deficit, the production problems resulting from contradictory effects of producer pricing policies, and increasing specula-tion in and reselling of subsidized produce on the parallel market, the subsidies were reduced, although administrative and operational costs would continue to be subsidized.[145] Prices for rice, maize, beans, sugar, and milk still remained below the government's purchasing prices and handling costs.[146] Due to pressures from the ever-increasing fiscal deficit, food subsidies were even more drastically reduced in February 1985, and it was announced that they would eventually be eliminated.[147] The 1985 economic plan designated 0.7 percent of government expenditure toward food subsidies, a significant decline from 6.3 percent in 1984.[148] The combined effect of these subsidy cuts and increasing prices can be seen in the fact that average prices in 1985 were 600 percent more than in 1984.[149] From May 1984 to May 1985, the price of the basic consumer basket, consisting of twelve essential foods and three nonfood items, had increased 462 percent.[150]

Employment and Wages. A third policy strategy designed to ensure access to food was to increase employment and raise wages in order to provide the poor more purchasing power. During the first year the government succeeded in cutting the unemployment rate by half, down to 17 percent.[151] Unfortunately, it also became the major generator of jobs, swelling the administrative payroll.[152] Despite the inefficiency and inflationary costs of such a policy, the government felt it was essential, given the dislocations of the 1979 war. The government decreed a 125-córdoba-per-month raise for all those earning less than 1,300 córdobas per month, which would benefit almost 40 percent of the urban population. They slashed housing rents, and transportation, education, and medical costs were strongly subsidized, allowing more of a family's income to be used for food.[153]

The increase in purchasing power resulting from these measures increased consumption expectations, putting an even greater strain on food supplies. With effective demand rising and production lagging behind, a serious disequilibrium between supply and demand resulted, stimulating high prices on the black market and encouraging speculation. In 1983 this disequilibrium became more acute, and, combined with the state's inability to control prices, it resulted in increasing inflation and a rising consumer price index throughout the 1983-86 period. Average prices in 1984 were 274.4 percent larger than in 1980. However, the wage increase during the same period was only 187.4 percent.[154]

In the face of a growing economic crisis and the need to cut the budget deficit, the growth of the public sector became fiscally unsustainable and the government was forced to eliminate many jobs, placing an even greater burden on the price controls and subsidies.[155] As a result, when subsidies were eliminated in 1985, consumers' purchasing power was damaged further. Any future increases in producer prices to stimulate production would now be passed on to them as well. In order to ameliorate the impact of the new pricing measures, the government included a massive wage increase among its policy changes and announced the Sistema Nacional de Ordenamiento de Trabajos y Salarios, known as SNOTS. This new system for organizing salaries attempted to peg wages to inflation, thus allowing for periodic salary increases.[156] As a result of three such increases in 1985, the average wage increased 272 percent between 1984 and 1985. After two similar wage increases in early 1986, by May wages were 931 percent above the 1985 average.[157] However, the SNOTS system has not worked as well as hoped, due to problems with incomplete coverage of the work force.[158] And salary increases did not match the rate of inflation. Although, the wage increases between 1985 and May 1986 appear incredibly large, they pale in comparison with the 3737 percent increase in inflation over the same period.[159]

The Impact of Policies on Consumption and Nutrition

As of 1985, few studies had been undertaken that would have facilitated the accurate evaluation of how these policies and policy changes have affected actual consumption levels. However, based on aggregate data, it appeared that national per capita consumption increased significantly between 1980 and 1982, despite considerable population growth during the first years after the Revolution. Consumption of eight of the eleven basic products selected in a CIERA survey in 1982 increased.[160] Per capita consumption of rice increased by over 75 percent between 1977 and 1983, but bean consumption was no higher and corn improved only slightly. In fact, by 1984, corn consumption had fallen below prerevolutionary levels. Further analysis indicated that pork consumption, despite an initial increase after the Revolution, was also below 1975 levels by 1984 and that beef consumption had never recovered to prerevolutionary levels.[161] Although MICOIN argued that these major protein sources had been replaced by increased consumption of eggs and beans by 1982, since 1983 that has not been the case.[162]

Increases in per capita consumption were more restricted in 1983, evidenced by the fact that nine of the eleven goods surveyed during a CIERA study declined or showed no increase.[163] However, as Collins pointed out, "unlike in most countries where per capita food consumption food statistics mark sharp differences between the well-off elites and an impoverished majority, the distribution of basic foods was improving by all accounts." Greater production and more equitable sharing of that production were "the hallmarks of the Sandinista revolution."[164] Despite the reversal of trends for many items in 1983, per capita consumption of eight of the basic products in the CIERA study still exceeded prerevolutionary levels.[165]

It is difficult to make generalizations about how policies to improve the standard of living and increased access to food have affected the various social groups because there are few data disaggregated by class, income, and region. However, it is assumed that the two-thirds of the rural population with access to land, those integrated into the cooperative movement, and those receiving credit and state services probably experienced the greatest relative improvement in consumption.[166] Urban workers who benefited from improved employment opportunities in construction and the state sector probably fared better.[167] With respect to regional differentiation, the cost of a consumer basket of twenty-one basic foods increased less in Managua than in any other region between 1984 and 1985. However, it has been argued that subsidized services to the other regions, which would free up more money for consumption, made up for this discrepancy.[168]

Although consumption data may be useful in making an overall assessment, the clearest indicator of the relative success or failure of a country's food policy is the level of nutrition. Again, precise estimates are not possible due to lack of data disaggregated by class, income, or region and because no national surveys of nutritional status were conducted from the start of the Revolution until August 1986. One can point to the significant drop in infant mortality, from 122 per thousand to 72 per thousand children under the age of one, between 1978 and 1984, as a significant nutrition-related indicator.[169] Although infant mortality rose to 86 per 1,000 in 1985, the level remained significantly lower than the prerevolutionary figure.[170] Overall, per capita caloric intake did not show a significant increase between 1979 and 1984, from 2,273 per day to 2,291 per day.[171] However, in every other Central American country, except for Panama per capita caloric intake dropped over the same period.[172] National averages may, unfortunately, mask nutritional differences among various social groups. For example, a 1982 CIERA survey of ten barrios around Managua revealed an average per capita consumption of 2,007 calories per day, lower than the national average and below recommended levels.[173] Furthermore, rural areas reveal significant differences in nutritional status in comparison to urban areas. A 1982 study of rural Nicaragua by the Nutrition Institute for Central America and Panama (INCAP) revealed that only 43 percent of the population had an adequate diet with respect to calories and that 33 percent consumed less than 75 percent of required calories.[174] A 1982 study by MED, the Ministry of Education, demonstrated that 70 percent of the school children surveyed in Region I showed significant levels of malnutrition.[175] A 1986 CIERA study of nine municipalities in Regions I and II was concerned that protein-caloric intake in both regions was significantly below recommended levels. It also indicated that corn represents the most important source of calories in both regions, thus justifying concern about falling levels of corn supply.[176]

Peter Utting has pointed out that strict nutritional criteria have not played an important part in the definition of food policy. Rather, the government has concentrated its efforts on, and directed its resources toward, the production and distribution of the products that have traditionally made up the local diet.[177] Thus, the main focus of the Nicaraguan Food Program (PAN) during the first six years of the Revolution was on increasing production of the traditional basic foods -- corn, beans, rice, and sorghum. In 1985 PAN began to shift its focus toward evaluating and addressing nutritional concerns, not just production.[178] The first major step in the new five-year nutrition plan, the Plan Quinquenal de Alimentación y Nutrición (PQAN) was taken in August 1986, when a national height-age survey was completed. Although this was only the first in a series of steps required to assess and address the nutritional needs of the population, by determining the most vulnerable areas of the country, it represents a significant advance in the direction of nutritional improvement. Much work remains to be done in this area, however, to evaluate and draw accurate conclusions about the nutritional consequences of Nicaraguan food policy.

Conclusion

Between 1979 and 1986, the revolutionary government of Nicaragua implemented major programs and restructured the production sector in order to stimulate production of basic grains, not only through land redistribution, but also through a restructuring of the country's pricing, investment, and credit policies. Concurrently, the government maintained an environment favorable to the continued production of agro-export goods. Although the "subject" of the new production strategy was clearly defined as the workers and peasants producing basic foods, the private export producers were also invited to cooperate in return for guarantees of profits and security of ownership, "so long as the law was obeyed and activities such as tax evasion, capital flight and speculation were avoided."[179]

It is also apparent in analyzing the evolution of both production and distribution policies between 1979 and 1986 that the government was willing to make significant alterations in its policies as new constraints, contradictions, and conflicts arose. Its willingness to allow the free market to play a larger role in the economy and to increase the amount of property in private, rather than state, hands demonstrates a commitment to a mixed economy and pragmatism in the face of economic pressure, in contrast to the common arguments that the Nicaraguan economy is becoming completely state-run. These new directions often created tensions within the government between those who favored centralized planning and control and those who supported a more decentralized and participatory process. For the moment, however, it appears that the latter group, responding to pressure from the mass organizations, will prevail.[180]

As a final note, it is important to recognize that all attempts by the Nicaraguan government to design and implement necessary food policies, as well as to formulate an appropriate overall development strategy, have been made increasingly difficult by the actions of the United States: its economic blockade, its attempts to close European markets, its efforts to impede the Contadora process, and its continued military aggression and support of the contra war. Estimates indicate that in 1985, 15 percent to 20 percent of the corn and bean production was either destroyed or abandoned as a result of contra attacks.[181] In addition, the U.S financial war has aggravated the foreign exchange crisis, reducing the funds available for allocation to the various agricultural sectors. The availability of foreign aid immediately following the Revolution had enabled the government to distribute funds to "priority areas," including both the food and the private export sectors. However, aid from the bilateral and multilateral lending institutions decreased as a credit blockade was set in motion by the United States. The IDB and the World Bank provided $238.1 million in loans between July 1979 and December 1981; this amount dropped to $92.1 million between 1981 and 1982, and continued to decline.[182] Therefore, despite attempts by the Nicaraguan government to create a viable mixed economy and to feed its people, the future success of this novel approach to development and the ultimate decision on future development strategy may depend significantly on the actions taken by international opposition, actions that are beyond the control of the revolutionary government.

Notes to Chapter 8

1.   For a discussion of the food problem, see William W. Murdoch, The Poverty of Nations: The Political Economy of Hunger and Population (Baltimore: Johns Hopkins University Press, 1980), pp. 98-166;

Alain de Janvry, The Agrarian Question and Reformism in Latin America (Baltimore: Johns Hopkins University Press, 1981), pp. 141-181; and Frances Moore Lappé and Joseph Collins, Food First: The Myth of Scarcity (Boston: Houghton Mifflin, 1977). For a summary of food and agriculture in Central America, see Tom Barry and Deb Preuch, The Central American Fact Book (New York: Grove Press, 1986), pp. 144-162.

2.	John C. Super and Thomas C. Wright, Food, Politics, and Society in Latin America (Lincoln: University of Nebraska Press, 1985), p. xi.

3.	Super and Wright, Food, Politics, and Society, introduction. Lappé and Collins agree that distribution is more important to the welfare of the majority than is the amount of food produced (Lappé and Collins, Food First).

4.	For an interesting discussion of the causes of land scarcity in Central America, particularly in El Salvador and Honduras, see William H. Durham, Scarcity and Survival in Central America: Ecological Origins of the Soccer War (Stanford: Stanford Univeristy Press, 1979).

5.	Carmen Diana Deere and Peter Marchetti, "The Worker-Peasant Alliance in the First Year of the Nicaraguan Agrarian Reform," Latin American Research Review 8, no. 3 (Spring 1981): p. 43.

6.	Charles Brockett, "Malnutrition, Public Policy, and Agrarian Change in Guatemala," Journal of Interamerican Studies and World Affairs 26, no. 4 (November 1984): p. 484. See also Phillip F. Warnken, The Agricultural Development of Nicaragua: An Analysis of the Production Sector (Columbia: Agricultural Experiment Section, University of Missouri, 1975), pp. 16-19.

7.	Deere and Marchetti, "The Worker-Peasant Alliance," p. 44.

8.	Brockett, "Malnutrition, Public Policy," p. 484.

9.	Solon Barraclough, A Preliminary Analysis of the Nicaragua Food System (Geneva: United Nations Research Institute for Social Development, 1982), p. 16.

10.	Joseph Collins, What Difference Could a Revolution Make: Food and Farming in the New Nicaragua (San Francisco: Institute for Food and Development Policy, 1985), p. 108.

11.	Programa Alimentario Nacional (PAN), Plan quinquenal de alimentación y nutrición (Managua: PAN, 1985), p. 1. Unless otherwise noted, all translations are mine.

12.	James Austin, Jonathan Fox, and Walter Kruger, "The Role of the Revolutionary State in the Nicaraguan Food System," World Development 13, no. 1 (January 1985): p. 20.

13.	PAN, Plan quinquenal, p. 1.

14.	Deere and Marchetti, "The Worker-Peasant Alliance," p. 45.

15. Michael E. Conroy, "External Dependence, External Assistance, and Economic Aggression against Nicaragua," Latin American Perspectives, Issue 45, 12, no. 2 (Spring 1985): p. 48.
16. Cited in Collins, What Difference, p. 137.
17. Cited in Centro de Investigación y Estudios de la Reforma Agraria (CIERA), El hambre en los países del Tercer Mundo (Managua: CIERA, 1983), p. 37.
18. Spalding, "Food, Politics," p. 224, n. 12.
19. Xavier Gorostiaga, Dilemas de la revolución popular sandinista a tres años del triunfo (Managua: INIES/CRIES, 1982).
20. John Weeks, The Economies of Central America (New York: Holmes and Meier, 1985), p. 171.
21. Rose Spalding, "State Economic Expansion in Revolutionary Nicaragua" (1984), manuscript, p. 3.
22. E. V. K. FitzGerald, "La economía nacional en 1985: la transición como coyuntura," paper presented at the Annual Congress of Nicaraguan Social Scientists (ANICS), Managua, August 1985. See also idem, "Notes on the Analysis of the Small Underdeveloped Economy in Transition," in Richard R. Fagen, Carmen Diana Deere, and José Luis Corragio, eds., Transition and Development: Problems of Third World Socialism (New York: Monthly Review, 1986).
23. Collins, What Difference, p. 108.
24. Austin, Fox, and Kruger, "The Role of the Revolutionary State," p. 19.
25. United Nations Research Institue for Social Development (UNRISD), "Urbanization and Food System's Development in Nicaragua," in Food Systems and Society: Problems of Food Security in Selected Developing Countries (Geneva: UNRISD, 1986), p. 206.
26. PAN, "Programa prioritario de la revolución: Programa alimentario nacional" (Managua: PAN, 1981).
27. PAN, Plan quinquenal, p. 2.
28. Ibid., p. 2.
29. Spalding, "Food, Politics," p. 206.
30. Conroy, "External Dependence," p. 53.
31. Carmen Diana Deere, Peter Marchetti, and Nola Reinhardt, "The Peasantry and the Development of Sandinista Agrarian Policy, 1979-1984," Latin American Research Review 20, no. 3 (1985): pp. 78-81.
32. Deere and Marchetti, "The Worker-Peasant Alliance," p. 47.
33. Deere, Marchetti, and Reinhardt, "The Peasantry," pp. 81-82.
34. Ibid., pp. 89-90.
35. CAHI, Envío 5, no. 20 (September 1985). "Idle" land was defined as being uncultivated for at least two consecutive years. Land was defined as "underused" when less than 75 percent was sown. Ranchlands were considered underused when there was less than one head of cattle for each thirty-five acres in the Pacific coastal region or five acres in the highlands (see Collins, What Difference, pp. 87-96). "Decapitalization" referred to disinvestment through such devices as allowing plant and machinery to run down while profits

were pocketed or taking out low-interest investment loans and converting the money into dollars to be banked abroad (see Dennis Gilbert, "The Bourgeoisie and the Nicaraguan Revolution," paper presented at the Congress of the Latin American Studies Association, Mexico City, October 1983, p. 44). This economic sabotage was often practiced by cutting back on land in cultivation, laying off workers, selling machinery and livestock, overinvoicing for imported goods, or paying inflated salaries to family members (see Collins, What Difference, p. 44).

36. Austin, Fox, and Kruger, "The Role of the Revolutionary State," p. 19.
37. Joseph R. Thome and David Kaimowitz, "Agrarian Reform," in Walker, ed., Nicaragua: The First Five Years, p. 304.
38. Eduardo Baumeister and Oscar Neira, "Economía política en las relaciones entre el estado y el sector privado en el proceso nicaragüense," paper presented at the Seminario sobre los Problemas de la Transición en Pequeñas Economías Periféricas, Managua, 1984.
39. Joseph R. Thome, "A Half-Decade of Agrarian Reform in Nicaragua," paper presented at the International Studies Association Convention, Atlanta, March 30, 1984, p. 9.
40. Thome and Kaimowitz, "Agrarian Reform," p. 308.
41. James Austin and Jonathan Fox, "Food Policy," in Walker, ed., Nicaragua: The First Five Years, p. 406.
42. CAHI, "Nicaragua's Agrarian Reform," Update 3, no. 2 (Jan. 13, 1984): 3.
43. Thome, "A Half-Decade," p. 13.
44. CAHI, "Agrarian Reform Undergoes a Change in Nicaragua," Update 5, no. 4 (Feb. 7, 1986): 4.
45. Mexico and Central America Reports (MCAR) (March 21, 1986): 2.
46. CAHI, "Agrarian Reform Undergoes a Change," Feb. 1986, p. 4.
47. MCAR (March 21, 1986): 3.
48. CAHI, "Agrarian Reform Undergoes a Change," Feb. 1986, p. 4.
49. Peter Timmer, "A Framework for Policy Analysis," in Charles K. Mann and Barbara Huddleston, eds., Food Policy: Frameworks for Analysis and Action (Bloomington: Indiana University Press, 1986), pp. 17-25.
50. Ibid., p. 20; see also DeJanvry, The Agrarian Question, pp. 152-157, and Murdoch, The Poverty of Nations, pp. 156-159, for more discussion of "urban bias."
51. Spalding, "Food, Politics," p. 212; see Saulniers, this volume, for a discussion of the prerevolutionary pricing policies.
52. For an in-depth anaylsis of ENABAS's role in the pricing, marketing, and distribution of food, see Alfred Saulniers, this volume.
53. CIERA data, cited in Austin and Fox, "Food Policy," p. 407.
54. Collins, What Difference, p.195.
55. Enríquez, "The Dilemmas," p. 280.

56. CIERA data, cited in UNRISD, "Urbanization and Food Systems," p. 198.
57. Mesoamerica (May 1986): 10.
58. Cited in UNRISD, "Urbanization and Food Systems," p. 198.
59. Interview with Sonia Aburto, coordinator of the 1,000-sample survey, CIERA, August 1986.
60. Peter Utting, "Domestic Supply and Food Shortages," in Rose Spalding, ed., The Political Economy of Revolutionary Nicaragua (Winchester, MA: Allen and Unwin, 1986).
61. Mesoamerica (May 1986): 2.
62. Interview with Peter Utting, policy analyst and adviser, CIERA, August 1986.
63. Ibid.
64. Barricada (August 12, 1986).
65. El Nuevo Diario (July 28, 1986); Mesoamerica (May 1986): 10.
66. Austin, Fox, and Kruger, "The Role of the Revolutionary State," p. 21.
67. Laura Enríquez and Rose J. Spalding, "Rural Transformation: Agricultural Credit Policies in Revolutionary Nicaragua," paper presented at the 12th Congress of the Latin American Studies Association, Albuquerque, April 18-20, 1985, p. 12.
68. Ibid., p. 13.
69. Ibid., p. 36.
70. Spalding, "State Economic Expansion," p. 7.
71. CIERA data, cited in Deere, Marchetti, and Reinhardt, "The Peasantry," p. 83.
72. Harold Sims, "Sandinista Nicaragua: Pragmatism in a Political Economy in Formation," p. 7. Institute for the Study of Human Issues Occasional Papers in Social Change, no. 5 (Philadelphia: ISHI, 1981).
73. Spalding, "State Economic Expansion," p. 7.
74. Sims, "Sandinista Nicaragua," p. 7.
75. Enríquez, "The Dilemmas," p. 275.
76. Spalding, "Food, Politics," p. 209.
77. Austin, Fox, and Kruger, "The Role of the Revolutionary State," p. 21.
78. CAHI,"UNAG Calls on Nicaraguan Government Cancel Debt Totaling 350 Million Córdobas Held by 43,000 Peasants." Updates 2, no.13 (June 24, 1983).
79. Collins, What Difference, p.195.
80. Interview with Richard Stahler-Sholk, research associate, Coordinación Regional de Investigación Económica y Social (CRIES), July 1986.
81. Mesoamerica (May 1986): 10.
82. Collins, What Difference, p. 196.
83. Interview with Peter Utting, CIERA, August, 1986.
84. Spalding, "Food, Politics," p. 210.
85. Enríquez and Spalding, "Rural Transformation," p. 34.

86. Austin and Fox, "Food Policy," p. 407.
87. Ministerio de Desarrollo Agropecuario (MIDINRA), Informe de Nicaragua a la FAO (Managua: MIDINRA, 1983).
88. Comisión Económica para América Latina (CEPAL), Notas para el estudio económico de América Latina, Nicaragua (Mexico City: CEPAL, 1983).
89. United States Department of Agriculture (USDA), "Attaché Report: Nicaragua Agricultural Situations Report," no. NU-4006. Guatemala City, 1984.
90. Barricada (Feb. 28, 1983), cited in Spalding, "Food, Politics," p. 215.
91. CEPAL, Notas para el estudio (1983).
92. United Nations Food and Agriculture Organization (FAO), "Production Yearbooks," various issues from 1977 to 1982.
93. Richard L. Harris, "Propiedad social y propiedad privada en Nicaragua," Cuadernos Políticos, no. 40 (April-June 1984): 53. For a discussion of the relationship between the export sector and the revolutionary government, see María Verónica Frenkel and Gregg L. Vunderink, "The Relationship between the State and the Private Agro-Export Sector in Post-Revolutionary Nicaragua," manuscript.
94. Thome, "A Half-Decade," p. 16.
95. Central America Report (CAR) 10, no. 31, p. 243.
96. Collins, What Difference, p. 41.
97. Washington Letter on Latin America (December 9, 1981), cited in Austin, Fox, and Kruger, "The Role of the Revolutionary State," p. 17.
98. Baumeister and Neira, "Economía política," p. 1.
99. Thome, "A Half-Decade," pp. 16-17.
100. Lappé and Collins, Food First, introductory chapter.
101. Brockett, "Malnutrition, Public Policy," p. 487.
102. Collins, What Difference, p. 119.
103. PAN, Plan quinquenal, p. 12.
104. Instituto Centroamericano de Empresas (INCAE), cited in Austin, Fox, and Kruger, "The Role of the Revolutionary State," p. 26.
105. Ibid.; see Saulniers, this volume.
106. Ministerio de Comercio Exterior (MICE) data, cited in UNRISD, "Urbanization and Food Systems," p. 208.
107. CEPAL, Notas para el estudio (1985).
108. MICE data, cited in UNRISD, "Urbanization and Food Systems," p. 208.
109. Peter Utting, "Limits to Change in a Post-Revolutionary Society: The Rise and Fall of Cheap Food Policy In Nicaragua" (1986), manuscript, p.17.
110. Collins, What Difference, p. 125.
111. CIERA/PAN/CIDA, Informe del Primer Seminario sobre Estrategia Alimentaria (Managua: CIERA, 1983), p. 22.
112. UNRISD, "Urbanization and Food Systems," pp. 198-199.
113. Utting, "Limits to Change."

114. Austin and Fox, "Food Policy," p. 402; Collins, What Difference, p. 127.
115. Austin, Fox, and Kruger, "The Role of the Revolutionary State," p. 21.
116. Utting, "Domestic Supply."
117. Collins, What Difference, p. 128.
118. Ministerio de Comercio Interno (MICOIN), Sistemas de comercialización, vol. 1 (Managua: MICOIN, 1983).
119. Unpublished ENABAS data; see Michael Conroy and Rolf Pendall, this volume.
120. Austin, Fox, and Kruger, "The Role of the Revolutionary State," p. 28.
121. UNRISD, "Urbanization and Food Systems," p. 200.
122. ENABAS data, cited in Conroy and Pendall, this volume.
123. Collins, What Difference, p. 220.
124. Interview with Richard Stahler-Sholk, CRIES, July 1986.
125. Spalding, "State Economic Expansion," p. 8.
126. Utting, "Domestic Supply."
127. Spalding, "State Economic Expansion," p. 15.
128. Thomas C. Wright, "The Politics of Urban Provisioning in Latin American History," in Super and Wright, eds., Food, Politics, and Society, p. 33.
129. Austin and Fox, "Food Policy," p. 400.
130. CAHI, Updates 2, no. 10, p. 2.
131. Collins, What Difference, p. 122.
132. Ibid., p. 228.
133. Interview with Hugo Cabiesas, August 1986.
134. By fall of 1986, two more items had been removed from the list of rationed goods.
135. Utting, "Domestic Supply."
136. Forrest Colburn, "Theory and Practice in Nicaragua: The Economics of Class Dynamics," Caribbean Review 12, no. 3 (1984): 2.
137. Timmer, "A Framework for Policy Analysis," p. 20.
138. USDA, "Attaché Report," p. 9.
139. Spalding, "Food, Politics," p. 212.
140. USDA, "Attaché Report," p. 9.
141. CIERA/PAN/CIDA, Informe del Primer Seminario.
142. Spalding, "Food, Politics," p. 212.
143. Ibid.
144. Data from the Secretaría de Planificación y Presupuesto (SPP), the National Budget and Planning Office, cited in UNRISD, 1986, p. 200.
145. CAHI, "Nicaragua Takes Emergency Measures to Ensure Food Distribution." Updates 3, no. 20 (June 27, 1874).
146. Austin and Fox, "Food Policy," p. 401.
147. Utting, "Limits to Change."
148. SPP data, cited in UNRISD, 1986, p. 200.
149. INEC data, 1986 biweekly statistical reports.
150. INEC data, cited in UNRISD, 1986, p. 202.
151. Collins, What Difference, p. 121.
152. Austin and Fox, "Food Policy," p. 401.

153. Collins, What Difference, p. 121.
154. INEC data, from 1986 biweekly statistical reports.
155. Austin and Fox, "Food Policy," p. 401.
156. Interview with Richard Stahler-Sholk, CRIES, July 1986.
157. INEC data, from 1986 biweekly statistical reports.
158. Interview with Richard Stahler-Sholk, CRIES, July 1986.
159. Ibid.
160. CIERA, Distribución y consumo popular de alimentos en Managua (Managua: CIERA, 1983).
161. Ibid.
162. MICOIN, Sistemas de comercialización, vol. 1.
163. Cited in Utting, "Limits to Change."
164. Collins, What Difference, p. 239.
165. Cited in UNRISD,"Urbanization and Food Systems," p. 203.
166. Austin and Fox, "Food Policy," p. 409; UNRISD, "Urbanization and Food Systems," p. 209.
167. UNRISD, "Urbanization and Food Systems," p. 209.
168. See Conroy and Pendall, this volume, for further discussion of regional differences in services.
169. Unpublished data from the statistical office of the Ministry of Health (MINSA).
170. Interamerican Development Bank (IDB), Economic and Social Progress in Latin America (Washington: IDB, 1986).
171. FAO, "Antecedentes sobre la situación en América Latina y el Caribe, paper presented at the 19th Regional FAO Conference, Jamaica, June 1986.
172. Ibid.; IDB, Economic and Social Progress (1985).
173. CIERA, El hambre de los países; PAN, Plan quinquenal, p. 6.
174. PAN, Plan quinquenal, p. 7.
175. Ministerio de Educación (MED), "Programa de nutrición integral: estado nutricional de la población escolar institucionalizada de las regiones I y II de la República de Nicaragua" (Managua: MED, 1982).
176. CIERA, "Estudio de ingreso-gasto de nueve municipios," internal document (Managua).
177. Utting, "Limits to Change."
178. Interview with Julio López, director of PAN, June 1986.
179. E. V. K. FitzGerald, "The Economics of the Revolution," in Thomas Walker, ed., Nicaragua in Revolution (New York: Praeger, 1982), p. 216. At the time of this writing, it was difficult to assess the impact of the new agrarian reform law on relations with the private export sector. One source maintained that the private landowners felt increasing insecurity about how the new clause "public use or social interest" would actually be implemented. Yet it also pointed out that they were, nonetheless, still producing export crops (see CAHI, Updates 5, n. 20 (May 7, 1986): 3). In a forthcoming article,

I shall examine more closely the particular question of the tension between food self-sufficiency and export production in Nicaragua, with emphasis on the impact of the 1985-86 changes in policy on that tension (see María Verónica Frenkel, "The Dilemmas of Food Security in a Revolutionary Context: Nicaragua 1979-1986," in Scott Whiteford and Anne Ferguson, eds., Food Security and Hunger in Central America and Mexico: Roots of Rebellion [Boulder: Westview, 1987, forthcoming]).

180. See Utting, "Limits to Change," for an interesting discussion of the relative importance of each of the mass organizations on changing food policy. For a more in-depth discussion of the changing role of the mass organizations, see Gary Ruchwarger, People in Power: Forging a Grass Roots Democracy in Nicaragua (South Hadley, MA: Bergin and Garvey, 1987); and Lawrence S. Graham, this volume.

181. Mesoamerica (May 1986): 11.

182. Enríquez and Spalding, "Rural Transformation," p. 49.

Biographical Information
on the Authors

Michael E. Conroy is Associate Professor of Economics and Associate Director of the Institute of Latin American Studies at the University of Texas at Austin. He has written in three areas relevant to Latin America: regional economic development, economic demography, and the political economy of Central America. He is Co-chair of the Latin American Studies Association's Task Force on Scholarly Relations with Nicaragua, and one of the co-founders of the Central America Resource Center in Austin.

Félix Delgado Silva is a member of the Economic Studies research staff INIES. He is a graduate of the <u>Facultad de Ciencias Económicas</u> at the National Autonomous University of Nicaragua. His research at INIES has focused especially on studies of industrial productivity, particularly in the textile and clothing industries, and he has worked intensively on the development of the INIES Socio-economic Data Bank. He collaborated on several of the chapters in this book, but especially on those by Michael Conroy and Alfred Saulniers.

Alfonso DuBois is a member of the research and publications staff at CRIES, and editor of the CRIES journal, <u>Pensamiento Propio</u>. A philosopher-historian from the Basque nation, he has published widely on themes that span the Nicaraguan revolutionary experience. He worked especially closely with Scott Whiteford and Terry Hoops on the research that is synopsized in Chapter 7.

María Verónica Frenkel is a graduate student in Government, with a concentration in Latin American politics, at the University of Texas, Austin. She served as Co-coordinator, with Joanna Chataway, of this research project in Managua. Upon completion of her MA thesis, entitled <u>The Dilemmas of Food Security and Agrarian Transformation in a Revolutionary Context</u>: <u>The Case of Nicaragua</u>, she will work at CIERA for a year before continuing her studies on agricultural policy, tenure structures and the peasantry.

Lawrence S. Graham is Professor of Government and coordinator of Outreach Programs at the Institute of Latin American Studies at the University of Texas, Austin. A faculty member of the University since 1965, he is a specialist in comparative politics and development administration whose field work has taken him to Latin America as well as to southwestern and southeastern Europe. His research on the state apparatus has included work in Brazil, Peru, Colombia, and Mexico, as well as Yugoslavia, Rumania, Hungary, and Poland.

Janine Hooker is full-time researcher in the Office of Planning of the Nicaraguan Ministry of Health. A graduate in mathematics from the National Autonomous University of Nicaragua, she worked on a wide variety of health-sector research problems, as counterpart to Chandler Stolp, for the entire six weeks that he was in Nicaragua.

Terry Hoops is an Instructor in the Department of Anthropology at Michigan State University. His research experience includes Mexico and Argentina. His focus of research has been on class structures and systems of power in Latin American societies. The title of his dissertation research project is entitled La Sente Dencente: A Study of Kinship Property and Class in an Argentine Oligarchy.

Martha Juárez is a member of the Economic Studies research staff at INIES. A graduate in sociology from the UCA (Univ ersidad Centroamericana), she has also worked in the INIES Centro de Documentación and in its Training Division. She is a member of the Board of Directors of the Nicaraguan Association of Social Scientists (ANICS). She worked with the project for the full three months in Managua as one of the cocoordinators, and she worked especially closely with Scott Whiteford and Terry Hoops on the study synopsized in Chapter 8.

Rolf Pendall is a graduate student in the Community and Regional Planning Program in the School of Architecture of the University of Texas at Austin. Pendall received his B.A. in Sociology and Anthropology from Kenyon College in 1984. He is presently concentrating on Latin American economic development planning, through the University of Texas joint program in Community and Regional Planning and Latin American Studies. He joined the research group in Nicaragua for six weeks, working with both Michael Conroy and Patricia Wilson.

Alfred H. Saulniers was one of the founders of the Office of Public Sector Studies at the University of Texas at Austin and its principal coordinator for most of its ten years of existence. A Ph.D. economist specialized in the economics of public enterprises, he has worked and written extensively on the public enterprises of Latin America and Africa, with special emphasis on Peru and Zaire, and has edited two comprehensive international annotated bibliographies on the theme. For the 1986-89 period he is working for the Harvard Institute for International Development as senior economic advisor to the Prime Minister of Morocco.

Chandler Stolp is Assistant Professor at the LBJ School of Public Affairs at the University of Texas. He holds a Ph.D. in social and decision sciences and public affairs from Carnegie-Mellon Universityand a BS in economics and engineering from Stanford University. He specializes in information management, particularly in the health sector and in Latin America. Other research interests include efficiency analysis, comparative technology assessment, computerized decision support systems, migration, Central America refugee policy, maternal and child health, and econometric techniques in poor data environments.

Herminia Valdes is a member of the Urban Studies research staff at INIES. She has two degrees from the National Autonomous University of Nicaragua, the first in Ciencias de la Educación and the second, earned in 1987, in Ciencias Económicas. Her prior (and continuing) research focus has been the "spontaneous settlements" that have burgeoned in Managua. She collaborated on, but did not necessarily agree with the conclusions of, the "regional outreach" research of Michael E. Conroy and Rolf Pendall.

Scott Whiteford is Associate Professor of Antrhopology and Director of Latin American Studies at Michigan State University. He has published extensively on issues related to the political economy, agrarian systems, and labor organizations in Latin America. An anthropologist trained at the University of Texas, he is perhaps best known for his work on "social impact analysis" of agrarian systems, government policies, and technological change, with special reference to Mexico and Argentina.

Patricia A. Wilson is Associate Professor in the Graduate Program of Community and Regional Plnning in the School of Architecture at the University of Texas at Austin. She directs the Joint Master's Program in Planning and Latin American Studies. She is best known for her publications on regional development planning in Latin America, especially Perú. She holds a doctorate in Planning from Cornell University and a B.A. in Economics from Stanford University.

Index

The Nicaraguan public sector has reflected some of the most innovative and potentially controversial dimensions of the Nicaraguan revolution, yet neither the evolution of that sector nor the many facets of its current organization and functioning have been studied systematically. In this book, contributors focus on problems of analyzing and implementing programs in the public sector, including evaluating the nature of the state apparatus and examining efforts to dramatically decentralize local administration. Also discussed are programs to improve food production and distribution systems, the efficiency of health care centers, and the implications of varying levels of participation by labor groups in state or privately controlled agriculture.

This book goes a long way toward correcting misunderstanding in the United States of the scope of public-sector activities and the consequences of their expansion for the Nicaraguan economy and society. Working in close collaboration with the Nicaraguan Institute of Social and Economic Studies (INIES), these researchers had unprecedented access to government data and selected the issues to be considered in conjunction with Nicaraguan scholars and policymakers.

Michael E. Conroy is associate professor of economics and associate director of the Institute of Latin American Studies at the University of Texas, Austin.

ISBN 0-8133-7438-3